The Open Society and its Enemies in East Asia

The ideas contained in Karl Popper's *The Open Society and Its Enemies* are relevant to anyone seeking to understand the recent history of the East Asian economies. Even though Popper wrote this tract to provide an explanation for both the rise and objectionable nature of totalitarian regimes in Europe in the twentieth century, many of the arguments that he advanced in this European context also explain the social, political and economic relationships that are seen in modern South Eastern Asian economies.

The narrative of the book that follows is necessarily inter-disciplinary in nature, since to make the link between the Popperian framework and East Asian socio-economic relationships the contributing authors needed to draw upon research fields as far apart as political philosophy and East Asian studies. With one or two exceptions, however, nearly all of the contributing authors have a background in economics, and this background is reflected in the way that they have sought to tackle the research question. This book is, in short, an inter-disciplinary exercise undertaken from an economics perspective, and hence it may best be described as an exercise in political economy rather than pure analytical economics.

The novelty of juxtaposing Popperian ideas with a discussion of social, political and economic development in South East Asia makes this narrative of interest to both political philosophers and specialists in South East Asian economies. The key insight drawn from the analysis is that although Karl Popper's *The Open Society and Its Enemies* was a product of a European time and place, it is also relevant to anyone seeking to understand the recent history of the East Asian economies.

Gregory C.G. Moore is Professor of Economics, University of Notre Dame, Australia.

I0894650

Routledge studies in the modern world economy

1 **Interest Rates and Budget Deficits**
A study of the advanced economies
Kanhaya L Gupta and Bakhtiar Moazzami

2 **World Trade after the Uruguay Round**
Prospects and policy options for the twenty-first century
Edited by Harald Sander and András Inotai

3 **The Flow Analysis of Labour Markets**
Edited by Ronald Schettkat

4 **Inflation and Unemployment**
Contributions to a new macroeconomic approach
Edited by Alvaro Cencini and Mauro Baranzini

5 **Macroeconomic Dimensions of Public Finance**
Essays in honour of Vito Tanzi
Edited by Mario I. Blejer and Teresa M. Ter-Minassian

6 **Fiscal Policy and Economic Reforms**
Essays in honour of Vito Tanzi
Edited by Mario I. Blejer and Teresa M. Ter-Minassian

7 **Competition Policy in the Global Economy**
Modalities for co-operation
Edited by Leonard Waverman, William S. Comanor and Akira Goto

8 **Working in the Macro Economy**
A study of the US labor market
Martin F. J. Prachowny

9 **How Does Privatization Work?**
Edited by Anthony Bennett

10 **The Economics and Politics of International Trade**
Freedom and trade: volume II
Edited by Gary Cook

11 **The Legal and Moral Aspects of International Trade**
Freedom and trade: volume III
Edited by Asif Qureshi, Hillel Steiner and Geraint Parry

12 **Capital Markets and Corporate Governance in Japan, Germany and the United States**
Organizational response to market inefficiencies
Helmut M. Dietl

13 **Competition and Trade Policies**
Coherence or conflict
Edited by Einar Hope

14 **Rice**
The primary commodity
A. J. H. Latham

15 **Trade, Theory and Econometrics**
Essays in honour of John S. Chipman
Edited by James C. Moore, Raymond Riezma and James R. Melvin

16 **Who benefits from Privatisation?**
Edited by Moazzem Hossain and Justin Malbon

17 **Towards a Fair Global Labour Market**
Avoiding the new slave trade
Ozay Mehmet, Errol Mendes and Robert Sinding

18 **Models of Futures Markets**
Edited by Barry Goss

19 **Venture Capital Investment**
An agency analysis of UK practice
Gavin C. Reid

20 **Macroeconomic Forecasting**
A sociological appraisal
Robert Evans

21 **Multimedia and Regional Economic Restructuring**
Edited by Hans-Joachim Braczyk, Gerhard Fuchs and Hans-Georg Wolf

22 **The New Industrial Geography**
Regions, regulation and institutions
Edited by Trevor J. Barnes and Meric S. Gertler

23 **The Employment Impact of Innovation**
Evidence and policy
Edited by Marco Vivarelli and Mario Pianta

24 **International Health Care Reform**
A legal, economic and political analysis
Colleen Flood

25 **Competition Policy Analysis**
Edited by Einar Hope

26 **Culture and Enterprise**
The development, representation and morality of business
Don Lavoie and Emily Chamlee-Wright

27 **Global Financial Crises and Reforms**
Cases and caveats
B.N. Ghosh

28 **Geography of Production and Economic Integration**
Miroslav N. Jovanović

29 **Technology, Trade and Growth in OECD Countries**
Does specialisation matter?
Valentina Meliciani

30 **Post-Industrial Labour Markets**
Profiles of North America and Scandinavia
Edited by Thomas P. Boje and Bengt Furaker

31 **Capital Flows without Crisis**
Reconciling capital mobility and economic stability
Edited by Dipak Dasgupta, Marc Uzan and Dominic Wilson

32 **International Trade and National Welfare**
Murray C Kemp

33 **Global Trading Systems at Crossroads**
A post-Seattle perspective
Dilip K. Das

34 **The Economics and Management of Technological Diversification**
Edited by John Cantwell, Alfonso Gambardella and Ove Granstrand

35 **Before and Beyond EMU**
Historical lessons and future prospects
Edited by Patrick Crowley

36 **Fiscal Decentralization**
Ehtisham Ahmad and Vito Tanzi

37 **Regionalisation of Globalised Innovation**
Locations for advanced industrial development and disparities in participation
Edited by Ulrich Hilpert

38 **Gold and the Modern World Economy**
Edited by MoonJoong Tcha

39 **Global Economic Institutions**
Willem Molle

40 **Global Governance and Financial Crises**
Edited by Meghnad Desai and Yahia Said

41 **Linking Local and Global Economies**
The ties that bind
Edited by Carlo Pietrobelli and Arni Sverrisson

42 **Tax Systems and Tax Reforms in Europe**
Edited by Luigi Bernardi and Paola Profeta

43 **Trade Liberalization and APEC**
Edited by Jiro Okamoto

44 **Fiscal Deficits in the Pacific Region**
Edited by Akira Kohsaka

45 **Financial Globalization and the Emerging Market Economies**
Dilip K. Das

46 **International Labor Mobility**
Unemployment and increasing returns to scale
Bharati Basu

47 **Good Governance in the Era of Global Neoliberalism**
Conflict and depolitization in Latin America, Eastern Europe, Asia and Africa
Edited by Jolle Demmers, Alex E. Fernández Jilberto and Barbara Hogenboom

48 **The International Trade System**
Alice Landau

49 **International Perspectives on Temporary Work and Workers**
Edited by John Burgess and Julia Connell

50 Working Time and Workers' Preferences in Industrialized Countries
Finding the balance
Edited by Jon C. Messenger

51 Tax Systems and Tax Reforms in New EU Members
Edited by Luigi Bernardi, Mark Chandler and Luca Gandullia

52 Globalization and the Nation State
The impact of the IMF and the World Bank
Edited by Gustav Ranis, James Vreeland and Stephen Kosak

53 Macroeconomic Policies and Poverty Reduction
Edited by Ashoka Mody and Catherine Pattillo

54 Regional Monetary Policy
Carlos J. Rodríguez-Fuentez

55 Trade and Migration in the Modern World
Carl Mosk

56 Globalisation and the Labour Market
Trade, technology and less-skilled workers in Europe and the United States
Edited by Robert Anderton, Paul Brenton and John Whalley

57 Financial Crises
Socio-economic causes and institutional context
Brenda Spotton Visano

58 Globalization and Self Determination
Is the nation-state under siege?
Edited by David R. Cameron, Gustav Ranis and Annalisa Zinn

59 Developing Countries and the Doha Development Round of the WTO
Edited by Pitou van Dijck and Gerrit Faber

60 Immigrant Enterprise in Europe and the USA
Prodromos Panayiotopoulos

61 Solving the Riddle of Globalization and Development
Edited by Manuel Agosín, David Bloom, George Chapelier and Jagdish Saigal

62 Foreign Direct Investment and the World Economy
Ashoka Mody

63 The World Economy
A global analysis
Horst Siebert

64 Production Organizations in Japanese Economic Development
Edited by Tetsuji Okazaki

65 The Economics of Language
International analyses
Edited by Barry R. Chiswick and Paul W. Miller

66 Street Entrepreneurs
People, place and politics in local and global perspective
Edited by John Cross and Alfonso Morales

67 **Global Challenges and Local Responses**
The East Asian experience
Edited by Jang-Sup Shin

68 **Globalization and Regional Integration**
The origins, development and impact of the single European aviation market
Alan Dobson

69 **Russia Moves into the Global Economy**
Breaking out
John M. Letiche

70 **The European Economy in an American Mirror**
Barry Eichengreen, Michael Landesmann and Dieter Stiefel

71 **Working Time Around the World**
Trends in working hours, laws, and policies in a global comparative perspective
Jon C. Messenger, Sangheon Lee and Deidre McCann

72 **International Water Treaties**
Negotiation and cooperation along transboundary rivers
Shlomi Dinar

73 **Economic Integration in the Americas**
Edited by Joseph A. McKinney and H. Stephen Gardner

74 **Expanding Frontiers of Global Trade Rules**
The political economy dynamics of the international trading system
Nitya Nanda

75 **The Macroeconomics of Global Imbalances**
European and Asian perspectives
Edited by Marc Uzan

76 **China and Asia**
Economic and financial interactions
Edited by Yin-Wong Cheung and Kar-Yiu Wong

77 **Regional Inequality in China**
Trends, explanations and policy responses
Edited by Shenggen Fan, Ravi Kanbur and Xiaobo Zhang

78 **Governing Rapid Growth in China**
Equity and institutions
Edited by Ravi Kanbur and Xiaobo Zhang

79 **The Indonesian Labour Market**
Shafiq Dhanani, Iyanatul Islam and Anis Chowdhury

80 **Cost-Benefit Analysis in Multi-level Government in Europe and the USA**
The case of EU cohesion policy and of US federal investment policies
Alessandro Ferrara

81 **The Economic Geography of Air Transportation**
Space, time, and the freedom of the sky
John Bowen

82 **Cartelization, Antitrust and Globalization in the US and Europe**
Mark LeClair

83 **The Political Economy of Integration**
Jeffrey Cason

84 **Critical Issues in Air Transport Economics and Business**
Rosario Macario and Eddy Van de Voorde

85 **Financial Liberalisation and Economic Performance**
Luiz Fernando de Paula

86 **A General Theory of Institutional Change**
Shiping Tang

87 **The Dynamics of Asian Financial Integration**
Edited by Michael Devereux, Philip Lane, Park Cyn-young and Wei Shang-jin

88 **Innovative Fiscal Policy and Economic Development in Transition Economies**
Aleksandr Gevorkyan

89 **Foreign Direct Investments in Asia**
Edited by Chalongphob Sussangkarn, Yung Chul Park and Sung Jin Kang

90 **Time Zones, Communications Networks, and International Trade**
Toru Kikuchi

91 **Miraculous Growth and Stagnation in Post-War Japan**
Edited by Koichi Hamada, Keijiro Otsuka, Gustav Ranis, and Ken Togo

92 **Multilateralism and Regionalism in Global Economic Governance**
Trade, investment and finance
Edited by Junji Nakagawa

93 **Economic Growth and Income Inequality in China, India and Singapore**
Trends and policy implications
Pundarik Mukhopadhaya, G. Shantakumar and Bhanoji Rao

94 **Foreign Direct Investment in China**
Spillover effects on domestic enterprises
Deng Ziliang

95 **Enterprise Forms and Economic Efficiency**
Capitalist, cooperative and government firms
Kazuhiko Mikami

96 **Diversity and Transformations of Asian Capitalism**
Edited by Boyer, Uemura and Isogai

97 **Knowledge Transfer in the Automobile Industry**
Global-local production networks
Dessy Irawati

98 **Exchange Rates and Foreign Direct Investment in Emerging Asia**
Selected issues and policy options
Ramkishen S. Rajan

99 **Singapore, the Energy Economy**
From the first refinery to the end of cheap oil, 1960–2010
Ng Weng Hoong

100 **China–India Economics**
Challenges, competition and collaboration
Amitendu Palit

101 **Case Studies on Chinese Enterprises**
Edited by Donglin Xia

102 **Argentina's Economic Growth and Recovery**
Michael Cohen

103 **The Korean Labour Market After the 1997 Economic Crisis**
Edited by Joonmo Cho, Richard B. Freeman, Jaeho Keum and Sunwoong Kim

104 **China and India**
The quest for energy resources in the 21st century
Zhao Hong

105 **Beyond the Global Crisis**
Structural adjustments and regional integration in Europe and Latin America
Edited by Lionello Punzo, Carmen Aparecida Feio and Martin Putchet Anyui

106 **The Global Economic Crisis in Latin America**
Impacts and responses
Edited by Michael Cohen

107 **The Processes and Practices of Fair Trade**
Trust, ethics and governance
Edited by Brigitte Granville and Janet Dine

108 **Regional Development through Ecological Business**
Unique cases in Japanese rural regions
Makoto Hirano

109 **Aging and Economic Growth Potentials in the Pacific Region**
Edited by Akira Kohsaka

110 **Crises of Global Economy and the Future of Capitalism**
An insight into the Marx's crisis theory
Edited by Kiichiro Yagi, Nobuharu Yokokawa, Shinjiro Hagiwara and Gary A. Dymski

111 **The Financial History of the Bank for International Settlements**
Kazuhiko Yago

112 **Freight Transport and the Modern Economy**
Michel Savy and June Burnham

113 **Thoughts on Economic Development in China**
Edited by Ma Ying and Hans-Michael Trautwein

114 **China's Ethnic Minorities**
Social and economic indicators
Rongxing Guo

115 **Globalization, Outsourcing and Labour Development in ASEAN**
Shandre Thangavelu and Aekapol Chongvilaivan

116 **The Role of Informal Economies in the Post-Soviet World**
The end of transition?
Colin C. Williams, John Round and Peter Rodgers

117 **Demystifying the Chinese Economy Miracle**
The rise and future of relational capitalism
Yongqin Wang

118 **Globalism and Regional Economy**
Edited by Susumu Egashira

119 **Russia's Changing Economic and Political Regimes**
The Putin years and afterwards
Andrey Makarychev and André Mommen

120 **Innovation and Regional Development in China**
Edited by Ingo Liefner and Yehua Dennis Wei

121 **International Trade Negotiations and Domestic Politics**
The intermestic politics of trade liberalization
Edited by Oluf Langhelle

122 **Emerging Knowledge Economies in Asia**
Current trends in ASEAN 5
Edited by Dessy Irawati and Roel Rutten

123 **The Internationalization of the Renminbi**
International Monetary Institute, Renmin University of China

124 **Financial Globalization and Regionalism in East Asia**
Edited by Takuji Kinkyo, Yoichi Matsubayashi and Shigeyuki Hamori

125 **Successful Business Dealings and Management with China Oil, Gas and Chemical Giants**
EurIng. Henry K. H. Wang

126 **State Building and Development**
Edited by Keijiro Otsuka and Takashi Shiraishi

127 **International Economic Development**
Leading issues and challenges
Edited by Fu Lai Tony Yu, Wai Kee Yuen and Diana S. Kwan

128 **Innovation, Globalization and Firm Dynamics**
Lessons for enterprise policy
Edited by Anna Ferragina, Erol Taymoz and Kamil Yilmaz

129 **International Remittance Payments and the Global Economy**
Bharati Basu with James T. Bang

130 **The Open Society and its Enemies in East Asia**
The relevance of the Popperian framework
Edited by Gregory C.G. Moore

The Open Society and its Enemies in East Asia

The relevance of the Popperian framework

Edited by Gregory C.G. Moore

Routledge
Taylor & Francis Group
LONDON AND NEW YORK

First published in paperback 2024

First published 2014
by Routledge
4 Park Square, Milton Park, Abingdon, Oxon OX14 4RN

and by Routledge
605 Third Avenue, New York, NY 10158

Routledge is an imprint of the Taylor & Francis Group, an informa business

Publisher's Note
The publisher has gone to great lengths to ensure the quality of this reprint but points out that some imperfections in the original copies may be apparent.

British Library Cataloguing in Publication Data
A catalogue record for this book is available from the British Library

Library of Congress Cataloging in Publication Data
A catalog record has been requested

ISBN: 978-0-415-73923-8 (hbk)
ISBN: 978-1-03-292879-1 (pbk)
ISBN: 978-1-315-81678-4 (ebk)

DOI: 10.4324/9781315816784

Typeset in Times New Roman
by Wearset Ltd, Boldon, Tyne and Wear

Contents

Contributors

William Coleman, Reader in Economics, Research School in Economics, Australian National University.

Ronald E. Findlay, Ragnar Nurkse Professor of Economics, Department of Economics, Columbia University.

Patrick Jory, Senior Lecturer in Southeast Asian History, School of History, Philosophy, Religion and Classics, University of Queensland.

Gregory C.G. Moore, Professor of Economics, School of Business, University of Notre Dame, Australia.

Jeremy Shearmur, Visiting Scholar, School of Philosophy, Australian National University.

Sean Turnell, Associate Professor in Economics, Department of Economics, Macquarie University.

Rod Tyers, Winthrop Professor of Economics, Department of Economics, University of Western Australia.

Peter Warr, John Crawford Professor of Agricultural Economics, Arndt-Corden Department of Economics, Australian National University.

Acknowledgements

The chapters that constitute this book, *The Open Society and its Enemies in East Asia: The relevance of the Popperian framework*, were either inspired by or delivered at the 2011 *Freedom to Choose* conference, which is an annual one-day conference devoted to placing free-market ideas in their historical context and held on the Fremantle Campus of the University of Notre Dame Australia. Each year a different sub-theme relating to free markets is chosen for review, and the invited speakers are encouraged to adopt a critical, scholarly and non-ideological stance when considering the associated issues. Dissent from, if not outright objection to, the proposition that free markets are beneficial is encouraged from both the floor and podium. The sub-theme chosen for the 2011 conference was "The Open Society and Its Enemies in East Asia". The speakers, all invited, were asked to consider the degree to which Karl Popper's 1945 two-volume work, *The Open Society and Its Enemies*, is relevant to the economies of Burma, Singapore, China and other East Asian Countries. Not surprisingly, each speaker took this brief in a different direction and the rich diversity of the narratives that follow reflects this.

General thanks are extended to the speakers for giving up their valuable time to attend this conference. Particular thanks are extended to the Mannkal Economic Education Foundation for sponsoring the *Freedom to Choose* conference each year. The generous seed donation from this foundation will allow this conference series to continue for many years yet. Finally, I wish to acknowledge the assistance provided by the University of Notre Dame Australia (UNDA) for providing the venue for the conference and, in particular, Debra Hoare and Leanne van der List, the administrative officers at UNDA who oversee the machinery of the annual conference itself.

Prefatory remarks

The context for the open society and its enemies in East Asia

Gregory C.G. Moore

1 Introduction

The two volumes of Karl Popper's *The Open Society and Its Enemies* were published in 1945. Although my central argument in these prefatory remarks is that Popper's book is of relevance to modern East Asian societies, I must first grant the fact, squarely and honestly, that it was a product of a specific time and place, if not a veritable Carlylesean tract for that specific time and place, which in many ways bears little resemblance to modern East Asia. Specifically, *The Open Society* must be interpreted as a systematic and rhetorically charged assault on the dominant political-cum-philosophical notions that occupied the middling intellectuals of *Mitteleuropa* in the middle decades of the twentieth century, namely the totalitarian isms: Nazism, Leninism, Italian Fascismo, Austrofascism, Stalinism and their many attendant, often equally vicious, forms. Popper admits as much in various prefaces and reflections, but the contention that this intellectual product was an issue of 'time and place' and a book of rhetoric for his wavering contemporaries is best driven home by considering the gestation period of the publication. Popper had, in fact, been brooding on the ideas contained in *The Open Society* for most of the 1920s and 1930s, even though his main occupation was, then and later, to crystallize his non-justificatory philosophy of science, a philosophy for which he has subsequently gained just and lasting fame. Indeed, it would have been strange if he had not so brooded on politics, as he was born in 1902 into a prosperous Viennese family of nominal Lutheran faith, but Jewish descent, that held the dominant liberal-humanist values of his cosmopolitan class in the last years of the Austro-Hungarian Empire, and thereby he had witnessed the unreason and bloodshed that accompanied the implosion of this world order and the rise of the hideous and brutish totalitarian edifices that replaced it. He was, in short, shaped by the better aspects of the late Hapsburg civilization (and let us also remember its worst), its death throes and the virus of violence that ensued, and hence he wished to use his considerable intellectual powers to understand this unfolding tragedy and, ultimately, to check its course.

My task in what follows, then, is to provide the context for the chapters that constitute *The Open Society and its Enemies in East Asia* by demonstrating that the ideas contained in Popper's *The Open Society* are both a product of a European time and place and relevant to anyone seeking to understand the recent history of the East Asian economies. As a historian of ideas who has previously been a consumer rather than a producer of all things Popperian (with at most cannibalizing his views on historicism for my research in the 1990s into Victorian methodological debates) and as someone who has formerly undertaken little research in East Asian economic, social and intellectual history for want of interest in these domains (a preference that, after the reading I have embarked upon for this project, I now realize was a prejudice), the exercise of providing the context for these chapters was, to say the least, challenging. The collision of two seemingly unrelated areas of research nonetheless warrants the fresh eye of the reasonably read journeyman, as the specialist in either area invariably presumes too much of the reader, with, in this case, the danger being the Popperian expert failing to grasp what is foreign to the East Asian specialist and the East Asian expert not comprehending what is unfamiliar to the Popperian philosopher. Thus, to this end, the narrative of this preface has three main sections. In the second section I provide an account of how Popper came to write *The Open Society* to show that this book was designed to resolve problems of a specific time and place. In the third section, the largest section, I delineate each of the themes of *The Open Society* that I believe has universal relevance and demonstrate how each is, in particular, germane to research in East Asian studies. In the fourth section I describe each of the chapters that constitute the current book and relate their narratives to the universal themes described in the previous section. The final section contains some concluding comments and draws the reader's attention to some of the limitations of the study.

2 *The Open Society and Its Enemies* as a book of time and place or 'problem situation'

The way in which the Hapsburg frame, its fracture and replacement shaped Popper's message in *The Open Society* is most strikingly, but sparingly, reported in his intellectual autobiography, *Unended Quest* (1974). More recent scholarly output has enriched, expanded and sometimes contradicted Popper's own sparse account, with some of the more eye-catching of these publications being William Warren Bartley III's incomplete biography, *Rehearsing a Revolution. Karl Popper: A Life* (1989), elements of which were reported at a meeting of the Mont Pelerin Society prior to Bartley's death; the opening chapters of Jeremy Shearmur's *The Political Thought of Karl Popper* (1996), even if these pages were designed to provide no more than context for his gentle critique of Popper's political thought; and, most importantly due to his meticulous research into the particulars of the environment that shaped Popper's early life, Malachi Haim Hacohen's *Karl Popper – The Formative Years, 1902–1945* (2000). These biographies, particularly the last, show the way in which the world view of the Viennese *fin-de-siècle* progressives, radical liberals and old liberals shaped Popper's vision of a tolerant and liberal empire – towards which some at one point mistakenly thought that the Hapsburg Empire was evolving – in which nationalist, racial and religious prejudices are suppressed in favour of a society of Kantian individuals, each of whom was presumed to have the same intrinsic worth and dignity (but also the same unfailing fallibility), and many of whom could be emancipated from their binding material constraints via piecemeal social reforms that were to be engineered by some sort of representative body in a voluntary and non-violent manner. The nature of the historical situation that induced Popper to choose this vision is itself re-created in a number of overlapping and heavily contested discourses that are all too often (as in, now) reduced to historiographical signposts through one-off references to *fin-de-siècle* Vienna and the *Mitteleuropa* project (both inspired by Carl K. Schorske's 1980 book *Fin-de-siècle Vienna: Politics and Culture*), Wittgenstein's Vienna (prompted by Allan Janick and Stephen Toulmin's 1973 book with this title) and the Late Viennese Enlightenment (pressed by Austrian authors I have not even read). My own prefatory remarks obviously cannot do justice to the associated voluminous literature, but I believe that, following Hacohen's lead, it is easy enough to understand why someone from Popper's intellectual milieu – in the face of rising nationalism and anti-Semitism and living in social settings in which progressive issues were discussed on a daily basis – would adopt this vision.[1] It was not, however, a trouble-free choice for Popper.

It is, in fact, important to represent Popper's eventual *choice* of vision as *understandable* rather than inevitable, especially as many of his contemporaries with similar social, intellectual and ethnic backgrounds chose entirely different world views and, moreover, chose world views (such as Marxism) that *The Open Society* was specifically designed to combat. My emphasized words are chosen carefully here. Popper himself was hostile to sociologies of knowledge and historicist historiographies in which the individual is an over-determined product of his or her paradigm, or superstructure sitting on a means of production, or any other variation of this theme one may wish to ponder. He believed that such historically deterministic frameworks were too often designed to belittle decision makers by portraying them as lackeys in the service of base interests or unthinking automatons, and, as single-exit games, missed the fact that the historical context of an episode is equivalent to a complex 'problem situation' that an historical actor has to resolve, which has more than one solution, and (invoking R.G. Collingwood) which the historian has to reconstruct in a rational manner to make the final decisions of the actors understandable – but not necessarily right (Popper 1994, 145–7)![2] Popper's own historical 'problem situation' became particularly complex with the unravelling of the Hapsburg Empire and his singular reading of the western canon over this period (from Kant to Kierkegaard), and hence his eventual resolution of the problem confronting him was meandering and time consuming. His liberal-humanist sensibilities were first shaken by his youthful ponderings on the loss of life on the multiple fronts on which the old Empire was fighting during the 1914–18 war, the elimination of the family's wealth in the inflation that followed, and the realization that the poverty of the Austrian rump that remained was the result of the Hapsburgs being the aggressors rather than the aggressees in that war. In revolt against the values of his upbringing, he quit the gymnasium he was attending and, as an effective drop-out, lived an austere and bohemian life, wearing a used-army uniform, in a disused military hospital. As an impetuous sixteen-year-old in search of a better view, he accidentally spilled on to the elevated portico on which the assembled ministers announced the 1918 revolution (and there is a photo of his likeness waving to the crowd), and then ducked behind a pillar when shots rang out. He subsequently worked as an apprentice cabinet maker, a road worker, a carer for underprivileged children and a school teacher, all the while studying and collecting degrees (including a doctorate in 1928) without the prospect of great material return and more for its own sake. He drifted in and out of the intellectual circles, such as Arnold Schonberg's Society for Private Musical Performance, and was actively restricted to the margins of others, such as the Vienna Circle. He revolted against any authority and was known as a difficult young man.

He was a socialist throughout this period and even flirted with communism in 1918–19. Acting as an office boy for the Austrian Communist Party, he interacted with the likes of Paul Lazarsfeld (who later revolutionized sociology in the US) and the Eisler siblings – namely Ruth Fisher (who later became leader of the German Communist Party in the 1920s, an anti-Stalinist and eventually an American agent who betrayed her unattractive brothers), Hanns Eisler (who later composed Hollywood films and the East German national anthem) and Gerhart Eisler (who was a sufficiently efficient Stalinist enforcer that he was deemed worthy to adorn an East German postage stamp). If we are to follow Popper's own account in *Unended Quest*, it was the callous remarks in 1919 by such communist leaders following one of the aborted communist putsches against the new Austrian republic (known as the *Hörlgasse* street battle), to the effect that the deaths of protesters were necessary for their ends, that induced him to reflect upon, and finally reject, communism. He realized that he could not brook the violent consequences of the end–means logic trafficked by the Austro-Marxists, nor the dogmatism of Party policy, nor the Marxist historicist laws of inevitability, and hence, against the tide of the prevailing sentiment of many of his contemporaries, he slowly and hesitantly turned (or possibly returned?) to a vision, described above, of rational and fallible Kantian individuals making choices with consequences and pursuing piecemeal reforms in a non-violent fashion within a liberal democracy. This, however, took time, and Popper, obviously unmoored, continued to drift in what became known as Red Vienna, in which the Social Democrats ran a socialist municipality in the face of an economically bankrupt and hostile wider Austria. He remained a (liberal-) socialist committed to social reform, but increasingly in a way that made him a Dantesque party of one when he debated politics with his radical friends. He read deeply in psychology for his teaching qualifications and, more importantly for this narrative, in philosophy in a singular way, and as shown in detail by Bartley (1989) and Hacohen (2000), in a way that shaped *The Open Society*.

It must be emphasized, however, that this period of intensive study and reflection was predominantly in the field of the philosophy of science rather than political philosophy, even though the latter was never far from his mind. This study led to Popper's revolutionary non-justificatory philosophy of science that turned on a new demarcation criterion between science and non-science – namely by which fallible individuals use the principle of falsification rather than verification to reject rather than prove conjectures – and which made his reputation when he presented it in *Logik der Forschung* (1934; republished in English as *Logic of Scientific Discovery* in 1959). This book was not only the product of the same environment that produced *The Open Society* (since it was, in part, inspired by Popper's reflections upon the unfalsifiability of Freudian psychoanalysis and Marxist historicism), but also fed into the later political tract (not least because its 'fallibilist' theme was at odds with totalitarian ideologies scrutinized in *The Open Society*). Popper eventually bound his philosophy of science with his political philosophy into a complex whole – and hence his philosophy of science figures in the next section – but the constraints of time meant that Popper naturally prioritized each in its turn. It was not, indeed, until the shelling of the *Karl-Marx-Hof*, the destruction of Red Vienna and the ascendancy of fascism in the mid-1930s that Popper was prompted to shift his focus from the philosophy of science to political rhetoric proper. The celebration of irrationalism and the cult of violence within fascist historicism was even more distasteful to Popper than Marxist historicism, which for Popper was invariably the naïve historicism of the Austro-Marxists, and hence, for all its wrongheadedness and totalitarian implications, was at least initially expounded by people with rational and humane goals. Indeed, like many of his generation, Popper initially baulked at criticizing Red Vienna's Social Democrats, one wing of which was Marxist to the roots, on the grounds that to do so would aid the groundswell of support for the Austro-fascists. He also presumably turned explicitly to political rhetoric once he realized that his position as an assimilated Jew and liberal who respected rational thought was more tenuous under the latter compared to the former regime. In the introduction to his *Myth of the Framework*, he stated that the seed of *The Open Society* may have been planted not long before 1933 when a Carinthian National Socialist declared to him: "What, you want to argue? I don't argue: I shoot" (1994, xiii). This story is strangely not presented in his autobiography, but there, as elsewhere, Popper emphasized the way in which such events shaped his political philosophy. He consequently fled Austria, via London, to the New Zealand University of Canterbury in 1937, and began writing what became *The Open Society* (and its companion *The Poverty of Historicism*) on the very day he received news of the *Anschluss* in 1938. It was largely completed by 1943, but due to wartime delays and rejections from publishers, was not issued into the public domain until two years later. It was his war effort, both as a rejection of the fascism that the allies were then fighting and as a warning against the communist-style planning that he feared would be embraced in the post-war reconstruction. In his words:

> *The Poverty* and *The Open Society* were my war effort. I thought that freedom might become a central problem again, especially under the

> renewed influence of Marxism and the idea of large-scale planning (or 'dirigism'); and so these books were meant as a defence of freedom against totalitarian and authoritarian ideas, and as a warning against the dangers of historicist superstitions. Both books, and especially *The Open Society* (no doubt the more important one), may be described as books on the philosophy of politics.
>
> ([1974] 1976, 115)

The writing of *The Open Society* did not end with its publication in 1945. After taking up a position at the LSE on the conclusion of the war, where his reputation grew slowly but surely, Popper repeatedly revised his narrative and responded to his critics in addendums and footnotes in multiple editions through to the 1960s. Although solitary in nature ("willing neither to be a leader nor to be led", as Paul Lazarsfeld remarked), known as the illiberal liberal of the LSE for being a ferocious interlocutor with students and colleagues (who jested that *The Open Society* was written by one of its enemies), and largely unbefriended and unbefriending (yet inspiring some loyal students), Popper still clearly responded to what was going on around him, and hence any examination of the 'problem situation' associated with the production of *The Open Society* would have to be edition-dependent. Embracing this tactic would, however, press my prefatory remarks beyond the conventional constraints imposed upon such things and hence the narrative that follows is based on the final 1966 edition largely as if nothing transpired in Popper's life between 1945 and 1966. The reader may have also noted that, in almost an artful dodge, I make reference to the voluminous literature that has sought to re-create Popper's 'problem situation' (now 'problem situations'), but largely confine myself to the particulars presented in Popper's own account in *Unended Quest*. This decision is problematic not only because Hacohen *et al.* provide relevant particulars by the 100-page load, but also because these historians on occasion question Popper's own recollections. And, admittedly, some of the pivotal events in Popper's account of his intellectual evolution may be either exaggerated or apocryphal. One wonders, for example, about the real weight played by the deaths in the *Hörlgasse* riot of 1919, the precise role the cod-sciences of Freudianism and (naïve) Marxism played in the formation of the demarcation principle in the 1920s, the actual date on which he gave up on induction as a demarcation criterion between science and non-science, the significance of the Carinthian thug demanding consent with menace shortly before 1933, and so on. Memories are naturally faulty and the importance of events is always twisted in retrospect – and there is, after all, the contested matter of Popper's famous verbal account of the Wittgenstein–Popper poker incident of 1946 in which Popper's memory may or may not have failed him (but probably did not!). I believe, however, that the secondary literature enriches rather than supersedes *Unended Quest* and hopefully this brief narrative simply inspires the reader to consult these and other tracts Popperian when considering East Asian themes.

3 *The Open Society and Its Enemies* as a book of universal relevance

It may therefore be accepted without too much controversy that *The Open Society* was a plea for rational thought, liberty, humanism, reform and democracy at a time when totalitarianism ideologies were in the ascendant; that it was a European product designed primarily to serve the pressing European needs of the day; and that East Asia was certainly not on Popper's mind at the time of its construction. The universality of certain aspects of Popper's message is, for all this, also patent to the naked eye, and, to drive home this point, as well as to create context for the chapters of this edited book, it is appropriate now for me to disentangle some of the key themes of *The Open Society* and to show how they are relevant to East Asia. For want of space I have restricted myself to considering, each under a numbered heading, what I believe are the six main themes. Other themes (especially essentialism and holism, which I wished to consider but felt obliged to drop) may be found in more formal accounts in the various scholarly tomes on this subject (see, e.g. Simkin 1993; Shearmur 1996; Hacohen 2000; Popper 2008). It is also essential that the reader consult Shearmur's more authoritative representation of the characteristics of a Popperian open society – which has a slightly different emphasis and was developed independently to the writing of this preface – in Chapter 1 of this book. In any event, it is appropriate to begin by considering the concept that drives the title of the book and the force of much of its narrative rhythm.

1 The closed society versus the open society

Popper argued that the stress individuals experience when the society to which they belong evolves from a 'closed society' to an 'open society' may induce them to support movements that ostensibly seek to re-create a strong notion of community, but often, instead, bring about totalitarianism. Specifically, a closed society is characterized by a hierarchical structure in which social interaction takes place within an unchanging daily routine that is governed by taboos, laws and customs, and in which events are regarded as inevitable as the sun rising (1966, i, 1, 57–9, 172ff.). Individuals in such societies lead a life governed by the familial or organic social relationships of the fixed tribal world and do not experience the stress of using their critical reasoning powers to make decisions that can alter the unfolding historical situation in which they find themselves. An open society, by contrast, is one from which what Popper calls critical dualism or critical conventionalism has emerged; that is, it is a society in which individuals realize that the taboos, laws and customs are relative to different tribes and hence that they are institutions which can be changed and improved (1966, i, 1, 60, 172ff.). Individuals in such societies are suddenly confronted with the strain of a life increasingly governed by impersonal (or what Popper calls "abstract") interactions within a world forever in flux and the terrible stress of using their critical reasoning powers to make decisions that can alter their unfolding historical situations, particularly in those dislocating times of war, famine, financial upheaval and commercial-cum-industrial surges. The associated trauma of this development (or what Popper calls the "strain of civilization") leads to the emergence of strong men who seek to strip the decision-making powers from the populace by reinstating the tribal system in the guise of a totalitarian regime, of philosophers who provide philosophical systems to justify the strong men taking command in this way, and of individuals abrogating their responsibility to make personal decisions by placing their fate in the hands of the strong men. Popper focuses his attention *in particular* on the role of philosophers in providing the philosophical justification for totalitarianism (usually via the use of some sort of historicism) and he makes this argument over two volumes, with the first volume devoted to the system presented by Plato (in order to throw light on Hitler) and the second devoted to the systems presented by Hegel and Marx (with passing reference to Aristotle). It is, however, in the first volume that Popper develops this argument most effectively by showing how Plato – believing that Athenian democracy had become a 'sick society' due to the strain imposed by its movement from a closed to an open society – sought to reinstate the authoritarian tribalism of the early Greek societies.[3]

Popper's central claim – that modern totalitarianism is predominantly the product of a 'civilization' never really overcoming the shock of its birth, namely the trauma of moving from a closed to an open society – is effectively a thesis that should be settled on an empirical level (although it should be stressed that Popper was explicit that his own falsification method should not be used, especially naively, in historical research). In other words, it is a thesis that should be critically appraised by considering the protocol statements presented by historians, anthropologists, sociologists and, due to the prominent role played by past philosophers in providing justifications for the reversion to the tribal past, intellectual historians. It should also be compared with competing explanations which appeared at the time, such as the hypotheses advanced in Friedrich A. Hayek's (1944) *The Road to Serfdom* (in which incremental steps towards a welfare state lead to a fully-fledged totalitarian state and from which Popper must partly dissent due to his support for the type of piecemeal engineering considered in point 5 below) and Hannah Arendt's (1951) *On the Origins of Totalitarianism* (which at the time seemed to usurp Popper's narrative in the educated reader's imagination, but, at least from my reading and in spite of the title, does not offer an explicit theory of the rise of totalitarianism). I personally believe that Popper's narrative holds up well in the face of this competition, particularly the way in which past philosophers from Plato to Hegel to Marx are presented as the midwives of totalitarianism, but, and I have to admit this, there is perhaps slightly more to the rise of totalitarianism than simply the way intellectual and political leaders feed off the citizen's stress from everyday decision making. Popper himself seems to imply this in asides, and, as discussed further below in this narrative, I believe he too would accept a more complex position if cornered. Still, it is a thesis with sufficient empirical content that the relevance of Popper's thesis for East Asia is almost self-evident. After all, the shock that the Asian societies experienced when moving away from their custom-bound closed societies was far more dramatic than in the West, partly because of the suddenness with which change was introduced with the arrival of European colonialism and partly because of the extreme dislocation caused by the advent of post-colonial arrangements, a process that was often accompanied by violent wars of liberation. The strong men of Asia, furthermore, had the luxury of bolstering their position by drawing upon both the philosophical systems of the Western world (and here the naked use of bastardized Marxist-Leninism in Mao Zedong's China and the often surreptitious mimicking of Plato's *Republic* in modern Singapore come to mind) and the intellectual ponderings of the East itself (from misconstruing the writings of Confucius to distorting the words of Mohammad, all finessed by some sort of reference to throwing off the Western 'intellectual' yoke and returning to Asian traditions). The existing academic literature devoted to Asia is replete with such appraisals of the political arrangements of this region, only not in the Popperian frame and without his vocabulary.

2 *Historicism*

Popper stated that his "attitude to historicism is frank hostility" (1966, i, 17). He believed that historicism was the most important means by which philosophers undermine an open society, and hence his critique of this philosophical framework is, not surprisingly, the main thread that holds the narrative of *The Open Society* together. Historicism entails harvesting historical events to construct either singular trajectories or universal laws of "inevitable" historical development, usually of a stadial form, that place restrictions on the capacity of individuals to make rational and moral decisions that can alter the course of their unfolding historical situation. The quest to construct such inevitable trajectories usually manifests itself in times of unsettling change, especially in those periods in which a closed society of repetition and unchanging customs gives way to an open society of rapid and ceaseless change. This is because historicism is a means by which individuals cope with the daily strain of facing the threatening Heraclitean flux and, further, it allows them to abrogate their responsibility to make stressful decisions within this flux, especially decisions that relate to combating social evils (1966, i, 4). These historical trajectories may also be so structured that they depict a society evolving to some perfect end (such as in the writings of Hegel and Marx) or moving away from some perfect form (such as in the writings of Plato), and in both cases they provide opportunities for strong men to come to the fore and to close any emerging open society. In the case of historicist trajectories evolving to a perfect end, strong men can present themselves as leaders who will oversee and hasten the evolution of society to its inevitable end (whether it be a Thousand-Year Reich or a working man's paradise), while in the case of historicist trajectories moving away from some perfect form, strong men can present themselves as gifted leaders, with inside knowledge, who can arrest the regression from the perfect form (as in Plato's quest to check the rise of Athenian democracy by harking back to the rigid caste system and authoritarian societies of the likes of Sparta). Popper (1966, i, 8) further argued that historicist trajectories can be theistic in form, in the sense that it is the will of God that events will unfold in an inevitable sequence (usually in a way that is to the advantage of a chosen people); or natural in form, in the sense that they are effectively laws of nature (such as Comte's stadial laws of thought); or spiritual in form, in the sense that there is some evolution of an essence (usually involving the manifestation of the spirit of a national group); or economic in form, in the sense that society is driven by laws of economic development (such as Marx's stadial theory of the means of production). But whatever the precise form, the key Popperian message is that historicism is a threat to an open society, while a secondary message seems to be that there is something *cowardly* and morally wrong when individuals baulk at engaging with a historical situation, say, by failing to pursue 'activist' lines of social reform on the grounds that they are constrained by the historicist trajectories and must resign themselves to this fate.[4]

The tension, if not the contradiction, between the acceptance of trajectories or laws of historical *inevitability* and great men presuming that they can *meddle* with these developments, at least by hastening or retarding the change within the fixed boundaries of the presumed trajectory, is, in the scheme of things, no more than a minor problem within the historicist's frame of mind. The myriad contradictions, paradoxes and flaws in the historicist framework are actually delineated by Popper with ruthless and sparse prose in the slim volume, *The Poverty of Historicism*, which was published in three parts in *Economica*, via Hayek's intervention after it was rejected from *Mind* in the 1940s, before appearing in a book much later in 1957. Indeed, *The Poverty of Historicism* was carved out of *The Open Society* project when Popper realized that he was trying to do too much with the latter, and hence the two books should be considered as companion volumes and read together. There is, however, a slight danger of reading *The Poverty* first, since the reader has a tendency to presume that *The Open Society* is no more than an anti-historicist tract and thereby, in the process of cannibalizing the passages that relate to this, letting the other themes fall into the background. The reference to the assistance provided by Hayek to Popper in his publishing endeavours also points to the wider reaction to historicism by European scholars at this time, as seen in Hayek's *The Counter-Revolution in Science* (1952) and Leo Strauss's *Natural Right and History* (1953), with the latter studiously not citing Popper. The 'time and place' of European historicism should nonetheless not blind us to the possibility of elites throughout the world also embracing historicism when confronted with the shift from a closed to an open society. East Asia is no exception. Not only did the strong men of Asia import European historicism to justify their illiberal actions in the post-colonial era – such as the earlier mentioned (mis-?) use of Marxist laws of history in Mao's China – it is also clear that most Asian countries are still in the process of emerging from closed societies of fixed status and repetition, and thereby all sorts of historicist logics are being deployed by strong men to justify controlling these unwieldy forces. The most common of these deployments is to make reference to a unique historical evolution of an Asian nation state or region that makes liberal democracy unsuitable. This veritable 'Asian way' argument is reflected in everything from the 1993 Bangkok Declaration to the utterances of Mahathir Mohammad and Lee Kuan Yew. Indeed, one could argue that, paradoxically, Robert Young (most dramatically in *White Mythologies*) and other members of the post-colonial movement who have dominated much of Asian Studies over the past twenty years have indirectly lent support to Popper's thesis by showing how Western philosophies of history – in the form of either unreformed Marxian historicism or W.W. Rostow's Vietnam-era pro-democracy development trajectories – were represented as having universal applicability and thereby straitjacketed the policies available to the intellectual elites in Asia. It is all laudable stuff, but one must raise the questions of why they do not draw upon Popper in the process and why sometimes they seem to surreptitiously reintroduce historicism by dwelling upon singular Asian trajectories. In any event, I contend that historicism, either imported or adjusted for local conditions, is often as imperialistic as a chinless youth made tall by a Sam-Browne belt and swagger stick.[5]

3 The engine of success: critical rationalism in liberal democracies

Popper presents his thesis of the rise of totalitarianism almost with the presumption that an open society is superior to a closed society, and, further, one has to read his two-volume narrative carefully and in conjunction with his other publications to determine the rather multi-layered justification for this presumption. It is sufficient to state here that, over and above the 'critical dualism' characteristic described earlier in this narrative, the Popperian open society is a liberal one in which all individuals are open to criticism; there is scope for non-violent change through some sort of democratic process; and individuals are 'protected' from exploitation within a pluralistic society that is subject to the rule of law. Popper, in other words, very nearly equates the fully evolved open society with Western liberal democracy, and this, admittedly, may make some Asian specialists – drunk on the admittedly nutritious brew of Edward Said's *Orientalism* (1978) – suspicious that this is yet another example of Western self-affirmation by establishing an oriental 'other'. I do not believe that this is the case, partly because the 'other' to *European* liberal democracy is *European* totalitarianism (and, indeed, Asia is barely mentioned in *The Open Society*) and partly because of the soundness of Popper's arguments in favour of an open society. As Shearmur emphasizes in Chapter 1, these arguments largely turn on humanitarian issues, such as the minimization of pain and an ability to embark upon peaceful social reform. But before turning to these important issues further below, it is convenient at this point to focus on an argument in favour of an open society that is less explicit in Popper's narrative and may only be properly grasped by considering *The Open Society* alongside his other writings, namely that an open society is required to create an engine of progress in which new ideas are systematically generated, criticized and expelled. This argument is important to consider first, even though it is not always at the very forefront in *The Open Society* itself, since it is dangerous to consider any publication in isolation from its author's other writings and, perhaps more importantly, because progress is of some importance to the economists who are contributing to this volume. In any event, Popper's logic is impeccable: a liberal society will outperform an authoritarian regime because the generation and critical appraisal of ideas are the key source of a society's scientific and social progress. This claim evolved out of Popper's path-breaking work in the philosophy of science alluded to earlier in this preface. Specifically, in *The Logic of Scientific Discovery* (1959), Popper exposed the poverty of using the verification principle (as deployed by the logical positivists of the Vienna Circle) to justify scientific theories. The problem with this approach had been identified before (most famously with Hume's problem), but it was Popper's stress upon the asymmetric nature of verification and falsification that revolutionized the thinking on this issue; that is, he showed that no number of white swans demonstrates that all swans are white, but one black swan demonstrates that not all swans are white, and thereby he showed that a scientific theory may be rejected but never proven. This gave rise to his science/non-science demarcation criterion, by which a science is defined not by one's ability to prove theories but by one's ability to falsify conjectures. More importantly, it gave rise to a different vision of the scientific process in which fallible individuals with imagination do not collect observations in a mind-numbing Baconian induction process, but instead propose conjectures that might be tightened into falsifiable hypotheses and subjected to attempted refutation (including the Kantian ideas that accompany them) by considering evidence that is open to inter-subjective assessment in the public domain. Popper (1966, ii, ch. 24) had, in short, used *The Open Society* to transfer a *variation* of this idea, which became known as critical rationalism, to the political arena by showing that liberal societies flourish because they allow fallible citizens to learn from their mistakes while totalitarian regimes become sluggish because they suppress criticism. Popper – without ever condoning naive falsificationism in the non-sciences – celebrated speculation and criticism whenever they could be brought to bear.[6]

The link between critical rationalism in the arena of political philosophy and the domain of the philosophy of science was largely lost on Popper's contemporaries when *The Open Society* appeared in 1945. This was because his *Logic of Scientific Discovery* was not translated into English until 1959 and his demarcation criterion was sufficiently innovative that even some of his German-speaking colleagues in the Vienna Circle mistakenly presumed that it was a mere finesse on the justificatory approach of logical positivism. Critical rationalism was nonetheless just as revolutionary in political philosophy as it was in the philosophy of science. As Bryan Magee (1997, 199) claims, Popper indirectly uses critical rationalism to advance a profoundly original argument in defence of liberal democracy that turns less on traditional moral considerations (which, as shown below, Popper valued independently) and more on the contribution a liberal democracy makes to achieving another end, namely progress. It is important at this stage to recognize that Popper at no time equated an open society with free-market capitalism and he certainly did not equate progress with mere economic progress, especially if it did not help those in greatest need.[7] But, at the same time, economists like myself do not do too much violence to the Popperian vision if the narrow focus on economic progress via the growth of ideas is accompanied with the rider that the resulting prosperity should be employed, via a discovery process that Popper called piecemeal reform, to provide the merit and public goods that are required for a civil society, and the institutional environment to help those in need. The Popperian engine of discovery is therefore, in this reworking along economic lines, designed to generate ideas that both contribute to the production process and lead to a better allocation of the surplus to humanitarian ends. Indeed, the end institutional product of this hyper-critical evolution need not even be a free market economy so admired by most economists. It is the laissez faire of ideas, not of goods and services, which is being emphasized (even if my personal view is that they are intertwined). In any event, the argument that a liberal democracy succeeds because it generates (and destroys) the most ideas should resonate with those economists who now believe that new ideas are the key contributors to economic growth (as reflected in Solow's slippery residual and, more recently, endogenous growth theory). In contrast, this pro-'liberal democracy' argument went against the considered opinion of the time in which it was proposed, especially after the democracies fell into disrepute in the 1930s due to the appeasement policies in the face of totalitarian aggression abroad and lame economic policies in the face of economic malaise at home.[8] Even those who had not embraced the noxious 'isms' of this time presumed that a democracy was inefficient compared to a benign dictatorship, and, further, that democracies were wealthy because such societies had accumulated sufficient wealth to afford the moral luxury of democracy, not because the very nature of democracies created this wealth (Magee 1973, 1997). The application of critical rationalism in the political domain, however, turned this conventional causal reasoning on its head: societies were not liberal democracies because they were prosperous, but rather they were prosperous because they were liberal democracies. All this is impressive stuff, but it is a proposal that should be critically appraised by considering the evidence and, due to the complex causal processes at play, this is a difficult task. The relevance of this hypothesis for Asia is in dispute for this reason, and hence, not surprisingly, the chapters that follow and the wider literature (indirectly and unknowingly) are preoccupied with this aspect of Popper's grand structure. The economic success of illiberal China is set against the failure of illiberal Burma, while the Asian Way argument (sometimes referred to as the Lee hypothesis after one of its chief advocates, Lee Kuan Yew) is buttressed by citing the growth of Singapore under less than liberal arrangements. The selective use of statistics and simple-minded null hypotheses to support the Lee hypothesis has, in turn, incensed economists such as Amartya Sen (1997, 2). The fact of the matter is that the cult of econometrics, when applied by journeyman hands to multiple causal relationships between non-operational concepts (such as freedom and liberty), is both questionable and only taken seriously in seminars within economics departments (and then really only as a means by which young researchers demonstrate that they have mastered a tool that they can pass down to others). Still, it is evidence that has to be thrown into the mix, particularly when an econometrician above the common ruck sometimes manages to isolate one of the many causal relationships between freedom and progress. Popper, however, never passes their lips and the debate itself is nothing more than a dog's breakfast.[9]

4 A liberal, non-violent and humanitarian democracy

It is important to emphasize that although Popper was a militant democrat, his advocacy was always for a democracy of a specific type. An unthinking, illiberal and uncritical democracy was obviously off the agenda, as this would not generate the engine of discovery described in the previous numbered point. His ideal open society is a *liberal* democracy defined by individualism, equalitarianism, faith in reason and love of freedom, not democracy per se (1966, ii, 199). Popper's historical template for such a democracy is the Athenian democracy in the time of what he called the "Great Generation", which existed in the fifth century BC just prior to and during the Peloponnesian wars (1966, ii, 185). Popper focused on this era of Athenian history because, as mentioned previously, Plato justified a return to a closed society on the basis of the supposed failings of this democracy and hence it was a means by which Popper could fight modern battles by historical proxy. Popper does not, however, present a broad historical review of all democracies across time and space (and the protocol statements that they would yield); nor does he really provide a logical-deductive explanation for why a democracy would necessarily yield the liberalism and critical rationalism that drives progress. His main rhetorical tactic seems to be that of delineating the illiberal nature of totalitarian societies and then implying that democracies will be liberal and critical in orientation because they are not totalitarian. This is not always convincing. There is, after all, the possibility of democracies giving rise to an intolerant collective (as in Ibsen's *The Enemy of the People*); the dysfunction and internecine bloodshed of the splintered collective associated with Balkanized groups (from the American to the Iraq civil wars); a public choice dynamic in which communities close in on themselves (via, say, sclerosis of the Olsen sort or, as Buchanan argued, poor policies arising from the ill-dispersion of the associated costs and benefits); and, most importantly since it is Popper's own argument, people voluntarily choosing to return to a tribal society due to the stress of decision making in an open society (such as post-1933 Germany). Popper is, of course, intelligent enough to consider many of these illiberal possibilities and to make explicit that his democracy would not operate along illiberal lines (1966, ii, 160ff.). Still, beyond contending that there must be some sort of Hayekian "planning for freedom" that entails imposing appropriate institutions to prevent the rise of a totalitarian democracy, he does not present a specific logic for why a democracy should become a liberal democracy in which ideas may be trafficked freely and in safety.[10] If anything, the most logically developed defence of democracy presented by Popper seems to be based less on the way a democracy yields a liberal and open environment and more on Popper's acute humanitarian sentiments. Specifically, while a liberal democracy makes a contribution to humanitarian ends via that part of the engine of discovery that produces civilizing reforms, it also makes a contribution to these ends by reducing the scope for violence. Popper effectively makes the moral injunction that to kill someone is usually bad and to kill people *en masse* is very often bad (and his personal distaste for inhumane acts is littered through his recollections, from his pacifism as a child to his aversion to the Viennese street shootings). The political system must therefore be arranged such that it minimizes mass killings, and since mass killings in particular take place in a quest for regime change, the political system must contain a non-violent mechanism for such change. True democracies have such a mechanism while totalitarian regimes do not, so the former system is preferred, *quod erat demonstrandum* (1966, ii, 151, 161). That Popper would advance this logic is perhaps not surprising, as he was an assimilated Jew living in an age in which to be old was, as the Polish poet Wislawa Szymborska would say, the "privilege of rocks and trees".

Popper, then, does not really provide a fully developed explanation for why a 'liberal' version of the many possible versions of democracy emerges, but the saving grace of his position is that he is always clear that he is in favour of a liberal democracy rather than just any 'garden variety' democracy. Popper's two justifications of liberal democracy – as a means to promote critical rationalism and to provide non-violent regime change – are also presumably connected. Specifically, if citizens recognize that critical rationalism is the best way to achieve progress towards a more civilized society (a big if), and if such progress is actually what they want (a bigger if), and if a regime with increasing totalitarian sentiment starts to curtail critical rationalism (not much of an if), then the citizens of such a society need a non-violent means (i.e. a democratic mechanism) by which to change the regime. Popper also dismisses the entirely plausible possibility of a benign dictator (or oligarchy) promoting critical rationalism to a greater extent than a liberal democracy with the equally plausible argument that there is no effective succession plan within totalitarian regimes, so that there is every possibility that a benign dictator will eventually be replaced with a short-sighted tyrant and, hence again, the regime change required to return to a liberal world would entail violence (1966, i, fn. 25, 269; 160). It is, I believe, these sorts of arguments that make Popper's analysis relevant to East Asia. The contention that unalloyed totalitarian regimes in Asia without peaceful mechanisms for regime change (whether they be the dystopias of Kim Il-Sung's North Korea and Ne Win's Burma or less oppressive regimes) do not reach their full potential owing to the eventual and violent curtailment of critical rationalism has much empirical content if one examines Asian history. This line of argument, of course, could always be made more nuanced by drawing on the frighteningly complex debates generated by Joseph Needham's multi-volume series on *Science and Civilization in China* (of which seven were written by Needham himself and none have been read by me) and the associated Needham Question of why the West took over from China in science and technology despite China being the first mover in these affairs.[11] It is nonetheless true enough in this cut-down form and, more importantly, it is not at odds with the fact that the dichotomy between brutish totalitarian states and tolerant liberal democracies is becoming less relevant in Asia in recent times, as the elites of the totalitarian societies seek increasingly to imitate the templates for liberal success by acting as benign dictators or oligarchies. For, according to Popperian logic, this Asian 'critical-rationalist spring' will last only as long as the benign dictators and oligarchies permit it to last, and if they ever retreat from this position, there will be no means by which to remove the regimes in a non-violent way. The citizens will have to yield to the new oppression or take actions that will lead to mass killings.

5 Piecemeal change to minimize suffering versus utopian dreams to maximize happiness

It is now appropriate to consider what Popper believed to be the most important purpose of an open society in a little more detail, namely the way in which it allows individuals to exploit that part of the aforementioned engine of discovery, via what he called piecemeal reform, to improve on free-market outcomes. Specifically, Popper rejected what he called "utopian engineering", which he associated with totalitarian regimes, in favour of "piecemeal engineering", which he associated with open societies. Utopian engineering effectively sits alongside historicism as a system of thought that philosophers intentionally or unintentionally use to usher in a closed society. Utopian engineering may seem a strange policy for philosophers to advocate if they are also inclined to believe in historicism, but, as mentioned before, there is no shortage of paradoxes within the historicist approach to modelling the social world and, further, Popper recognizes that there are two strands of historicism: one in which an actor cannot alter the inexorable laws of history, and another in which he or she can alter the historical trajectory at the margins (1966, i, 157). It is also the case that utopian engineering is *embraced* by some philosophers who *reject* historicism for a world in which actors can make meaningful change and, as in the case of Marx's legendary contempt for utopian socialism, *rejected* by those who *embrace* a pure form of historicism in which potential policy makers are locked in by the rhythms of history. This, however, simply implies that, within the Popperian frame, philosophers who facilitate the rise of totalitarianism are not confined to historicists. In any event, utopian engineering is defined as the pursuit of an ideal state that is mapped out by a social engineer in a complex blueprint and in which some grand utilitarian goal is to be achieved, whereas piecemeal engineering is defined as the implementation of 'trial-and-error' policies that are designed not to maximize human happiness at some distant 'ideal' end, but to minimize pain and suffering by solving more immediate and pressing problems (1966, i, 158). The former approach sets society along a path to tyranny by a series of logical mechanisms that is reminiscent of, but nonetheless different to, Hayek's *Road to*

Serfdom. Specifically, utopian engineering requires a "strong centralized few" to implement a complex blueprint; the centralized few, even if setting out as a benign oligarchy, need to crush dissent and curtail critical discussion to implement a blueprint to which not all citizens subscribe; such dissent (and the violence needed to suppress it) will be magnified in utopian engineering settings, since people find it difficult to comprehend a complex utopian blueprint that leads to a distant end, while they can readily see the sense of relieving immediate suffering by achieving a limited end via piecemeal change; and complex blueprints take more than one generation to implement and, without a successor plan, the centralized few may be succeeded by tyrants (1966, i, 158–61). Popper also believed that piecemeal engineering was more likely to achieve its prescribed goals than utopian engineering. Specifically, the absence of criticism that ensues from the aforementioned suppression of dissent makes it difficult to determine the efficacy of the utopian policy; well before utopian engineers achieve their ideal end, new ends will be deemed desirable; powerful interests become attached to the grand ends set out in the blueprint and thereby dogmatically pursue them despite evidence that the plan is failing; and, unlike utopian engineering, faltering piecemeal engineering may be reversed without much suffering (1966, i, 158–63). Underlying all of these arguments in favour of piecemeal engineering is Popper's humanitarian mission – which is always present in his narrative and punctuated in the anecdotes relating to his life – to minimize pain rather than to maximize utility, an approach he termed negative utilitarianism.[12]

This analysis indicates that, like Hayek, Popper did not believe that free-market capitalism necessarily yielded results that were in any way good, fair or just, but unlike Hayek (who famously argued that the state could rarely improve on these free-market outcomes for want of every individual's local knowledge), Popper believed that, through the trial-and-error process of piecemeal engineering, the state could improve on free-market outcomes. Popper was therefore never an Austrian economic libertarian in the Hayekian sense. His road to totalitarianism is built by those who embrace utopian engineering and/or historicist philosophies rather than, in the case of Hayek's road to serfdom, incremental steps towards state planning. Popper was appreciative of Hayek as a like-minded interlocutor and correspondent, and readily acknowledged the similarities between his and Hayek's criticisms of grand state interventions (1966, i, 159; fn. 4, 285–6), as well as his and Hayek's views on historicism and simple-minded "scientism" (see Hayek 1952).[13] The fact of the matter is, however, that Popper followed Marx closely in condemning the inequities of the unrestrained capitalism of the Victorian age. Invoking the paradox of economic freedom (namely that unlimited economic freedom defeats itself by allowing the strong to enslave the weak), and by drawing upon the Marxist distinction between formal and material freedom, he believed that the state should create freedom by elevating the economically weak (1966, ii, 123–5; Magee 1973, 78). To this end, Popper supported piecemeal engineering both to minimize pain (as dictated by his negative utilitarianism) and to provide the type of economic interventionism required to resolve the paradox of economic freedom. The state should be small, its policies should be implemented within the rule of law rather than through bureaucratic edict (1966, ii, 130–2), and its sole purpose should be to protect both the economic and political freedoms of the individual, but it has interventionist and civilizing roles nonetheless.[14] This may perhaps disenthrall some libertarians (including the generous sponsors of the conference from which this book springs) – and disabuse others who dismiss Popper as an extreme neoliberal member of an undifferentiated Mount Pelerin Society – but once one interprets Popper from his own critical rationalist stance it is a perfectly sensible proposal: one needs to see if state intervention improves on the market outcomes through trial and error rather than to reject it outright from the start. Popper himself would have also presumably been in a position to cast judgement on the success of the piecemeal engineering with which he sympathized, as he lived through to the age of Thatcher in which many of the incremental changes associated with the rise of the welfare state were reversed (on the grounds that they had failed) in the fashion that he proposed; that is, with the Brixton riots, a decade of depressing British cinema and the tragedy of high unemployment, rather than gulags, Leni Riefenstahl documentaries and mass killings. And, of course, the relevance of all of this to East Asia is sadly all too clear, with Popper's model of utopian policy formation confirmed with the failures of the blueprints associated with Saloth Sar's (aka Pol Pot's) year zero of 1975; Ne Win's "Burmese Way to Socialism" of 1962 (in which the call for "self-improvement by way of self-criticism" was not what Popper meant by forming policy via trial and error); and Mao's Great Leap Forward of 1956 to 1961 (where everything failed, from backyard pig-iron production to Lysenko-style food experiments).[15] The success of more recent "piecemeal" experimentation with "market socialism" (*sic*) under Deng Xiaoping and his successors contrasts neatly with these fiascos. Indeed, a consensus has now formed to the effect that the Chinese leadership stumbled towards market reform, in a piecemeal fashion, rather than adhering to a grand blueprint (see Perkins (1994) for an early statement of this).

6 *Intellectual history*

It cannot be emphasized enough that *The Open Society* is, above all else, an intellectual history. As stated in the previous numbered points, Popper is interested less in the cut and thrust of the rise of the totalitarian regimes and more in showing how philosophers have acted as midwives for these regimes. He therefore not surprisingly spends the lion's share of the book analysing the writings of Plato, Hegel and Marx to show how they deployed historicism and attendant philosophies to justify, in Popper's eyes, the unjustifiable (and remember that, in the original parable, the lion's share is the entire share). Popper, in particular, sets the philosophers in the dislocating times in which they wrote their works, and, to this extent, adheres to his own historiographical approach of *situational logic* that was touched upon in the second section of this chapter; that is, eschewing cheap psychologizing and sociologies of knowledge in which social causes impact on an agent as if he is an automaton, and, instead, explaining an agent's behaviour as a rational response to an 'objective' problem situation, which is captured by reconstructing the context in which the problem is set. The more specific problem situation that dominates *The Open Society* is, of course, a society's inability to cope with the strain of civilization as it moves from a closed to an open society. Popper therefore seeks to present Plato's call for a return to a society ruled by aristocratic oligarchs as a rational (but definitely not the right) reaction to this strain and dysfunction in the Athenian democracy; Hegel's position as an apologist for the Prussian absolutism as a reaction to the devastation of the German states in the Napoleonic era; and Marx's sponsorship of collectivist rule by the proletariat as a reaction to the tumult of the Industrial Revolution. This historiographical approach, which closely resembles Collingwood's "question-and-answer" logic, is more complex than one imagines at first reading, and justice has certainly not been done to it here.[16] It was, however, the less than perfect execution of this method, rather than the method itself, that drew the ire of his contemporaries. This was mainly because, in contravention of the scholarly etiquette of the day and unlike the modern contextualists of the Sussex and Cambridge schools, Popper allowed his "presentist" objectives (his war aims!) to dominate in such a way that he did not always provide sympathetic or temperate readings of the texts. Thus, by quoting others or through his own words, Popper labels Hegel a "charlatan", Fichte a "windbag", oracular philosophers "clowns" and so on, in a veritable bayonet charge in which no prisoners are taken. The important qualification to this is his free admission that although the Marxist historicism leads to tyranny, Marx himself should be celebrated as a rational humanist who provided many powerful insights – which is true enough and makes the narrative devoted to Marx in the second volume the most measured (but therefore in some ways more cold and ruthless) of his critiques.[17] The violence of this language was distasteful enough to scholars who had devoted a lifetime to studying Plato and Hegel line by line and as 'greats' – not to mention for the Marxists who, in the shadow of Stalingrad and the fall of Berlin, still had confidence in this philosophical frame – but it was Popper's occasional slipshod readings of the original texts (and misrepresentations of his fellow exegetes) that spurred them to counter Popper's position with effect. Giants in the field such as Isaiah Berlin and Gilbert Ryle may very well have declared that Platonic and Marxist exegesis would never be the same after Popper, but other critics used his occasional exegetical failings to marginalize his larger message.[18] Popper himself excused the lapses on the grounds that he was isolated and without access to key texts while writing *The Open Society* in New Zealand (where the university library was not much bigger than his father's), and he used footnotes and addendums in later editions to defend his textual interpretations. The general verdict now seems to be that Popper's textual assessments are more right than wrong, even if they originally rest on some poor readings (Klosko 1996). The first critiques of Popper's exegeses nonetheless provided a reasonable excuse, especially for the children of 1968, to dismiss Popper's narrative.

Popper's use of intellectual history as a means to convey his philosophical arguments – a tactic that pervades most of his writings – also irritated some of his greatest (but never uncritical) admirers. A young Bryan Magee (1997, 188ff.), then unknown to Popper, rather presumptuously and with some fury wrote Popper a letter stating that he only confuses the issue when he makes a contribution to the solution of a philosophical problem by examining it within an intellectual history of past philosophers, since this allows modern philosophers to ignore the former and focus on Popper's errors as a historian of ideas. Magee is, of course, right, but also wrong, since Popper's use of intellectual history has the indirect and useful effect (even if Popper was perhaps unaware of this fact) of inducing many to read his work who would otherwise not have done so, and, more importantly in my eyes, allowing him to tease out novel ideas over which he did not yet have complete control. The latter strategy is perhaps the most underestimated use of intellectual history and it is certainly relevant to Popper's *The Open Society*, where all of the side considerations, detours from the main message and qualifications appear to be the product of someone who knows the general direction, but not the precise route and final destination, when setting out on a journey. The concise and analytical *The Poverty*, which recall was carved out of *The Open Society* project, also shows how he could boil down his findings after completing the hard yards of studying the intellectual history, while the notoriously long gestation periods of most of Popper's works would presumably have been longer if he had not used this strategy. All of this, of course, points to the way in which this theme is relevant to anyone working within Asian studies. Not only does it signal the way intellectual historians can show how the strong men of Asia exploit ancient and not-so-ancient texts to justify their actions in the face of the strain of civilization, as in Popper's original thesis, but, presumably through a more sympathetic reading of the original texts than that adopted by Popper (and in the eavesdropping tradition of the Sussex School in particular), they can show how these strong men usually distort these texts for their ends. This was precisely Sen's (1997) tactic in the Morgenthau Memorial Lecture devoted to the exceptionalism underlying the Lee hypothesis; namely that in the same way that there are non-freedom traditions in the European tradition (Plato, for example), Asia is far more diverse than many think and, within this diversity, there are freedom traditions in what perhaps may be called the Asian canon. There is, for example, a respect for diversity and tolerance within Buddhism (even though Buddhists paradoxically seem to have a rapacious appetite to kill each other) while Confucianism is more complex, humanist and not solely authoritarian (a point emphasized in recent years by Simon Leys).

4 The chapters that follow

Popper, then, uses *The Open Society* to present a complex and multi-layered structure of principles of universal relevance and, indeed, a number of other themes could have been presented in addition to the six delineated in the previous pages. Every thematic thread, however, cannot be disentangled in a preface such as this and, in any event, my goal is less to provide a critical analysis of *The Open Society* and more to show how it is relevant to East Asia, and thereby to provide context for the narratives of the chapters that follow, of which there are eight in total. All but the first chapter were delivered in an earlier form at a one-day economics conference in 2011 called *Freedom to Choose*, which (and as stated in the Acknowledgements) is held each year on the Fremantle campus of the University of Notre Dame Australia and sponsored by the Mannkal Economics Economic Foundation. This conference is designed to create a forum in which undergraduate, honours and postgraduate students in economics can interact with senior academic and industry economists to discuss their career prospects. Each year this conference has a different theme, but it is always related to a libertarian topic. The theme for 2011 was to consider the extent to which Popper's concept of an open society is relevant to the East Asian economies. Seven scholars from a range of backgrounds were invited to deliver papers. Some speakers had no formal background in things Popperian while others could be described as authorities on both Popper and his philosophy, but all had an interest in discovering the extent to which the Popperian framework is relevant to the East Asian economies.

The opening chapter by Jeremy Shearmur is introductory in nature and is devoted to describing the key characteristics of Popper's vision of an open society. Shearmur was, for a period of eight years, Popper's personal research assistant and subsequently the author of two books that were drawn upon by me in the preparation for writing my own narrative, namely *The Political Thought of Karl Popper* (1996) and, along with Piers Norris Turner, the edited volume of Popper's unpublished and uncollected writings, *Karl Popper, After the Open Society* (2008). He therefore writes with some authority on what Popper meant by a functioning open society both in the two volumes of *The Open Society* and in Popper's voluminous comments on this matter in the lifetime of writings that followed. According to Shearmur, Popper believed that an open society is one in which individuals, but government officials in particular, are open to criticism via Popperian critical rationalism; there is a mechanism for non-violent change through some sort of democratic process; there is social and political pluralism; the rule of law is present; and there is an understanding that individuals must be 'protected' from economic and political exploitation. Some of these characteristics have been briefly commented upon in the themes I addressed above, but Shearmur's chapter was written quite independently from my own prefatory remarks and his agenda is clearly different to mine, as he is less interested in disentangling the themes of *The Open Society* (and thereby does not consider Popper's anti-historicism and singular historiography) and more interested in describing what Popper's open society would actually look like in a concrete setting. It is an admirable outline and serves well as context for the references to such a society in the subsequent chapters in which this concept is used in relation to specific East Asian countries.

Chapters 2 and 3 are devoted to considering Popper's vision in relation to Thailand. Chapter 2 by Patrick Jory is entitled 'Karl Popper and Thailand's political crisis: the monarchy as the problem for an "open society"'. It considers the way in which many Thai scholars and politicians use historiographical techniques – which in many ways resemble the historicism so detested by Popper – to claim that Thailand's less than transparent 'democracy' is the result of a 'special' historical trajectory and hence is immune from criticism. Jory, who is a noted cultural historian rather than an economist per se, focuses in particular on the way in which these techniques are used to justify Thailand's *lèse majesté* law that prevents criticism, a key element in Popper's open society, of the Thai crown. Jory's narrative is, of all the chapters, the most explicit in its use of Popperian categories to explain (and, I would add, successfully explain) an Asian phenomenon. Chapter 3, by contrast, takes a more indirect and critical line with regard to the Popperian framework. Entitled 'Thai populism and the middle-income trap' and written by Peter Warr, who is the head of the Research School in Pacific and Asian Studies at ANU, it shows that an open society of the Popperian sort does not necessarily provide a defence against politicians using inefficient economic policies to manipulate the electorate to ensure that they are re-elected. Warr, in particular, focuses on the various rice floor schemes implemented in Thailand. Popper wrote *The Open Society* prior to the rise of public choice modelling and hence prior to the demonstration of how the liberal democratic process could be manipulated to suit special interests. We therefore cannot be too hard on Popper for not addressing these issues at length, at least in his early writings, even if he did briefly consider (and dismiss) Marxist arguments that similarly turned on the influence of vested interests. In any event, it is a sound criticism of the liberal democratic version of an open society and Warr strikes it home well.

Chapters 4 and 5 are occupied with the problem of Burma. Sean Turnell, who is a long-term Burma watcher and author of *Fiery Dragons*, considers the economic consequences of Burma's closed society in a chapter entitled 'Least free: the economic consequences of fifty years of totalitarian rule in Burma'. Turnell traces the sorry tale of Burma's decline under junta rule from one of Asia's most prosperous nations to one of its most impoverished (and least free). In the context of the themes discussed above, but without at all times explicitly stating this, Turnell is effectively showing how an uncritical, illiberal and unfree Burma has failed dismally to live up to its full social and economic potential (Popperian point 3 above), and that utopian engineering both fails economically and bolsters the power of the centralized few (Popperian point 5 above). Next, Ron Findlay, who is a Professor of Economics at the University of Columbia and of Anglo-Burmese decent, provides a personal account of recent Burmese history in a chapter entitled 'Development and Freedom in Burma'. He traces the tumultuous history that led up to the colonial age of George Orwell's *Burmese Days* and *Shooting the Elephant*, the great exodus following the Japanese occupation of 1942, the promise of the Democratic Republic in the 1950s, and the entrenchment of the juntas following the 1962 coup d'état. For all of the tragedy that accompanied these episodes, Findlay provides a sympathetic reading of the history of his times prior to achieving academic success in the USA, including touching on the (mixed) advantages of Empire (and I would add that there were some advantages, even if we remember that Eric Blair was at one time a police officer at Insein, now the largest prison in Burma, and that he shot an elephant for the wrong reasons). Findlay also gives the impression that reading *The Open Society* as a precocious Anglo-Burmese youth (while being subject to threatening forces equal to those experienced by Popper as a youth) somehow had more meaning for him than for the Western reader of today.

Chapters 6 and 7 are devoted to questioning some of the Popperian conclusions in the broader East Asian arena. Rod Tyers, who is a Professor of Economics at the University of Western Australia, considers the recent economic success of China in a chapter entitled 'The rise and robustness of economic freedom in China'. China is, of course, the elephant in the room for those who adhere to a narrow reading of Popper's *The Open Society*, as it seems to be a totalitarian success story. Tyers provides an admirable survey of the recent economic literature that tracks this economic success, but shows how this both threatens and supports the Popperian frame depending on how one interprets the deeper reasons for this success. If one interprets modern China as an anti-democratic and anti-liberal closed society, then it does indeed pose a challenge to Popper's vision. If, however, one puts to one side Popper's own tendency to use false dichotomies and realizes that China has actually undertaken the 'trial-and-error' policies associated with piecemeal engineering that have allowed elements of an open society (of sorts) to emerge, then it is not necessarily at odds with the Popperian vision. This chapter is followed by another by Jeremy Shearmur, but this time devoted to Singapore and entitled 'Singapore: Plato's other republic?'. As the title of the chapter suggests, Shearmur considers the extent to which the apparent social and economic success story of the island state of Singapore may be attributed to the authoritarian structures that in some ways resemble those advocated by Plato in *The Republic*. The gains are compared to the considerable losses, mostly in the form of curtailed freedoms not seen to the Western visitor, but the final tally is rather inconclusive. It seems to be a case of wait and see.

In the final chapter, entitled 'Popular despotism: an economist's explanation', William Coleman of the Australian National University provides a more analytical challenge to the Popperian frame by considering sound economic reasons for why individuals would, at times, voluntarily form syndicates with a totalitarian head to achieve certain objectives. Drawing an analogy with pirate syndicates, Coleman suggests that, a priori, totalitarian regimes may not only be formed on rational grounds, but may also achieve certain goals with great success. The extent to which one wishes to treat this approach as a real challenge to the Popperian vision largely turns on whether one supports Popper's own rhetorical inclination of holding to strict dichotomies (such as totalitarianism versus democracy, open societies versus closed societies, and so on) and brooking no half-way houses (such as a liberal dictatorship or a democracy that cannot quite be called liberal), or if one interprets Coleman's syndicates as exceptions to the rule in a sea of possible exceptions to Popper's narrative, which is deemed sound enough, but does not provide the whole story of what makes a successful society. The chapter provides a neat ending to the proceedings.

5 Concluding remarks

The main failing of the book chapters that follow is that they do not collectively constitute a complete survey of the East Asian countries. Two chapters on Thailand, two chapters on Burma, one chapter on Singapore and one chapter on China, and a few contextual chapters do not 'East Asia' make. Japan, Taiwan, North Korea, South Korea, Malaysia, Vietnam and Kampuchea are, at most, mentioned as asides for illustrative or comparative purposes. The limited range of countries chosen for review was predominantly due to the fact that this edited book is a product of a one-day conference, and that there is simply a limit to the number of papers that one can fit into one day, and partly a function of the restrictions on the number of chapters that one can fit into a book of standard length. The soundest defence to the charge that the project has insufficient sweep is, however, that the purpose of the exercise is to illustrate the way Popper's world view is relevant to East Asian studies and thereby to induce specialists in this area to consider how Popper's writings may shed light on their areas of research. It is an illustrative, not a definitive, study. A second possible criticism of the studies which follow is that some authors engage directly and at length with how Popper's vision is relevant to their case study, while other authors simply make passing reference to one or two of Popper's insights in the process of considering the social and economic success or failure of a country with totalitarian inclinations. I believe, however, that this too is exactly what is wanted in a project with an objective of illustrating the relevance of a philosopher's frame. The goal, after all, is not to construct an army of parroting Popperian epigones (which rather goes against the whole principle of critical rationalism), but to show how Popper's vocabulary, philosophical ideas and historical conjectures may add value to any narrative devoted to East Asia. It may simply be a matter of drawing upon the concept of negative utilitarianism or the paradox of freedom, or using the Popperian view of historicism to question an officially sanctioned trajectory of a nation's history, or to consider the consequences of utopian engineering, and so on. Indeed, the way practitioners draw upon Popper after reading this volume is of less concern to me than achieving a greater goal of making readers aware that Popper was not just a philosopher of the first rank, but one of the great minds of the twentieth century. He is worth reading.

Notes

1 The recent announcement by the New Zealand Nabokovian scholar, Brian Boyd, that his official biography of Popper is once again in preparation, after being put to one side in the 1990s, leaves one with expectation that this flurry of scholarship will be added to soon. The biographies listed in the text above, which perhaps reflects the cult of the book, may be supplemented by very good 'essay' obituaries by David Miller (1997) for the *Biographical Memoirs of the Fellows of the Royal Society* and John

Watkins (1997a, 1997b) for the *Proceedings of the British Academy* and *American Scholar*. Hacohen's (1996, 1999, 2009) many journal articles also include valuable insights into Popper's life. Good character portraits of Popper are contained in Magee (1997) and, even though eccentric, Raphael (2000).

2 Popper's hostility to sociologies of knowledge and historicist historiographies on the grounds that they strip people of the capacity to make rational and moral choices that have meaningful consequences (as well as on the grounds that these conceptual frameworks have internal contradictions) occupies much of *The Open Society* and *The Poverty of Historicism* and is described in detail in the next section. Popper himself articulated his own problem-based historiographical position, which he called *situational logic*, in these and other books (see, e.g. 1966, ii, 97, 265), but specifically for the overlap between Popperian and Collingwoodian visions of intellectual history, see a paper he wrote in the late 1960s and later revised as "A Pluralist Approach to the Philosophy of History" (Popper 1994). In this publication he makes clear that, unlike Collingwood, he believes that the historian's sympathetic re-enactment of the inaccessible thought processes of the actor confronted with the problem is unimportant compared to making sense of the agent's decision by analysing the objective knowledge related to the 'problem situation' that can be critically analysed in the public domain. Popper's proposal that the historian needs to build the historical context in order to create a problem situation that an historical actor has to solve nonetheless bears a close resemblance to the stance of the Collingwoodian school (and thereby, to a lesser extent, to the modern Sussex and Cambridge contextual schools). The similarities between, and the failings of, the Popper and Collingwood positions are described in detail in Skagestad (1975) (see Moore (2010) for contextualism more generally). Needless to add, and this cannot be emphasized enough, the historiographical approach I deploy to understand Popper's decisions in the above narrative is driven by the modern contextualist traditions rather than every specific of Popper's situational logic, no matter how much they overlap. I am certain, for example, that Popper's strict reading of his own 'situation logic' approach would make him leery of any reference to his 'Jewish heritage' in an account of his intellectual choices, even if, in the context of my narrative above, the occasional reference to this heritage is to highlight the influence of the broad intellectual milieu of the Austro-Hungarian Jewish elite rather than any outrageous claim that 'we think with our blood' (and I would like to thank a referee for making this point). Finally, Popper himself reported that his approach was inspired by his Viennese mathematics professor, Hans Hahn, who treated the subject historically by considering each advance in infinitesimal calculus as a problem that an actor of the time had to solve (Hacohen 2000, 104).

3 The concept of totalitarianism is problematic, as it has formal properties within political philosophy that are not only contested in that discipline, but also diverge from the properties reflected in Popper's use of the term. I nonetheless follow Popper by using this concept broadly to mean an authoritarian, anti-democratic, anti-liberal, hierarchical and closed society: "what we call nowadays totalitarianism belongs to a tradition which is just as old or just as young as our civilization itself" (1966, i, 1). I do so all the while realizing that it is not quite a satisfactory use of the term.

4 Although modern economists may find this sort of analysis foreign, they should note that the discipline went a long way down the historicist route in the Victorian era following its advocacy by the historical schools of economics in the English, American and German *Methodenstreits* (or battles of method), and it was a near-run thing (partly attributable to some deft footwork by Alfred Marshall and John Neville Keynes) that the discipline did not take a more radical and permanent historicist turn. Also note that economic historicism is effectively a subset of the natural historicism in Popper's list in the above narrative, as economists presented them as laws of nature or singular trajectories by drawing upon Social Darwinism, Marxism, Comtism, Mill's Book IV

of *A System of Logic*, and Scottish and German stadial theories of growth (see Moore 1995, 1999, 2003). I am therefore bemused why Hacohen (2000, 352–8) would follow some of the contemporary reviewers of *The Poverty* in stating that it was an attack on a straw man, especially as he proceeds to examine the historicists targeted by Popper in the pages that follow this claim. There is, I grant, a problem with labelling Plato a historicist (see Klosko 1996). The historicism of Marx (made more problematic by asking which Marx, young or old?) is also clearly a very different matter to the more open and reformed Marxist historicism of the late twentieth century. The popular representation of Marxism in the 1930s was, however, largely as Popper presented it, and, as mentioned in the previous section, it was Popper's personal witnessing of the fatalism of the Austro-Marxists between the wars that drove his contempt for this approach. Finally, stadial theories (including Marxist theories) are still worthy of attention (a view I hold strongly) from a Popperian perspective if they are reinterpreted as trends that are dependent on initial conditions rather than historical laws or inevitable trajectories.

5 A good example of non-Marxist historicism, and mentioned in passing above, is W.W. Rostow's use of *The Stages of Economic Growth: A Non-Communist Manifesto* (1960) as a means to engineer a "Rostovian" take-off stage during the Indochinese wars so that Vietnam would imitate the European trajectory to liberal democracy. But see Young (1990, 2000, 53), Tucker (1999) and the later writings of Said for post-colonial critiques of historicism in orthodox Marxism, development economics generally, and other discourses engineered in the West and imposed on the East. Tucker (1999, 1) contends that development discourse, which is imperialist and based on myth, "portrays development as a necessary and desirable process, as human destiny itself", and hence is in need of deconstruction. Young (1990, 6–10) argues that the orthodox Marxist historicism prevents people from acting as agents of change (which was precisely Popper's point, but in relation to his support for piecemeal activism rather than revolutionary change) and, following Althusser and Mao, calls for an opening up of this historicism to allow multiple trajectories (but then what is left of Marxism?). In response to Tucker *et al.*, I would argue that Popper has already "deconstructed" and "opened up" historicism, and, further, the danger of taking this post-colonial line is a tendency to embrace historicism in another form, namely a singular Asian (or African or South American) trajectory. I am bewildered why there is only one reference to Popper (in a footnote in Young (1990) on a subject unrelated to historicism) in the books cited above. I can only presume that this lack of reference is because these advocates incorrectly presume Popper to be a neo-liberal. Such scholars would also no doubt reject the call for the universal applicability of an open society as another imperialist 'discourse' imposed by the 'ethnocentric' leaders in the dominant 'centre' on the 'others' residing in the 'periphery', and hence in need of 'deconstruction'. This post-colonial riposte to the concept of an open society should be taken seriously by Popperians even if one believes that the argument is taken too far and objects to the now dated postmodern jargon in which it was advanced. (And not all of these narratives are driven by what I call, after the indecipherable post-colonialist Homi K. Bhabha, Bhabharisms; Young's work, for example, is for the most part written in clean English). Finally, note that post-colonial criticism of essentialism is also anticipated by Popper.

6 Economists should, in particular, be alerted to the fact that Popper's critical rationalist framework is a complex and imposing edifice, since they, more than most, have tended to misrepresent Popper's contribution as no more than identifying the asymmetry between falsification and verification (even if they do occasionally make reference to the Duhem-Quine hypothesis or add a Lakatosian twist to this interpretation). As I have conveyed in the narrative, it is a neo-Kantian world in which conjectures spun out of our minds are constrained and adjusted via conflict with an independent objective reality that is derived by inter-subjective consent. The science/non-science

dichotomy also does not constitute a sense/non-sense dichotomy, since metaphysical and allied speculations are a source of the conjectures. Finally, it is again important to emphasize that although Popper did not believe that the falsification method, in its purest form, was suitable for non-scientific domains, he did hold that inspiration and conjectures held in check by a critical attitude informed by external objective knowledge were universally beneficial when they could be brought to bear.

7 It needs to be emphasized here that Popper's defence of an open society did not turn on greater economic growth (even though his narrative is heavy with implications for such growth), but on progress towards a humanitarian society. In an effort to demarcate his position from the Hayekian defence of such a society, he even once stated: "I consider it entirely wrong to base the rejection of tyranny on economic arguments.... It is not the inefficiency of communism that we are fighting, but its lack of liberty and of humanity" (Popper 2008, 34).

8 As Arendt (1951) reported, most European democracies voluntarily decided in favour of totalitarianism in the 1930s. The banality of evil was largely ushered in by the electorate.

9 As Solow (1994) suggests, the tangles of the causal processes that drive the creation of ideas and thereby growth are sufficiently complex that economic, political and cultural historians are at times better placed to make a contribution to this debate than econometricians and high theorists. The tenuous empirical studies that mount in the development journals are frightening to behold. Just think of the endless competing threads. First, the notions of freedom, democracy and liberty are too ill-defined to be captured in operational variables by statisticians. Second, it is possible to have some sort of freedom or liberty in one domain (such as in an economic transaction or the artistic act of a musical innovation) and not in another (such as in the choice of a political leader via the voting box or the artistic act of making a film), indicating that so-called closed and open societies are not so one-dimensional as they were in the 1930s. Third, economic historians put aside Leonard Read's *I Pencil* at times and grant that 'command-and-control' regimes in which free thought is frowned upon can actually outperform liberal democracies in producing a *limited* number of objects *en masse* (such as Moscow flats and hydro-eclectic projects) and even in an innovative way, especially when a commissar has a revolver at the nape of one's neck. China seems to have taken this one step further by holstering the revolver and out-sourcing this activity to state-owned businesses to produce objects (and innovations) *en masse*, which, because of the size of the population, collectively seem to mimic the myriad private businesses harnessing the array of resources to indirectly serve the myriad ends sought in the Western world. Fourth, the success of China is patently due to the fact that it is operating within the boundaries of the production frontier and harvesting the technology of the West (from secure property rights to the corporate form); that is, they are harvesting the spill-over effects of new technology so admired by the new growth theorists. The real test for such a country is whether or not it can out-compete the Western liberal democracies once it is located on the production frontier. Fifth, Popper failed to foresee the capacity for liberal democracies to descend into a sclerosis for the reasons outlined by the likes of Buchanan, Olsen and Stigler, nor the capacity of governments, such as the Thatcher government, to engineer Schumpeterian-style creative destruction as an antidote. Sixth, the short-term success of the Asian regimes may be attributed to benign dictators, and, as indicated by Popper, if there is no way of peacefully removing them via a democratic process when a short-sighted tyrant or oligarchy takes the helm, then short-term success is followed by long-term failure. And ... the list is endless. As stated in the narrative above, the debate is a dog's breakfast. Not surprisingly, those testing for the role played by democracy and liberty find a "mixed and confusing picture" "subject to much discussion" (see de Haan and Sierman (1996) and Sirowy and Inkeles (1990) for typical surveys).

10 Popper accepted that liberal democracies may fail, but in *The Open Society* at least, he was confident that they could succeed and, in response to the Marxists (and therefore the public choice theorists in our day), that the democratic leaders could make decisions without being manipulated by vested interests. See Shearmur (1996) for a lengthy, but gentle, critique of Popper's support for a liberal democracy, in which he contends (among many other arguments) that an open society may naturally implode through an internal dynamic that is Hayekian in nature. Specifically, he argues that the application of Popperian critical rationalism to construct liberal democratic institutions may erode the very institutions that allow critical rationalism and the open society to exist. In later years, Popper seemed to be even more explicit that democracy could fail. In a 1965 lecture entitled "Freedom: A Balance Sheet", he argued that if we choose freedom, we must be prepared to perish with it, as there is no guarantee that it will flourish (Shearmur 1996, 32).

11 It would be interesting to discover what Needham (a noted chemist, sinologist and fellow traveller) thought of Popper's philosophy of science. An early copy of Popper's manuscript devoted to the logic of discovery was sent to Needham in 1932 (see Hacohen 2000).

12 Slipping in this particular Popperian moral injunction within a broader account of piecemeal engineering may, in the reader's mind, suppress its importance within Popper's complex structure, and hence it should not pass without comment (and, indeed, for many reasons it should be another numbered theme in my list). Popper rejected the utilitarian scheme of a continuous and symmetrical pleasure–pain scale in which units of pleasure and pain are weighted equally. He contended that there is an asymmetry between pleasure and pain, which was metaphorically similar to the asymmetry between verification and falsification within the philosophy of science, and that minimizing pain is more important than maximizing net-pleasure. In other words, he wanted to model the decision making "negatively", just as in the philosophy of science. Popper called this approach "negative utilitarianism" and the term has stuck (and, given that he labels this important idea in no more than a footnote (1966, i, ch. 5, n. 6), it yet again reflects the richness and multi-layered nature of *The Open Society*). Popper also believed that unavoidable pain, such as in times of famine, should be relieved by assisting those suffering in equal measure (i, fn. 2, 284–5). It is also important to note that piecemeal engineering may be interpreted as the pursuit of 'low target' policies, but this does not quite capture what Popper meant, as he granted that some policies could be bold, only their boldness would be relative to the 'trial-and-error' history that allowed the complexity of the problem to be mastered (i, fn. 3, 285). Finally, negative utilitarianism should be considered alongside yet another Popperian moral injunction, moral egalitarianism, where all individuals are equally valuable, but space does not permit me to consider this.

13 Shearmur (1996, 22, 27) de-emphasizes the role played by Hayek in shaping Popper's views prior to the first edition of *The Open Society* and reports that Popper was surprised that Hayek had come to similar conclusions (from different premises) in *The Road to Serfdom*. The Hayekian influence on Popper in subsequent editions was, however, another matter, with Popper taking up Hayek's call for all government action to be implemented under the rule of law rather than through commissar edict. He never, however, really engaged with Hayek's criticisms of calculating values in socialist environments and, unlike Hayek, he believed that the concept of social justice was both useful and had a meaning which most people understood (Shearmur 1996, 12, 35). If anything, in relation to piecemeal engineering, Popper's stance was probably more influenced by his New Zealand colleagues, the New Zealand social welfare system and the social justice sentiments he paraded in his Red Vienna days. Indeed, it is interesting to note, at least for Antipodean economists (the majority of the authors in this volume), that the templates given by Popper for sound piecemeal engineering are C. Simkin's articles in the 1940s in the *Economic Record*. Simkin was one

of Popper's chief interlocutors during his New Zealand years and, by acting as Popper's sounding-board, arguably provided a greater contribution to knowledge than any of his contemporaries in economics.

14 In relation to that historical juncture, it should be emphasized that Popper's extended defence of a liberal democracy (theme 4 above), his critique of historicism (theme 2) and his promotion of piecemeal engineering (this theme) are all interconnected by his objection to Marxism and the dangers it posed in the postwar reconstruction of Europe. Specifically, and as stated at many points in this preface, his support for piecemeal engineering is largely an extended attack on Marx's historicist prophesy that capitalism would sow its own seeds of destruction and be replaced, inevitably, with a dictatorship of the proletariat. Popper objected to this line of thought, in chapters 19 through to 23 in volume two of *The Open Society* (but see also chapter 9), on the grounds that it encouraged individuals to resign themselves to historical forces rather than to pursue meaningful reform. He, in contrast, believed that individuals control their own destiny via a liberal democracy and could implement, via democratically determined piecemeal engineering, a more constrained capitalism in which workers were not exploited. Indeed, it is easy to detect Popper's controlled fury at his contemporaries in the Austro-Marxist movement for both baulking at supporting interventionist policies and not standing up to the fascists on the grounds that such actions would just delay the revolution, as dictated by the march of history (1966, ii, 182). He also rejected the associated Marxist proposition that the manipulation of political power by economic power cannot be checked, pointing out that the (piecemeal) welfare reforms which preceded the Great War showed not only that there was an alternative to naked capitalism which did not entail communism, but also that political acts can control the economic base rather than the reverse (1966, ii, 126–9). The link between Popper's 'conjecture and refutation' philosophy of science (theme 3) and his 'trial-and-error' piecemeal engineering should also be clear to the naked eye (1966, i, 163). The intermingling of the different ideas can only be really captured by reading the driving narrative of Popper's *The Open Society* in one sitting.

15 The reference to Pol Pot above points to a key utopian objection (and remember that once, many happily presented themselves as engineers of human souls) to piecemeal engineering; namely that a change of a piecemeal nature does not change the environment in which an actor is situated sufficiently to allow for a change in human nature or world view that is required for a utopian dream to be realized. Pol Pot noted the ease with which liberated Cambodian villages and towns returned to non-socialist ways after his soldiers passed through them in his early campaigns, and hence, in Year Zero, ruthlessly sent all urban individuals into the countryside, subsequently called the killing fields. The horror of Pol Pot's solution is indisputable, but the above-stated utopian objection to piecemeal engineering is sound enough.

16 The complexity of Popper's historiography is judiciously appraised in Peter Skagestad's *Making Sense of History* (see also Simkin 1993). Interestingly enough, Skagestad (1975, 38) also happens to illustrate the 'problem situation' method by focusing on the way in which Popper explained Plato's philosophizing as a rational response to a society's inability to cope with the strain of a society as it moves from a closed to an open society. Skagestad also makes it clear that this approach does not differ markedly from that proposed by Collingwood, in spite of Popper's own claims that Collingwood's calls for empathetic and sympathetic treatments of the historical agent, as well as stepping inside the historical agent's mind, amount to the sort of psychologizing he rejects.

17 Popper's self-confessed use of *The Open Society* to achieve his war aims is, of course, the main reason for this ruthless language. It may have also been simply an extension of Popper's legendary disposition to converse in a dominating, illiberal and ruthless manner. Magee (1997, 191) stated that Popper "pursued relentlessly, beyond the limits of acceptable aggression in conversation", and reported that Ernst Gombrich

likened it to arguing a case until the dissenter "put his signature to a confession that he was wrong and Popper was right". As mentioned earlier, Raphael (2000, 376) stated that academics gossiped that "*The Open Society* had been written by one of its enemies". The contradiction between Popper's critique of totalitarianism and his illiberal wish to subjugate others in conversation merely provides the historian with yet another insight into the complexities of human character.

18 Plamenatz (1952) is a good example of the umbrage taken at Popper's exegeses among his first reviewers. It also captures the aversion of the early reviewers to the shrillness of Popper's tone. Even the sympathetic reviews, such as Ryle (1947, 171), took exception to the excessive rhetoric of Popper's narrative: "it is hard tactics in a champion of the freedom of thought to use the blackguarding idioms characteristic of its enemies". Ryle thought the "verdicts" just, but that they would exert a greater influence if they had a more judicial tone. Given that Plamenatz and Ryle were Oxford men and reflected the tone of their institution, it is not surprising that Popper's later request for a position at Oxford was knocked back (Magee 1997, 73). The problem of Popper's shrill tone was compounded by the fact that Popper's liberal message was not in tune with the outlook of the 1940s. As in the case of Orwell's *Animal Farm*, Popper found it difficult to find a publisher (Raphael 2000, 376). *Poverty*, which was rejected in its article form by *Mind* (issued out of Oxford), was published in *Economica* via Hayek's role as editor of that journal, while *The Open Society* was repeatedly rejected until, once again through the work of Hayek, it was published by Routledge.

Bibliography

Arendt, H. 1951. *On the Origins of Totalitarianism.* New York: Harcourt, Brace and Co.

Bartley, W.W. 1989. *Rehearsing a Revolution. Karl Popper: A Life; Selection Entitled Music and Politics. Mimeo.* Written for the Mont Pelerin Society. Available at: http://thephilosophyofscience.files.wordpress.com/2011/07/rehearsing-a-revolution.pdf.

de Haan, J. and C. Siermann. 1996. "Political Instability, Freedom, and Economic Growth: Some Further Evidence". *Economic Development and Cultural Change* 44(2): 339–50.

Giannaras, A. and F. Eidlin, 1996. "Plato and K.R. Popper: Toward a Critique of Plato's Political Philosophy". *Philosophy of the Social Sciences* 26 (December): 493–508.

Hacohen, M.H. 1996. "Karl Popper in Exile: The Viennese Progressive Imagination and the Making of *The Open Society*". *Philosophy of the Social Sciences* 26(December): 452–92.

——. 1999. "Dilemmas of Cosmopolitanism: Karl Popper, Jewish Identity, and 'Central European Culture'". *Journal of Modern History* 71(March): 105–49.

——. 2000. *Karl Popper – The Formative Years, 1902–1945: Politics and Philosophy in Interwar Vienna.* Cambridge: Cambridge University Press.

——. 2009. "The Culture of Viennese Science and the Riddle of Austrian Liberalism". *Modern Intellectual History* 6(2): 369–96.

Hayek, F. 1944. *The Road to Serfdom.* Sydney: Dymocks.

——. 1952. *The Counter-Revolution in Science: A Study in Abuse of Reason.* Glencoe, IL: Free Press.

Janick, A. and S. Toulmin, 1973. *Wittgenstein's Vienna.* New York: Simon & Schuster.

Klosko, G. 1996. "Popper's Plato: An Assessment". *Philosophy of the Social Sciences* 26(December): 509–27.

Magee, B. 1973. *Popper.* London: Fontana.

——. 1997. *Confessions of a Philosopher.* London: Weidenfeld & Nicolson.

Martin, S. 2002. "Orwell's Burma". *Time Magazine*, New York.

Miller, D. 1997. "Sir Karl Raimund Popper, C.H., F.B.A. 28 July 1902 – 17 September 1994: Elected F.R.S. 1976". *Biographical Memoirs of Fellows of the Royal Society* 43: 367–409.

Moore, G. 1995. "The Role of Cliffe Leslie in the Early Stages of the English *Methodenstreit*". *Journal of the History of Economic Thought* 17(spring): 57–77.

——. 1999. "John Kells Ingram, the Comtean Movement, and the English *Methodenstreit.*" *History of Political Economy* 31(1): 53–78.

——. 2003. "John Neville Keynes and the English *Methodenstreit*". *Journal of the History of Economic Thought* 25(1): 5–38.

——. 2010. "Donald Winch in Context: An Essay on Wealth and Life". *History of Economics Review*. 52 (Summer): 77–109.

O'Hear, A. 2006. "Hayek and Popper: The Road to Serfdom and The Open Society". In E. Feser (ed.) *The Cambridge Companion to Hayek*. Cambridge: Cambridge University Press, pp. 132–47.

Perkins, D. 1994. "Completing China's Move to the Market". *The Journal of Economic Perspectives* 8(2): 23–46.

Plamenatz, J. 1952. "Review Article of The Open Society and Its Enemies by K.R. Popper". *The British Journal of Sociology* 3(3): 264–73.

Popper, K. 1945[1966]. *The Open Society and Its Enemies*, 2 volumes. London: Routledge.

——. 1957. *The Poverty of Historicism*. London: Routledge.

——. 1959. *The Logic of Scientific Discovery*. London. Hutchinson & Co.

——. 1974[1976]. *Unended Quest. An Intellectual Biography*. Revised Edition. Glasgow: Fontana Collins.

——. 1994. *The Myth of the Framework*. London: Routledge.

——. 2008. *After the Open Society: Selected Social and Political Writings*, edited by J. Shearmur and P.N. Turner. London: Routledge.

Raphael, F. 2000. "Popper". In R. Monk and F. Raphael (eds) *The Great Philosophers From Socrates to Turing*. London: Weidenfeld & Nicolson, pp. 369–406.

Revolutionary Council, The. 1962. *The Burmese Way to Socialism*. www.burmalibrary.org/docs/The_Burmese_Way_to_Socialism.htm.

Rostow, W.W. 1960. *The Stages of Economic Growth: A Non-Communist Manifesto*. Cambridge: Cambridge University Press.

Ryle, G. 1947. "Review of *The Open Society and Its Enemies* by Karl Popper". *Mind* 56(222): 167–72.

Said, E. 1978. *Orientalism*. New York: Vintage.

Schorske, C. 1980. *Fin-de-siècle Vienna. Politics and Culture*. New York: Vintage.

Sen, A. 1997. "Human Rights and Asian Values: What Lee Kuan Yew and Le Peng Don't Understand About Asia". *The New Republic*, 14 July: 1–9.

Shearmur, J. 1996. *The Political Thought of Karl Popper*. London and New York: Routledge.

Simkin, C. 1993. *Popper's Views on Natural and Social Science*. Brill: Leiden.

Sirowy, L. and A. Inkeles. 1990. "The Effects of Democracy on Economic Growth and Inequality: A Review". *Studies in Comparative International Development* 25(1): 126–57.

Skagestad, P. 1975. *Making Sense of History: The Philosophies of Popper and Collingwood*. Oslo: Universitetsforlaget.

Solow, R. 1994. "Perspectives on Growth Theory". *The Journal of Economic Perspectives* 8(1): 45–54.

Strauss, L. 1953. *Natural Right and History.* Chicago, IL: Chicago University Press.

Tucker, V. 1999. “The Myth of Development: A Critique of a Eurocentric Discourse.” In R. Munck and D. O’Hearn (eds) *Critical Development Theory: Contributions to a New Paradigm*. London: Zed Books.

Watkins, J. 1997a. “The British Academy: Obituary of Karl Raimund Popper: 1902–1994”. *Proceedings of the British Academy* 94: 645–84.

——. 1997b. “Karl Popper: A Memoir Magazine Article by John Watkins”. *American Scholar* 66(spring): 205–19.

Young, R.J.C. 1990[2004]. *White Mythologies: Writing History and the West.* 2nd edition. Abingdon: Routledge.

——. 2001. *Postcolonialism. An Historical Introduction.* Oxford: Blackwell.

1 Karl Popper and the idea of an open society

Jeremy Shearmur

1 Introduction

People in Western societies often think of the societies in which they live as being 'open societies' – at least in aspiration – and for an explication of the idea of an open society they may well refer to Karl Popper's *The Open Society and Its Enemies*. While the term 'open society' was used before Popper by Henri Bergson, in what Popper indicates is a rather different sense, the idea did receive its classic exposition in Popper's work.[1] The key idea is in some ways best understood as a statement and defence of what is involved in a modern, individualistic and abstract society, made in the face of nostalgia, of various kinds, for the values of community. It is important here to note that while Popper was, emphatically, a democrat, he did not simply equate an open society with democracy, and one can see important aspects of his analysis as warning democratic populations about the problems of certain ideas that they may find all too appealing. At this level, Popper's argument is that, while communitarian ideals, and the idea of a society in which people would not be subject to the strains and tensions that arise in an individualistic and abstract society, might be attractive, there is no going back to them from the kind of social arrangements with which we are now living. For Popper argues that, rather than the restitution of some kind of *Gemeinschaft*, the attempt to do so would produce not a community of the kind that its proponents would find attractive, but, rather, a kind of tyranny.

Popper's account was written with an eye to the situation of societies undergoing problems associated with certain particular kinds of modernization in the first part of the twentieth century. However, beyond talking in this context about the problems of a 'fatherless society', and of 'the strains of civilization' as an ongoing problem facing those living in such societies (something that I will discuss below), Popper did not offer a detailed sociological analysis of the issues with which he was concerned.[2] But it is interesting that he suggested that there were certain similarities between the situation against which Plato was writing, in Classical Greece, and his own analysis – as well as between Plato's response to them, and those of whom Popper was critical in mid-twentieth century Europe.[3] The contemporary situation in the various – and very different – countries of South East Asia is itself somewhat different; not least because, if they are aspiring towards the ideal of a commercial and open society, they are typically doing so against an authoritarian backdrop. That is to say, the problem situation in those countries may more typically be that of people aspiring towards life in open societies, rather than that of people in open societies aspiring towards goals that may be problematic for the continued existence of such societies as open societies.

Popper's ideas, however, still seem to me to be very pertinent. First, Popper places emphasis on the significance of individual responsibility for what occurs in politics and history. Such a stress is not incompatible with an appreciation of the importance of institutions (and of the difficulties that arise, if appropriate institutions are not in place). It is also, obviously, compatible with the idea that we act in the setting of problems which no one intended to bring about, and which may be difficult to tackle. But Popper stresses the difference between an appreciation of these things, and the idea that what happens in history is inevitable: that there is no option for us but to go with the flow, or to adopt what we take the outcomes of social trends to be, uncritically, as normative goals that we should further.

My concern in what follows, however, will be with how Popper characterized an open society and also with some of the problems he highlighted about such societies. Popper, as I have mentioned, discussed what he called 'the strains of civilization': the way in which our societies thrust the need to make decisions, and for people to take responsibility for the decisions they make, onto people whether they like this responsibility or not. He also described such societies as 'fatherless', by which he meant that, in them, there were no 'natural' authorities such that if, within them, we wished to give over decision making to some authority, it is still our decision so to do. Popper's *Open Society* also contains an interesting discussion of the way in which, within such societies, life can take on highly anonymous characteristics. We can live much of our lives doing work for people whom we do not know, consuming products made by people whom we do not know, and could, indeed, live for considerable periods without any direct contact with other people at all – while at the same time, benefiting from the products that many, many people have worked on. It is easy enough to understand how, in the face of this, people may look back with longing to life in settings which involved them in stronger notions of community; in which, in effect, the kinds of relationships that people now may enjoy only in families, and close friendships at their best, may come to define society more generally.

Popper's book, however, was not concerned just to explore this issue. He was also critical of various ideas which, at the time, seemed to suggest that it would be both possible and good to move away from an open society towards arrangements which were more communitarian, while still enjoying the kinds of freedoms characteristic of an open society. In addition, he offered a positive characterization of an open society, and an account of how he believed it could most usefully conduct itself. I will discuss this positive characterization first, and then turn to ideas that he believed could call such an open society into question should we respond to them in ways that he thought inappropriate. I will, in conclusion, discuss some problems that face an open society.

2 The idea of an open society

There are, it seems to me, six particular characteristics of an open society in Popper's sense: (at least) minimal democracy; pluralism; openness to criticism; the rule of law; markets; and what Popper called 'protectionism'. Let me discuss them in turn.

Popper was, emphatically, a democrat, and he was also strongly egalitarian in sentiment. His work is scathing about those who consider others to be lesser than themselves. At the same time, Popper's concern, here, is not with factual claims about people – say, about their intelligence and capacities – but with moral claims that they all deserve to be respected. There is, here, a strong if unorthodox Kantian influence upon Popper's sensibilities, if not upon his arguments. At the same time, Popper is convinced that in a society of any size, it makes little sense to say that everyone should rule. Indeed, he is well known for having argued that we should not ask 'Who should rule?' – as positive answers to this can generate paradoxes (as when, say, democratic citizens vote to transfer power to a 'strong man') and more substantively invite us to contemplate ideas that are utopian, or simply call for the domination of some over others. Instead, he suggests that we should address the question: How can we design our institutions so that those with political power can do least harm? It is in this context – and indeed, in a very limited way – that Popper strongly favours democracy. His concern, here, is that the population should be able to get rid of bad rulers by means of elections, and without bloodshed. He also favoured the idea that governments should be clearly accountable, and was critical of forms of proportional representation which would dilute the extent to which voters could be sure of being able to get rid of people and governments whom they felt had done a bad job.[4] Such an idea of democracy, while important, is obviously fairly limited in its scope. It is striking that Popper did not supplement it with more extensive notions concerning participation. Popper's minimalist characterization of democracy led Carlos Verdugo to criticize his account,[5] as being compatible with a regime like that set up by General Pinochet in Chile. In our present context one might ask: But does this not mean that Singapore, say, is democratic in this restricted sense of Popper's? To this, one would have to respond: Democratic, yes; but this does not mean that it is a fully open society. I will return to this issue later, when I consider Popper's ideas about the scope of the activities of government in an open society and what he says about openness to criticism.

Second, there is pluralism. Popper does not say much about this, although he does, in his 'Of Clouds and Clocks', refer to:[6]

> one of the characteristics of an open society [as being] that it cherishes … the freedom of association and that it protects and even encourages the formation of sub-societies, each holding different opinions and beliefs.

Popper's discussion of this is brief, and is – in terms of what we are used to in 'Western' societies – conventional. However, it is worth noting that there is a difference between two ways in which such organizations may be understood. One would be for them simply to be voluntary groups, which people form to pursue common aims or concerns. A second, which is more controversial, concerns the role such groups may have as vehicles for the pursuit of people's political interests; i.e. where a key concern of theirs is seen as making representation of their concerns to the government. Two points may be noted about pluralism in this latter sense. First, pluralism of this kind is not necessarily to be found in all societies which are 'democratic' in Popper's minimalist sense. In particular, while in Singapore there are certainly competing political parties, and people can form all kinds of organizations, there is a sharp line between social organizations and political activity, such that many of the quasi-political roles played by such groups in Western societies are there ruled out. Second, while ideas about politically related pluralism are deeply engrained in Western societies – ranging from the competitive pluralism of Britain and the United States, to the corporatism of some European countries – and while the freedom to form such organizations is deeply cherished, it is not so clear that their operation is necessarily in the public interest.

One might, here, highlight two issues. The first – to which we will return – concerns how the operation of such organizations relates to other aspirations Popper has for an open society. The second relates to the body of critical literature that developed concerning American pluralism. Here, to cut a long story short,[7] as a corrective to the idea that such arrangements allowed for the articulation of the interests of those whose concerns were not being adequately satisfied by society as it currently operated, it was argued that such arrangements systematically advantaged some people and disadvantaged others. While anyone was free to combine with others to pursue their shared concerns, issues of wealth, education, and the structural role of different bodies in the organization of countries, to say nothing of the kinds of issues which were raised in the 'community power debate',[8] may well suggest that such a pluralism is, to say the least, a mixed blessing. Corporatism also poses problems: it may serve to entrench particular interests to the exclusion of others, or particular conceptualizations of what people's interests are, and how they are best pursued.

Both Popper and his friend Friedrich Hayek, while democrats, stressed what seems to me the important point that democracy needs to be judged instrumentally, rather than being taken as something that is good in itself. But if this holds good in respect of democracy, we should also, surely, take the same view about pluralism and its character. While those of us who have grown up in societies in which such organizations are familiar typically favour them, and cherish our right to form them, what social organizations we have a right to form should, surely, be considered in the light of their consequences. It would seem, for example, perfectly reasonable that some of what had become the rights of trades unions should have been limited when they started to be exercised in ways that adversely affected the operation of society as a whole. Similarly, it would seem to me at least arguable that the influence the AARP has gained in the United States may equally be judged problematic; for example, in limiting the discussion of the possibilities of the reform of the Social Security system.[9]

Third, there is openness to criticism. This plays a key role in Popper's work. First, it is significant because of his epistemological fallibilism – his view that even the best of our theories may be flawed, and may have content of which their originators will not be aware – and also because of his view that our actions typically have unintended consequences, many of which we cannot anticipate, and some of which may be problematic. These ideas are linked, in Popper's argument, to the idea that anyone may be a pertinent source of criticism. Clearly, in ideas to do with theoretical knowledge, people may need to have appropriate capacities and also an appropriate training in order to be able to understand what is going on, and to make a contribution to its critical discussion. But in the sphere of political and social affairs, Popper in *The Open Society* stresses – developing his argument with the aid of interesting quotations from Pericles and Burke – that while not everyone may be able to initiate proposals as to how societies should be conducted, anyone may be able to criticize them. Perhaps the most obvious way in which we can cash out this idea is in terms of thinking that each individual typically knows their own situation best – that of themselves, and of those immediately around them – and if there are unexpected and undesirable consequences of the actions of other people or of government, each individual may have valuable potential input to social decision making with regard to these matters, and in this respect may be on a par with everyone else. Popper, here, refers to the Kantian notion of the 'rational unity of mankind', and it is worth noting that in Popper's work, rationality is to be understood in terms of the potentiality to offer criticism.

Ian Jarvie (2001) has argued, I think persuasively, that Popper's approach to the philosophy of science is best understood as a normative social theory (see also, on this theme, Shearmur 1980, 1985). Popper himself, however, tended to be impatient about the exploration of issues to do with the normative sociology of knowledge.[10] However, there is an obvious sense in which the idea of the importance of individuals being able to offer criticism may suggest political and social consequences. Compare, for example, the way in which John Stuart Mill, in his *Subjection of Women*, is critical of the social and political arrangements of his time which gave women less than full liberal rights, in part because of the way in which they led to the suppression of women's voices, and thus limited the discovery of truth. I have elsewhere suggested that one might, from these notions of Popper's, develop ideas about what may be called 'dialogue rights' – i.e. requirements for the according of people a certain kind of autonomy, in order to enable them to contribute to the discovery of truth, or the correctness of claims of moral validity.[11] There is an obvious enough parallel here with the use that Jürgen Habermas makes of (somewhat different) epistemological ideas, for the sake of social criticism.

Popper's own emphasis is much more practical. He is concerned with the idea that the views of those holding power may be incorrect, and that their actions may give rise to suffering. He is concerned that there be effective critical feedback, and to this end that social policy take an experimental form, but of a 'piecemeal' kind such that, if things go wrong, we can learn that there are errors, and put things right.[12] This idea plays a key role in Popper's view of an open society, and may be described as giving it one of its most important characteristics. However, as I recall one of those who was particularly enthusiastic about Popper's ideas, Tyrrell Burgess, pointing out, it is an idea that those who are involved in politics, the public service, or more generally running institutions seem particularly reluctant to embrace. It is interesting, in this context, that in Popper's old age he warmly received some suggestions, offered by the sociologist Ralph Dahrendorf, to the effect that it would be good to have, within the public service but distanced from political control, a body the key task of which was to assess the extent to which legislation in fact achieved what it had aimed to do.[13]

Popper, as I will explain, was concerned with the protection of individuals within an open society, and had ideas – upon which it seems to me that the Kantian tradition exercised an influence – about what may be termed their rights. But how he saw these rights was far from the Lockean and American tradition. This may be seen in terms of some of the concerns of his old age. For Popper, a key social concern should be the prevention of suffering, and he became worried about the way in which the sensibilities that underpinned this might be undermined by the effects of television. Popper, for many years, had no television, and seems to have been really shocked when he finally got to see it. (One wonders what his reaction may have been to the development of highly sophisticated computer games, often themed around the exercise of extreme violence.) Popper was worried about whether this would lead to people becoming desensitized to violence and suffering, and was concerned to bring home to those involved with the making of television programmes their responsibility for the likely effects of their work. He mooted the idea that there should be some form of licensing – after a training in which the character of these issues was brought home to those involved, and where the licences might be taken away.[14] I do not wish to try to evaluate the merits of Popper's suggestions here, about which I have some doubts; but they were a real concern of his, in the sense of something upon which he was working, up until the very point of his death. More important, I think, than the specifics of his suggestions, was the way in which his concerns here related to the idea that we should constantly be on the lookout for the problematic social consequences of the actions of ourselves and of others, and be ready to scrutinize them critically. While Popper was – as I will explain – concerned about the freedom of individuals, and concerned with the rule of law, he did not see this in terms of people having particular formal rights which could not be called into question, should they generate problematic consequences.

Next, there is the issue of the rule of law. In his *Open Society*, Popper developed ideas about what he called 'piecemeal social engineering' – which I will discuss shortly – which was to be directed towards the remedying of issues concerning which there was general agreement that they were problematic.[15] He stressed, however, that this activity should take place by means of institutionalized procedures, rather than personal discretion on the part of the public service. While Popper stressed institutionalization – and responded warmly to his friend

Hayek's suggestions about the importance of this – Popper does not offer much by way of detail concerning how such a society should operate. (It would, perhaps, be churlish to press this, as the book was long – to the point of his encountering huge problems in getting it published at all – and contained a vast amount of material, from critical engagements with those he took to be enemies of the open society, to discussion of many philosophical and historical issues.)

It is, however, interesting that when Popper returned to the themes of *The Open Society* in his old age (e.g. when he had the opportunity to add material to a Russian edition after the fall of the Soviet Union) a key concern of his was with the introduction of an adequate legal system, and with the retraining of Russian judges and other officials concerned with the administration of law, in Western countries.[16] Popper suggested – here drawing a parallel with Japan's introduction of the German civil code – that the introduction of a new system of law, and also the introduction of new officers of the courts trained in the ideas of law in an open society, was a key priority. Indeed, it is striking that, for Popper, it is this, rather than economic ideas about privatization, that was really the key step.

Popper, it should be noted, is sometimes assimilated to the 'New Right' – to economic liberalism. This seems to me to be a mistake (although I have argued in my *Political Thought of Karl Popper* that there are arguments as to why he should have been closer to such ideas than he was). Popper both knew and shared the concerns of many who were deeply involved with such matters, such as his friend Hayek. But while Popper favoured a market economy, it played a relatively minor role in his work.[17] It is striking but characteristic that when Popper was approached about the 'Principles of Freedom' series – a series of semi-popular books, the publication of which was subsidized by a number of large US companies – he was critical of the fact that the books seemed to stress only economic liberties.[18] Indeed, in correspondence with Rudolf Carnap after the Second World War, Popper, while explaining that he was no longer a socialist (as he had been in Vienna), indicated that he was willing that there be experimentation with the nationalization of monopolies – provided that there could be effective critical scrutiny of their performance. And as late as 1974, in correspondence with his friend and at that time Labour Member of Parliament Bryan Magee, Popper was willing to contemplate the partial nationalization of industry.[19] At the same time, more conservative and market-orientated ideas are also to be found in some of his writings, and he considered bureaucracy to be a massive unresolved problem for any form of socialism.

All this brings me to what Popper called 'protectionism' – and the relation between this and his more general ideas about politics. For these, I believe, along with fallibilism and the importance of critical scrutiny, lie at the heart of his ideas about an open society.

Popper places considerable emphasis on what he calls 'protectionism'. By this, however, he meant not economic protectionism – in the sense of an opposition to free trade – but, rather, the idea that the individual should be protected by law, with the power of the state behind it. It is important to bring out two things.

First, what was to be protected? Here, Popper's concern was with the kinds of things that liberals had stressed in terms of individual rights. But Popper's account also included protection from economic exploitation. Popper did not spell out in detail what he favoured here, but he was concerned with protecting people from having to make agreements which exploited them, and he was sympathetic to ideas about a guaranteed basic income, financed from taxation.[20] Second, how was all this conceptualized? Popper, as I have mentioned, did not think in terms of 'natural rights'. By contrast, he stressed the notion of laws which protect people being the creation of the state. It would seem to me that his ideas, here, are best understood in terms of Kantian influences, and that the result brings him close to what has, more recently, been written up as a 'republican' notion of freedom. (It is, in this context, telling that Popper has described as unsatisfactory a situation in which people enjoy toleration because of the kindness, or even angelic qualities of the strong; by contrast, he insists on the importance of a 'legal claim to be protected against the power of the strong', and 'that we need a state that protects the rights of all'.[21]) Indeed, the theme of each individual's enjoyment of liberty as a legal right, and the security of his or her freedom by this means from domination by others, plays a characteristic role in Popper's work. However, this is only part of Popper's approach; the other side of it relates to his ideas about the wider agenda for governmental action – something that should, it seems to me, be seen as operating within a framework of legally guaranteed rights, understood in the 'republican' sense indicated above.

A key theme in Popper's *Open Society* is thus his proposal of an agenda for governmental action, to be formulated in terms of consensually agreed ideas about evils that may in principle be remedied. Popper was writing at a time when there was considerable ideological disagreement. He took the view that while argument about political ideals and ideologies could take place, and while we might learn in discussion, we were not likely to be able to reach agreement. There was a risk that some would end up trying to impose their ideals upon other people, and to inflict a lot of suffering for the sake of the achievement of long-term – and fallible – ideals. Popper was also critical of political approaches which gave up on rational discussion, because it seemed to him that the alternative to reason was violence. And he was led to set out an approach which he offered as an alternative to both the liberalism and the socialism which were influential when he was writing.[22]

Popper's idea was that if one asked people about their ideals they might be found to disagree a great deal, and the very things that some people found particularly attractive others might find unattractive, or regard as utopian and unrealizable. If, by contrast, you asked them what concrete things were problematic they might find themselves much more able to agree. And it was what they could agree to be unacceptable that would, in Popper's view, generate the agenda for political action. These ideas have been referred to as 'negative utilitarianism'; but this seems to me to be misleading as a description, since Popper himself was perfectly happy to refer to cases of injustice as something that people might agree were unacceptable. It is in this context that the issue with which I have earlier reported Popper as being concerned – that violent television might dull our sensibilities – becomes significant. Popper also refers – in connection with the work of Trollope, an author of whom he was particularly fond – to the role that was played in public debate by the moral sensitivity of public opinion, and to people's intuitions about injustice; but he also expresses concern about the degree to which Trollope's points would hold good in other societies, or whether they would necessarily continue to hold good in Britain (see Popper 1963, 348–9).

One might put Popper's point in more contemporary terms in the following way. Robert Nozick (1974, 310), as part of his argument in the 'utopia' section of his *Anarchy, State, and Utopia*, wrote as follows:

> Wittgenstein, Elizabeth Taylor, Bertrand Russell, Thomas Merton, Yogi Berra, Allen Ginsburg, Henry Wolfson, Thoreau, Casey Stengel, The Lubavitcher Rebbe, Picasso, Moses, Einstein, Hugh Heffner, Socrates, Henry Ford, Lenny Bruce, Baba Ram Dass, Gandhi, Sir Edmond Hillary, Raymond Lubitz, Buddah. Frank Sinatra, Columbus. Freud, Norman Mailer, Ayn Rand, Baron Rothschild, Ted Williams, Thomas Edison, H. L. Mencken, Thomas Jefferson, Ralph Ellison, Bobby Fischer, Emma Goldman, Peter Kropotkin, you, your parents. Is there really *one* kind of life which is best for each of these people?

Popper's point would be that while there is no positive ideal upon which they could agree, there may nonetheless be things that they can all agree are undesirable. (Although, clearly, once one turns to *what* should be done and *how*, one might still face problems. For while, say, there might be agreement that people living in dire poverty other than as a result of their own positive decision is bad, what needs to be done, who the appropriate actors are, and what means they should use might reopen disagreements which could prove intractable.)

What, in *Popper*'s view, should then occur? For Popper – and in this his views are in line with most people today, other than strongly market-inclined libertarians, and certain socialists and anarchists – there should be public discussion about what is unacceptable, and presumably about what our priorities should be. (Positive ideals, and those things which people judge to be unacceptable but in respect of which they find that others do not agree, become matters for non-coercive private action; while Popper does not discuss the idea, his approach would seem to me to be compatible with the idea of the private provision, to members of particular communities, of various things on a collective basis, after the fashion of Nozick's 'utopia'.) The development of a rough consensus about such things, and their relative priorities, would presumably be something in which an intellectual elite, as well as various organizations, would have a role, as would be the suggestion of measures which might be taken to address the problems. Such ideas would then be open for general appraisal, as would what occurs when action is taken upon them.

Popper did not address the issue of what institutions would be needed for such purposes, and of how they might function. If people find Popper's approach attractive, this is clearly an issue which they might then address. To a degree, we have institutions which perform such functions in our own various societies – but they often face problems of various kinds, to the point where we might be led to scepticism about them. Just because the issues are diverse and complex, I will not discuss them here (but see Shearmur 2002, 2011). But there is a sense in which Popper's concerns pick up on concerns which are more widely shared,[23] and which pose some interesting questions for us at the time of writing. It is, however, worth noting that Popper stressed the degree to which we may need to limit our concerns to a negative and limited agenda if we are to hope for agreement.[24] He has also argued that while rational discussion is of key importance, we must not overestimate what we may expect it to achieve, stressing the difficulty – but also the potential fruitfulness – of argument between people whose viewpoints are very different, provided that they are in principle willing to learn from one another.[25] At the same time, and in a manner which might serve to limit the expectations of some of those who favour 'deliberative democracy', he has pointed to the way in which there were extensive discussions between Niels Bohr and Albert Einstein, which did *not* lead to agreement, but which were, nonetheless, fruitful. Above all, Popper argues for the importance of rationality, a willingness to learn from what others have to say, and modesty about our own ideas.

3 Some problems for open societies

Our concern, in looking at Popper's ideas, was in part to see what his explication of the idea of an open society amounted to; in part to use this as a lens through which to look at our own societies, and at ideals which we might wish to commend to those in societies geographically close to our own. Popper's ideas have a pertinence here, as a central concern of his was with life in an extended, commercial society; one in which the social bases of older ideas of community have fallen apart, and in which, in our day-to-day lives, we depend on the activities of countless other people with whom we do not, and cannot, have personal relationships.[26] Certain of the kinds of social change that our ancestors went through in Europe are now being experienced by people in the region with which this volume deals – although, obviously, under different conditions. In addition, some – but not necessarily all – of the features of 'modern' Western societies are ones to which people living in the countries of our region may well aspire, and others of them could well be things they are likely to get, whether they aspire to them or not, because of their connection with other things to which they aspire.

I will, with this in mind, survey some of the problems that open societies may themselves face. I will, again, do this using Popper's work as a point of entry.

One obvious problem concerns our knowledge. Popper was critical of those attracted to arrangements which looked rather like a modernized version of Plato's *Republic*, in which philosopher-kings ruled for the benefit of the entire society. Such ideas echoed through history, and were often found attractive by intellectuals who thought that the societies in which they lived would be better if they held a more powerful position – consider, in the Western tradition, Moore's *Utopia*, Sir Francis Bacon's *New Atlantis*, the ideas of the Saint-Simonians and the young Auguste Comte,[27] and the way in which these themes were taken up by some of the Fabians, and defended explicitly in the writings of H.G. Wells. Popper, by contrast with this, stresses the fallibility of those with political power, and the idea that they are in need of critical feedback from all citizens.

One might, however, pose two problems here. First, can people offer effective leadership if they admit the fallibility and openness to criticism which Popper is after? While this is a general sociological problem, it is striking that Popper himself was not strong on this point. It was reportedly said of Popper, by Paul Lazarsfeld, who knew him in Vienna, that Popper would be neither a leader nor a follower (cf. Hacohen 2002). And when, later, Popper himself had followers they were often seen as being uncritical, Ernest Gellner – in many ways sympathetic to Popper's approach[28] – being led to reflect on the dynamics of their relationship by referring to 'The Open Society by one of its enemies'. Popper, in his old age, was to write of a politics that he would like, as being one in which different politicians competed in telling of the errors they had made, and how they had learned from them. But this is a far cry from politics in Western countries today – in which active politicians seldom admit that they have ever been mistaken, and if they do, are seldom allowed to forget it by their opponents.

Second, we may ask: How, within an open society, are we to make best use of what knowledge we in fact have? Clearly, our knowledge is fallible; but it may be difficult to understand, let alone appraise correctly, our current theoretical ideas. There is a real risk that in our role as ordinary citizens we may reject unwelcome ideas, and instead choose to accept ideas that are more convenient, and fit better our moral notions, but which, in fact, are incorrect. (In this context, consider, for example, the problems of the popular appraisal of claims about the safety or otherwise of nuclear power, issues about global warming and problems about macroeconomics.) As I write, the United States faces some particularly difficult problems emerging from the global financial crisis: measures were taken which it was claimed were necessary to maintain the stability of the financial system, but which looked, to many people, as if the rich were being assisted – and often rewarded for morally problematic behaviour – at the expense of ordinary citizens. This, understandably enough, led to moral revulsion – but there this took two opposed forms, in terms of the Tea Party and the Occupy Wall Street movement, the emergence of which in turn may well have disruptive effects upon the longer term operation of the American political system. Scepticism may lead to real problems – especially if, indeed, we need to face expensive and difficult adjustments in the face of economic and environmental changes. Yet a credulous willingness to believe whatever those in power are saying also has its obvious difficulties (as perhaps our willingness to accept recent limitations on liberty for the sake of security may illustrate!).

There are also problems with the operation of political pluralism. Organized interest groups – whether of powerful industrialists or of large groups of citizens with a common concern – may make rational policy making difficult. Politicians may find that it is not possible to get elected without buying off different interests in their regions or constituencies. But this may well mean that the most pressing problems go unaddressed. One may all too easily set up arrangements – such as the US Social Security system – which may develop in ways that are unfair, and problematic for national well-being, but which it becomes almost impossible, politically, to change, while secret interactions between government and powerful commercial operations may lead to their being granted deals that are also far removed from the public interest. Popper's ideal of people coming to a consensual agreement as to what problematic issues are most urgent is attractive; but it is not clear how we can achieve it within anything like the political systems to be found within Western democratic countries.

There are also some interesting problems about *us*. The societies in which we live accord us a high degree of free consumer choice. I have recently spent some time in the United States where I was struck by just how powerful the spell is of advertising – and also by just how beguiling are all the varieties of easily available fast food. I have for much of my life been overweight. It was striking to be in a country in which I by no means stood out as fat, and in which I was able to purchase clothes *well* below the largest sizes on offer in ordinary stores. It is striking that it has been estimated that, as of 2010, 15.5 million people in the US were classified as 'morbidly obese' (i.e. as having a BMI of over 40); see Sturm and Hatori 2013. All this, it seems to me, points to a problem about how we may behave in situations in which we are free to make decisions for ourselves. Societies like the United States and Australia are ones in which people really are free to make choices for themselves; in which one can easily get into a situation like that feted by Mill in his *On Liberty*, where people can enjoy their individuality, without suffering from 'the tyranny of the majority'. But will we, in such situations, make *good* choices?

One important issue, here, would seem to me to be a product of other kinds of freedom of choice. It is striking that people in Western countries now have easy access to the internet, to a plethora of information, and to (virtual) communities of our own choosing, by way of social networking sites. We are doubtless influenced by others. But the others by whom we choose to be influenced are increasingly up to us. There is a sense in which a shift away from domination by our betters, to say nothing of by Mrs Grundy, is liberating; and for those who have the resources and the ability to handle these matters effectively, the result may be a real enhancement of life. But there is equally a risk that those people who are less resilient, and who have fewer resources – financial, intellectual or emotional – may face real problems if their choices are unwise. Indeed, it is worth noting that the very choices we are making are in some ways weakening institutions upon which we have depended in the past. The fact that many of us obtain our news from Google News rather than from quality newspapers has had dramatic consequences for the operation of those newspapers – and has led to the loss, notably in the United States, of a number of quality papers, and to the emasculation of others. What remains may simply not be able to undertake the kind of detailed investigative reporting, or to offer the kind of expertise, that it did in the past. Television networks are suffering in similar ways, while there is a risk that news-only television programmes play to our preconceptions, and offer us the entertainment we find attractive, rather than the hard analysis of our views and preconceptions which we need.

All this leads on to two issues about us. Consider the issue of people's moral sensitivity. This clearly plays an important role in the kind of account that Popper gives of how an open society should work – it requires that we be open to being moved by the suffering of others, and by injustice. But, as Popper noted in his 'Public Opinion and Liberal Principles' (in Popper 1963), what is involved is hardly something that is universal. In addition, as he indicated in his concerns about television, it is surely the case that it may be affected by the cultural context in which we operate. We may point to significant achievements here – to our revulsion for slavery, to our concern for equality across the sexes, to our concern for the rights of homosexuals, and to the striking changes that have taken place, also relatively recently, in our attitudes towards animals. In all these areas, and more, there may surely be much room for improvement. Yet are we unaffected by what we choose by way of entertainment? Does it really make no difference to us if we live in wonderfully constructed fantasy worlds of sheer brutality, in which moralized violence conquers all, and in which there are no moral dilemmas? And what of the creeping, not just explicitness but sheer brutality, of easily available commercial pornography? Just what will we make of ourselves through our choices and the impact of what we choose upon us?

The second issue, however, points in a rather different direction. One of the concerns of Karl Popper's friend Friedrich Hayek was with a theme which had been stressed in the work of David Hume. One might, in terms which address a contemporary open society, put the issue thus. An open society stands in need of a system of property rights, and an associated legal system, which has a certain systematic character. Within such a system, people can tell what will happen if they make a contract and the other party fails to fulfil it. This, in turn, means that they can engage in large-scale activities which involve bringing together many different things, to accomplish particular purposes which may be of key importance for the economic functioning of such a society, and for the well-being of the people within it. Yet, as Hume stressed, if we consider the individual case, what takes place may seem really unfair: goods, or real estate, may be taken from someone who desperately needs them, and given to someone who in any ordinary sense does not, but who has legal title to them. More generally, as Hayek himself was to stress, markets reward people for providing what other people want at the right time and place, not on the basis of what they might merit.[29]

All this may seem morally reprehensible; but it may well be the case that we need such arrangements in place: that we may not be able to operate a market-based society unless we accept the occurrence of such things. But this is yet another piece of theoretical knowledge which it is difficult for us to appraise. If we accept it, should we also accept *any* claim that those who are rich and powerful are making?[30] Yet if we do not, there is surely a risk that we will demand that the legal system does not disadvantage those whom Hume suggested would be disadvantaged by the legal system required by a commercial society. We can easily be influenced by appeals to our sentiments, in settings in which it is not clear what the longer term consequences of our actions will be. An open and commercial society seems to require certain kinds of characteristics on the part of its citizens if it is to function well – or, indeed, to function at all. But what, if anything, serves to foster those characteristics within an open society in which we have now what are almost unimagined freedoms of choice, and in which people are all too happy to sell us what we want, however bad the consequences may be for us individually, or for the societies in which we live?

Notes

1 This has an element of contingency to it, not least because Popper was unsure what his book should be called, and there was a risk that it might have ended up entitled *A Political Philosophy for Everyman.*

2 It would, I think, be interesting to explore these issues in the context of ideas about historical path-dependency of the kind associated with Barrington Moore Jr. (e.g. Moore 1966) and Theda Skocpol (e.g. Skocpol 1979); but that is clearly an issue for an occasion other than this.

3 See not just Popper's *Open Society*, but also his 'Theory of Totalitarianism', now published as chapter 14 in Popper (2008) *After The Open Society.*

4 He was critical, in this context, of proportional representation of kinds where the leading figures in unsuccessful governments might well turn up again in the next government, because they were high on their party's 'list'. See his 'On Democracy' (1988), now chapter 41 in Popper (2008) *After The Open Society.*

5 In a paper 'Popper on Democracy', delivered at a conference on Popper's work in Vienna in 2002 but which has not, to my knowledge, been published.

6 See 'Of Clouds and Clocks', now in Popper's (1972, 209) *Objective Knowledge.*

7 See e.g. Theodore Lowi's (1979) *The End of Liberalism.*

8 See, for a useful if partisan guide, Lukes (2005).

9 The AARP (American Association of Retired Persons) is a large lobby group which represents Americans over 50 years old, and is claimed, with some 37 million members, to be the largest lobby group in the United States (www.gwumc.edu/sphhs/departments/pch/phcm/casesjournal/volume1/sponsored/cases_1_15.cfm). It charges low membership fees, but has a considerable income from its large membership (membership giving access to all kinds of discounts), and also from product endorsement; cf. Ross Kaminsky (2011) for one hostile assessment.

10 See, in this context, Popper's (1995) dismissal of the anthropologist's concern for the social dynamics of knowledge in 'The Logic of the Social Sciences', in his *In Search of a Better World.*

11 See, on this, my *Political Thought of Karl Popper* (1987a), and also my *Hayek and After* (1987b).

12 As I suggested in my *Political Thought of Karl Popper*, there may be problems here, when – as occurs later in Popper's work – he places emphasis upon the significance of tradition. For a problem with traditions is that once things are changed, it may be difficult to restore how things were done before. However, it is possible that we may, here, learn a perhaps unexpected lesson from Hobsbawm and Ranger (eds) *The Invention of Tradition* (1983); namely that it may be possible for us to successfully create or possibly even re-create traditions.

13 See Karl Popper, 'On The New Liberty', now in Popper (2008) *After The Open Society.*

14 See 'The Power of Television', now in Popper (2008) *After The Open Society.*

15 There is more to this issue than I can discuss here; briefly, it may be seen as a

non-foundationalist attempt to provide an approach in normative political theory, in which people coming to the table with different perspectives are asked to explicate what they take to be unacceptable, and to take what could be consensually agreed about this as an agenda for remedial action by the government. See, on this, his 'Public and Private Values', in Popper (2008) *After the Open Society*.

16 See, on this, 'A Letter to my Russian Readers [of the translation of *The Open Society*] (1992), now in Popper (2008) *After the Open Society*.

17 I have discussed this issue in my *Political Thought of Karl Popper* (1987a).

18 See, on this, Popper to Hayek, 10 December 1972; Hayek Archive, Hoover Institution Archive, Box 44–1.

19 His letter to Magee on this theme is now included in Popper (2008) *After The Open Society*.

20 It is interesting that, in the (somewhat rough) record of the first meeting of the Mont Pelerin Society, Popper seemed in discussion to favour the idea that provision should be relatively generous – his suggestions contrasting with those of Mises and of Hayek. See Mont Pelerin Society Archive, Hoover Institution Archives.

21 This material is from Popper's (1963, 353) 'Public Opinion and Legal Principles', in his *Conjectures and Refutations*. He said much the same thing in even more graphic terms in his (unpublished) Emory Lectures of 1956 (a poor-quality recording of which is held in the Popper Archive at the Hoover Institution Archive).

22 This is to be found in his *Open Society* and in essays such as 'Utopia and Violence', in his *Conjectures and Refutations*, but comes out, I think, particularly clearly in his 'Public and Private Values', now available in Popper (2008) *After The Open Society*.

23 Not least, say, those of people concerned with 'deliberative democracy', or who have been influenced by certain of Habermas's works.

24 See also on this the important points made by Hayek (1944) concerning the limitations of the degree of agreement we can expect within democracies in his *Road to Serfdom*.

25 See, on this, 'The Myth of the Framework', now in Popper's (1994) *The Myth of the Framework*.

26 Popper, in this context, talked about the 'abstract' character of an open society; this, it seems to me, is best cashed out in terms of the kinds of social transformations associated with what Adam Smith and his contemporaries referred to as 'commercial society', and with the social transformations which then took place within them. It is, in this context, useful to consider the way in which, when Adam Smith and David Hume were writing, the social background against which they were writing was hierarchical and characterized by deference. Popper discussed the open society as a 'fatherless' society – in which this kind of deference had disappeared, and in which people were, willy-nilly, responsible for their own choices.

27 See Friedrich Hayek's ([1952] 2010) *The Counter-Revolution of Science*, now in volume 13 of *The Collected Works of F.A. Hayek*.

28 Gellner's (1993) brief study, *The Psychoanalytic Movement*, to me resembling the kind of study which a 'Popperian' approach called for, but which no one closely associated with Popper ever produced.

29 Cf., on all this, Shearmur (1987b) *Hayek and After*.

30 It was striking, in the Republican Presidential debates in 2011, that it was frequently claimed that taxing the rich was a tax on those who are responsible for creating jobs, and so would add to unemployment.

Bibliography

Gellner, E. 1993. *The Psychoanalytic Movement* (2nd edn). London: Fontana.

Hacohen, M. 2002. *Karl Popper: The Formative Years*. Cambridge: Cambridge University Press.

Hayek, F. 1944. *Road to Serfdom*. London: Routledge.

——. 1952 [2010]. *The Counter-Revolution of Science*. In B. Caldwell (ed.) *Studies on the Abuse and Decline of Reason. Volume 13 of The Collected Works of F.A. Hayek*. Chicago, IL: University of Chicago Press.

Hobsbawm, E. and T. Ranger (eds). 1983. *The Invention of Tradition*. Cambridge: Cambridge University Press.

Jarvie, I. 2001. *The Republic of Science*. Amsterdam and Atlanta: Rodopi.

Kaminsky, R. 2011. "AARP Is Killing Entitlement Reform". *American Spectator*, 14 October: http://spectator.org/archives/2011/10/14/aarp-is-killing-entitlement-re.

Lowi, T. 1979. *The End of Liberalism* (2nd edn). New York: W.W. Norton.

Lukes, S. 2005. *Power: A Radical View* (2nd edn). Basingstoke: Palgrave.

Moore, B. 1966. *The Social Origins of Dictatorship and Democracy*. Boston, MA: Beacon Press.

Nozick, R. 1974. *Anarchy, State, and Utopia*. New York: Basic Books.

Popper, K. 1963. *Conjectures and Refutations*. London: Routledge.

——. 1972. *Objective Knowledge*. Oxford: Clarendon Press.

——. 1995. "The Logic of the Social Sciences". In his *In Search of a Better World*. London: Routledge.

——. 2008. *After The Open Society*, ed. J. Shearmur and P. Turner. London: Routledge.

Shearmur, J. 1980. "The Religious Sect as a Cognitive System". *Annual Review of the Social Sciences of Religion* 4: 149–63.

——. 1985. "Epistemology Socialized?". *Et cetera* 42(3): 272–82.

——. 1987a. *Political Thought of Karl Popper*. London: Routledge.

——. 1987b. *Hayek and After*. London: Routledge.

——. 2002. "Popper e il consenso negative". In *Karl Popper 1902–2002: ripensando il razionalismo critico (II); Special issue of Nuova Civiltà delle Macchine* 20(2): 98–105.

——. 2011. "Popper and the Problem of the Public Sphere". In Andrea Borghini and Stefano Gattei (eds) *Karl Popper oggi. Una riflessione multidisciplinare*. Livorno: Salomone Belforte.

Skocpol, T. 1979. *States and Social Revolutions*. Cambridge: Cambridge University Press.

Sturm, R. and A. Hattori. 2013. "Morbid Obesity Rates Continue to Rise Rapidly in The United States". *International Journal of Obesity (London)* 37(6): 889–91: www.ncbi.nlm.nih.gov/pubmed/22986681.

2 Karl Popper and Thailand's political crisis

The monarchy as the problem for an 'open society'

Patrick Jory

1 Introduction

The problem this chapter seeks to address is the return to a 'closed', illiberal society in Thailand since the coup of 19 September 2006. This sudden change took place after fourteen years of apparent political liberalization since the pro-democracy protests of May 1992, and a much longer period of economic expansion. According to some versions of democratization theory, Thailand's rapid economic development and the formation of a sizeable middle class should have pushed Thailand firmly down the path towards a liberal democracy. Between the mid-1980s and mid-1990s Thailand's economic growth was, according to some measures, the fastest in the world, averaging around 10 per cent per year. Pro-democracy protests led by the Bangkok middle class in 1992, which resulted in an apparent retreat of the army from parliamentary politics and the promulgation of a new, relatively more democratic Constitution in 1997 following widespread public consultation, seemed to be proving the theory. Since the 2006 coup, however, there has been a dramatic reversal of what, only a few years ago, appeared to be Thailand's confident march towards the "End of History", to use the phrase from Fukuyama's (1992) famous argument in the book of that title.[1]

The question why such a democratic reversal should have taken place goes beyond the realm of abstract academic debate. Since the 2006 coup Thailand has been in the midst of a profound political crisis. In April/May 2010 the government ordered armed troops onto the streets to suppress pro-democracy demonstrations, resulting in the deaths of at least ninety-one people and injuries to thousands. The country remains deeply polarized. The general election of July 2011, won yet again by a party controlled by the exiled politician Thaksin Shinawatra and led by his sister Yingluck, should be viewed not as a resolution of the crisis but rather as one battle in a longer ongoing political war. To a certain extent this war may be understood as a struggle to establish in Thailand an "open society", as described in Popper's classic work, *The Open Society and Its Enemies*.

This chapter will attempt to explain the reasons for this apparent democratic reversal. Its argument is straightforward. For many years there has been a lingering misunderstanding about the problem of political liberalization in Thailand. The misunderstanding derives primarily from a misreading of the country's history which lays the blame for Thailand's authoritarian politics primarily on the military. Thailand has often been conveniently grouped along with other modernizing states in East Asia where the military has dominated politics for much of the post-independence era, such as South Korea, Indonesia and Myanmar. Such comparisons, often favoured by political science theorists, obscure the particular character of the political system in Thailand.

In fact, the military in Thailand is one element of a bigger problem; that is, the political status of the Thai monarchy since the overthrow of the Absolute Monarchy in 1932. The argument this chapter seeks to present is that it is the monarchy that poses the major obstacle to an open society in Thailand today. Unless the problem of the monarchy is dealt with, Thailand cannot develop into the kind of open society that Popper described. I will explain the reasons for this misunderstanding of Thailand's political predicament, and how the monarchy and the political order it legitimizes presents such a problem for an open society.

2 Thailand and Popper's theory of the 'open society'

> What damn good is this country –
> you can't compare it with anything!
>
> (Attributed to David Wilson; Popularized by Benedict Anderson (1978, 193))

It is first necessary to address the question as to the extent to which Popper can help us understand the problem faced by Thailand today. Popper was, after all, writing in the 1940s, attempting to explain the apparent appeal and success of totalitarian regimes of both the left and the right in much of Europe. His argument in *The Open Society and Its Enemies* drew attention to the danger of Hegelian thought about laws of historical development which Popper terms 'historicism', and how such thought provided a philosophical justification for totalitarianism. Hegel's ideas drew on a much older philosophical tradition dating from classical Greek philosophy, in particular the thought of Plato. Popper also argued, as Shearmur has shown in Chapter 1, that an open society was dependent upon a level of rationalism that was the product of the freedom to criticize. Can Popper's argument be applied to Thailand and the East Asian region more generally, which have experienced, at least up until the time of European imperialism, a separate historical development to that of Europe, and which are informed by different philosophical and religious traditions?

This question raises the bigger issue of the comparability of political development in different countries. In Thailand there is a long tradition of scholarship arguing that Thailand's historical development was different to that of the West. The Oxford-educated Thai aristocrat and one-time prime minister, Seni Pramoj, argued in the 1940s that Thailand had enjoyed democracy since the *thirteenth century* – well before the Europeans – and that its people had had a 'Constitution' which was superior to the Magna Carta because the king had bestowed it upon the Thai people of his own volition (ณัฐพล ใจจริง 2005, 96–7; Jory 2011,

546–7). One of the reasons underlying the belief that Thailand has experienced a different historical development was that it was the only country in Southeast Asia not to have been colonized by the West. As Benedict Anderson (1978, 197) argued in one of the best-known articles on Thai history in the past thirty years, this has led to a view that Thailand is unique in the region. The idea of Thai uniqueness is a staple of state propaganda in Thailand. The argument goes that Thailand is so different from anywhere else that it cannot be compared to other countries. Its feudalism was different from Western feudalism (คึกฤทธิ์ 1986).[2] Its form of democracy is a 'Thai-style' democracy.[3] And so on.

Thailand's lack of the historical experience of colonization has produced another problem: the fact that English is relatively poorly spoken and understood. In international surveys of English-language proficiency Thailand consistently rates as having one of the lowest rankings in the world. English-language discourse, particularly in the humanities and social sciences, and the ideas of political and historical universalism that they convey, have had until recently relatively limited influence or understanding beyond the university faculties. Indeed, for a long time government support for the learning of English was neglected in favour of the heavy promotion of the Thai language in the interests of cultural unity and even 'national security' (Reynolds 2006, 271–2). The language of intellectual and political debate in Thailand, is therefore, Thai. This would not have been such a problem in itself except for the fact that since the late 1950s Thailand has been dominated by a succession of conservative regimes, with the result that 'royalist-nationalist' ideas (ธงชัย วินิจจะกูล 2001) about Thailand's 'uniqueness' have been disseminated through the schools and mass media in the Thai language to become the 'ruling ideas'. As a result, Thai universities, which one might expect to be hotbeds of liberal, progressive thinking, are instead bastions of intellectual support for the royalist political order. This hegemony of a conservative discourse of uniqueness has not, however, gone unchallenged. Today it is under great pressure. For example, in the media and websites of pro-democracy groups outside the intellectual mainstream (especially the so-called 'Red Shirts') there are frequent comparisons between the situation in Thailand today and that in France in 1789, or Russia in 1917.[4]

If we, therefore, reject such ideas of Thai uniqueness, it is remarkable how much can be found in Popper's *The Open Society and Its Enemies* that is reminiscent of the debate taking place – mostly in the Thai language – in Thailand today. The royalist-military-controlled 'bureaucratic polity', which has dominated the Thai state since the late 1950s (see Riggs 1966), appears uncannily similar to the 'best state' described by Plato, as summarized by Popper (2010, 47):

> Plato distinguishes three classes in his best state, the guardians, their armed auxiliaries or warriors, and the working class. But actually there are only two castes, the military caste – the armed and educated rulers – and the unarmed and uneducated ruled, the human sheep; for the guardians are no separate caste, but merely old and wise warriors who have been promoted from the ranks of the auxiliaries.

While it has been almost two centuries since Thai kings actually personally led military campaigns, the current Chakri dynasty came to power in 1782 by means of a military coup d'état against the warrior king Taksin, who had restored the Thai kingdom after expelling a Burmese invasion that had sacked the royal capital of Ayutthaya. Early Chakri kings spent much of their energies fighting ongoing Burmese invasions and expanding the Thai empire on the Southeast Asian mainland through military conquest. The Thai word for king, กษัตริย์, derives from the Sanskrit term *kshatriya*, the military caste of the four castes of classical Brahmanism. Militarist strains of Thai historiography that are still influential in school textbooks and the military academy exalt the monarch as a warrior king (see Jory 2011). The King is recognized constitutionally as the Supreme Head of the Thai Armed Forces (จอมทัพไทย), and for much of the Cold War era he appeared publicly in military uniform. Thai Armed Forces Day takes place on the anniversary of the victory of the great Thai king Naresuan over his rival, the Burmese prince, in 1592. Such a militaristic conception of the monarchy is particularly strong in military circles. As for the 'ruled' or Popper's 'human sheep', the argument mounted repeatedly by royalists against the democratically-elected government overthrown in the 2006 coup, and more generally the legitimacy of elections themselves, was that the Thai working class lacked the education needed to elect morally upright politicians.

But it is in Popper's description of the open society that the analogy with Thailand's current predicament is clearest. In one evocative passage, Popper (2010, xvii–xviii) describes the origins of the open society:

> civilisation has not yet recovered from the shock of its birth – the transition from the tribal or 'closed' society, with its submission to magical forces, to the 'open society', which sets free the critical powers of man.

Popper (2010, xii–xiii) describes what he calls "perhaps the greatest of all moral and spiritual revolutions of history" which (in Europe) began three centuries ago as

> an attempt to build up an open society which rejects the absolute authority of the merely established and the merely traditional while trying to preserve, to develop, and to establish traditions, old or new, that measure up to the standards of freedom, of humaneness, and of rational criticism.

In Thailand this 'shock' corresponds directly with the overthrow of the Absolute Monarchy in 1932. This was the historical event which symbolized the rejection of 'absolute authority' and 'the merely traditional', the beginning of the breakdown of 'tribal society' and the building of an open society. The People's Party, a group of civilian and military officials, subsequently attempted to establish a constitutional democracy in which the powers of the monarch were to be subject to the will of the people. Only through the curbing of royal authority could the 'critical powers' of Thai citizens be set free and a more rational society develop.

Yet within fifteen years the leader of the People's Party, the left-leaning liberal lawyer Pridi Phanomyong, was forced into exile and a royalist-backed military coup overthrew the government, beginning the restoration of many of the monarchy's powers that had been lost in 1932.

The problem that the monarchy in Thailand poses to 'freedom', 'humaneness' and 'rational criticism', described by Popper as attributes of an open society, is extremely extensive and requires much fuller treatment than can be offered in this short chapter. But for our purposes here it may be demonstrated through an examination of one crucial aspect of the monarchy's wide-ranging powers, the *lèse-majesté* law.

3 The problem of *lèse-majesté*

> I wanted to "flick on the lights and flush out the ghosts".
>
> (Thaksin to the US Ambassador, July 2006)[5]

It was stated above that there has been a misunderstanding of the political problem in Thailand due to a misreading of Thai history. Why has this history been so badly misread?

There are two, related reasons. The first is the failure to acknowledge the centrality of the monarchy – not the military (as in Myanmar today, or Indonesia under the New Order between 1966 and 1998) – to Thailand's political system today. Thailand is a constitutional monarchy in name only. In fact, the formal Thai term for the country's political system – "**ระบบประชาธิปไตยอันมีพระมหากษัตริย์ทรงเป็นประมุข**" – does not mention the word 'constitutional' at all; the literal translation is "Democratic System with the Great, Holy King as the Head of State".[6] Under the present king the monarchy has managed to regain many of the vestiges of absolutism which it lost following the overthrow of the Absolute Monarchy in 1932. The king and the royal family exercise real political power both directly and behind the scenes. This has been clearly shown in scholarship over the past decade, in English and in Thai (although the latter is much more careful given the necessity of having to skirt the boundaries of the *lèse-majesté* law).[7] In 2005 the head of one of the king's royal foundations published a book in Thai called *Royal Power* (ประมวล 2005) in which he argued that the King *legitimately* exercised a form of political power that was outside the formal powers permitted to him in the Constitution. An indication of the influence of such views was that the book became a bestseller, and was promoted and widely discussed in the mass media. It contained a revealing preface written by Piya Malakul, a close confidante of the king, in which Piya wrote that upon reading the work the king had given it his seal of approval: "I like it a lot. It is well-written and correct" (ประมวล 2005). Most recently the interventions of the monarchy in the current political conflict have been confirmed by the controversial Wikileaks cables – the leaked diplomatic cables of the US Embassy in Thailand – a number of which were originally released by the former Reuters journalist, Andrew MacGregor Marshall.[8]

The second reason why Thailand's present political situation and its history have been misread is the extreme difficulty within Thailand of critically discussing the role of the monarchy in Thailand's political system due to the existence of the *lèse-majesté* law – Article 112 of the Thai Criminal Code. It cannot be emphasized enough how important this law is to understanding both the current political conflict in Thailand and the history of the monarchy. As Shearmur points out, openness to criticism is one of the basic characteristics of the open society. The development of rationality within a society, the growth of what Popper (2009, 250–1) calls the 'rational unity of mankind' where everyone is a "potential source of argument and reasonable information", is dependent upon the freedom to criticize. In a way that is perhaps unique to Thailand in the world today the obstacle to the development of such rationality is centred upon the monarchy.

The *lèse-majesté* law forbids criticism of the king, the queen, the crown prince or the regent. The offence carries a maximum penalty of fifteen years. Multiple offences may mean that persons convicted under the law can receive an even heavier sentence.[9] It is the harshest such law in the world. Besides prohibiting rational discussion of the monarchy's role in the current political system, the law also makes the writing of history in Thailand a difficult task, especially the history of the present king's long reign (since 1946). It effectively renders criticism of the present king by historians a criminal offence, and in theory it may also be regarded as treason, since the king is also protected from criticism by Article 8 of the Constitution.[10] Not surprisingly, a long list of books deemed critical of the monarchy are officially banned in Thailand. Controversial events of the past sixty years involving the king are dangerous territory for Thai historians to tread and are treated with a high degree of self-censorship. For example, the leading critical historian of the monarchy, Somsak Jeamteerasakul, was in 2011 summoned to a police station to hear the basis of the charge of *lèse-majesté* made by the military against him. Another historian, Thanapol Iwsakul, editor of one of the leading political science journals in Thailand, *Fa Dio Kan*, has faced charges of *lèse-majesté* for material published by the journal deemed to be critical of the monarchy. A third historian, Sutthachai Yimprasert, was arrested and detained by the military for several weeks following the government's crackdown on Red Shirts protesters in May 2010. An American citizen of Thai descent, 'Joe Gordon' (Loephong Wichaikhammat), was jailed under the law for two and a half years for merely translating into Thai and distributing on the internet sections of Paul Handley's critical biography, *The King Never Smiles*.

The *lèse-majesté* law thus inhibits a rational understanding of the monarchy in the political system. Scholarship has shown that the monarchy has regularly intervened in politics, both directly and through proxies in the Privy Council, the military, the judiciary and bureaucracy – the so-called "network monarchy", as McCargo (2005) describes it. However, one risks a lengthy jail sentence for actually stating the fact publicly.

The centrality of the monarchy to the political conflict in Thailand since 2005 is demonstrated by the increased frequency with which the law has been used during this period to silence criticism of the monarchy's apparent involvement in the conflict. Although the law has existed in various forms and with different penalties for over a hundred years (Streckfuss 2011), in the four years since the coup of 2006 there was a massive increase in the number of arrests and convictions for *lèse-majesté*. The former Democrat-led government presided over the greatest number of *lèse-majesté* cases in the history of the law.[11] The conviction rate is close to 100 per cent. Trials are closed to the media, and reporting on convictions in the mainstream media is muted. Criticism of the verdict risks a charge of contempt of court. According to figures presented by David Streckfuss (2011, 205), by 2011 there may have been as many as 170 political prisoners in jail in Thailand convicted under the *lèse-majesté* law. Most of these prisoners remain unknown to human rights organizations and the general public because *lèse-majesté* cases are so sensitive that they are rarely reported. Worse, *lèse-majesté* trials are often conducted in secret. That this appalling statement on the standard of human rights in Thailand is not more widely known is itself an indication of the power of the *lèse-majesté* law and the pervasive fear that silences critical discussion of the monarchy in Thailand. The Thai government itself has admitted to blocking more than 100,000 websites, mostly because they contain material that the government considers either insulting to the royal family or advocating republican ideas.[12]

To back up the older *lèse-majesté* law in an era when much of the criticism of the monarchy now takes place on the internet, following the September 2006 coup the military-installed government enacted the new Computer Crimes Act. While the new law covers various offences committed on the internet, it has been used primarily to crack down on criticism of the monarchy. The most egregious case was that of an elderly Thai-Chinese man sentenced in 2011 to twenty years in jail for allegedly sending four SMS messages to the secretary of the then prime minister, Democrat leader Abhisit Vejjajiva, judged to be defamatory of the queen. The man died in prison in 2012.

As a result of the explosion of censorship and intimidation of anyone expressing critical views of the monarchy, Freedom House downgraded Thailand's media rating to 'not free' – a humiliating rating for a country that was once regarded as the most open and liberal in the region (see Jory and Montesano 2011).

It should be pointed out that in Thailand one may freely criticize politicians, the military, even Buddhist monks; it is only criticism of the monarchy that is forbidden. Meanwhile, Thais are subject to a relentless barrage of propaganda about the virtues of the present king and the royal family through the mass media on a daily basis. The upshot is that millions of words in books and articles and newspaper columns have been written criticizing the role of the military in Thai politics, but only a tiny fraction of that has been written on the monarchy. The political role of the monarchy has been for all intents and purposes close to invisible.

4 'Sufficiency economy' and the closed society

Popper argued that in order to maintain the unity of the ruling class in a closed society, besides using "training and psychological influences" (i.e. through propaganda and state control of the education system), it was necessary to "eliminat[e] … economic interests which may lead to disunion". But economic dangers to the position of the ruling class came in different forms:

> It is important to avoid prosperity as well as poverty. Both are dangers to unity: poverty, because it drives people to adopt desperate means to satisfy their needs; prosperity, because most change arises from abundance, from an accumulation of wealth which makes dangerous experiments possible.
>
> (Popper 2010, 49)

Similarly, challenges to the unity of Thailand's 'ruling class' and the place of the monarchy at its apex have come from both the left, in the form of an insurgency led by the Communist Party of Thailand during the Cold War, when Thailand was a close US ally and bulwark of anti-communism in Southeast Asia, and from the neo-liberal, globalizing capitalism of the post-Cold War era, symbolized in the person of the deposed prime minister, telecommunications tycoon Thaksin Shinawatra.

King Bhumibol represents himself as many things, among them a future Buddha[13] as well as a great economist. The king has expounded an economic theory which he has called "sufficiency economy" (ทฤษฎีเศรษฐกิจพอเพียง). The "theory" or "philosophy", such as it is, supposedly teaches a mix of "moderation, reasonableness and self-immunity" and "sustainable development". It urges Thais to live within their means and to eschew rampant materialism and capitalist accumulation.[14] In fact, post-colonial theories of self-reliance[15] have not been uncommon in the developing world, but Bhumibol's "sufficiency economy" surely counts as one of the most inane[16] – and politically motivated. The king first enunciated it as coherent "theory" during the Asian Financial Crisis in 1997 to 1998, which affected Thailand's economy particularly severely, as well as the monarchy's own massive business interests. The theory was more or less forgotten following Thailand's economic recovery until relations between the then PM, Thaksin Shinawatra, and the Palace began to run into problems. In 2005 the king resurrected his "sufficiency economy" theory and it was effectively relaunched by the royalist forces as an attack on Thaksin, who was portrayed in the royalist media as a hyper-capitalist megalomaniac, intent on pursuing economic growth at all costs.[17] In doing so, Thaksin's enemies skilfully coopted the politically influential network of left-leaning NGOs and their academic supporters, some of whom had roots in leftist movements or even the Communist Party of Thailand in the 1970s, into the anti-Thaksin cause.

Popper's (2010, 41–2) paraphrasing of Plato's explanation of the rise of class conflict "between virtue and money, or between the old established ways of feudal simplicity and the new ways of wealth" aptly describes the conflict between Thaksin and the Palace as it developed from 2005. The breakdown in relations between the king and Thaksin is vividly recorded in the Wikileaks cables. The then American ambassador, Ralph Boyce, recounts a meeting with Thaksin in July 2006 in which

> Thaksin launched into an attack on the King and his vaunted 'sufficiency economy' model. Thaksin said that he was proud of his origins as 'a peasant', he had gotten ahead by managing debt and risk, and this was what the rural population needed to do. [...] Thaksin claimed that the policies advocated by the King kept the people poor, while TRT's policies had changed the countryside, making the people 'smarter and richer' and less dependent on the King. This was part of the reason for the King's opposition to Thaksin.[18]

Following the September 2006 royalist coup and the appointment of the king's own privy councillor, General Surayud Chulanont, as prime minister, 'sufficiency economy' became at least rhetorically the official economic policy of the new regime. It was the underlying idea informing the tenth five-year National Economic and Social Development Plan, announced in 2007.[19] The new economic philosophy was presented as an alternative to Thaksin's supposed 'neoliberalism'. Indeed, the leader of the royalist-backed junta which carried out the coup on 19 September 2006, General Sonthi Boonyaratglin, had referred to the Thaksin government he had overthrown as a 'capitalist dictatorship'.[20] Schools and universities were forced to disseminate the king's economic philosophy by setting up new curricula and teaching new courses on it, the bureaucracy established pilot projects around the country to apply the new philosophy, and the state media were obliged to promote it by featuring stories on its successful implementation. A few months after the coup the military-installed regime, with the support of the Thailand office of the Economic and Social Commission for Asia and the Pacific (ESCAP), even invited an economist of the stature of Nobel Prize winner Amartya Sen to lend support to the king's economic theory. In so doing, the theory was given the aura of international academic legitimacy.[21]

It is an irony that while the king and the Thai government were promoting the virtues of economic moderation, *Forbes* magazine in its annual list of the world's richest rulers ranked King Bhumibol as the world's wealthiest monarch, surpassing the rulers of oil-rich states like Saudi Arabia, the UAE, Brunei, and the United Kingdom's Queen Elizabeth, with a net worth estimated at US$35 billion.[22] That this statistic is not more widely known is itself an indication of the degree to which the monarchy's image of moderation has been manipulated. For a long time the Crown Property Bureau, the agency which manages the monarchy's assets, has been the largest corporate group in Thailand, yet staggeringly it has been "virtually ignored in economic literature on Thailand".[23] The simple reason is that at least within Thailand it is almost impossible to publicly criticize the business affairs of the monarchy, since that would be interpreted as an attack on the king and hence run the risk of a charge of *lèse-majesté*.

In this way an economic theory supposedly propounding moderation, living within one's means, and a rejection of the path of capitalist modernization was proposed by an unelected, immensely wealthy political figure, the de facto head of the largest corporate group in Thailand, who is protected from criticism by the very people who are directly affected by the implementation of his theory on pain of a fifteen-year jail sentence. The theory became state policy following a coup d'état launched by royalist generals and the establishment of a royalist-military dictatorship. Such a disturbing, mutually beneficial relationship between the international development bureaucracy and its academic supporters, and an untouchable king heading a royalist regime installed at the barrel of a gun, is indicative of the failure of the open society in Thailand. Indeed, this atmosphere of irrationality and fear of criticizing anything in which the monarchy has an interest is reminiscent of a passage written by Popper's friend and colleague Friedrich Hayek (1994, 167) in his classic work, *The Road to Serfdom*:

> The general intellectual climate which this [atmosphere of totalitarianism] produces, the spirit of complete cynicism as regards truth which it engenders, the loss of the sense of even the meaning of truth, the disappearance of the spirit of independent inquiry and of the belief in the power of rational conviction [...] are all things which one must personally experience – no short description can convey their extent.[24]

5 Modern Thai history and the struggle for an open society[25]

It was pointed out earlier that the current political crisis has been poorly understood partly as a result of an inadequate understanding of Thailand's political history, and in particular the place of the monarchy in that history. This misunderstanding is in turn due to the hegemony of the royalist-nationalist version of Thai history. This hegemony has, however, not gone unchallenged.

From its inception, history writing in Thailand has been dominated by the presence of the monarchy. In traditional historiography the kings enjoyed divine status as *avatars* (earthly incarnations) of the Hindu god Vishnu. Indeed, until the early decades of the twentieth century the term by which history was known in the Thai kingdom was *phongsawadan*, literally, 'lineage of the *avatars*'. Pre-modern historical discourse also represented the kings as *bodhisattas*, or future Buddhas, whose accumulated merit from their achievement of perfect virtue (*barami*) performed over countless previous lifetimes was greater than that of anyone else (see Jory 1998). This Theravada Buddhist theory of power provided intellectual legitimacy for a political and social hierarchy in which one's place in the hierarchy was understood as a function of one's store of merit. In traditional Thai historiography, therefore, there is a close nexus between conceptions of morality and power. One is struck here again by the obvious similarity to Plato's theory of the state ruled by the philosopher king, which Popper (2010, 40) attacked in his *The Open Society* for its assertion of the principle that "the 'best state', is a kingship of the wisest and most godlike of men".

In the tumultuous modern era, Thai kings acquired a new significance. While European colonization was the great historical rupture that thrust other Southeast Asian kingdoms into modernity, Siam was not directly colonized. Under the absolute monarchy credit for the modernization of the Thai kingdom and the preservation of formal political independence, two central ideas in the formulation of Thai nationalism, was written into official history as being due to the genius of the kings. Thongchai Winichakul (2001) refers to this conception of Thai history as "royalist-nationalist history", in which the monarchy is the embodiment of the nation.

This representation of the monarchy in Thai history was, however, fundamentally upset by the overthrow of the Absolute Monarchy in 1932. The question of the contemporary role of the monarchy in Thai politics goes back to this key event in modern Thai history. In the Thai context democracy began with the end of the Absolute Monarchy – by contrast with the other colonized countries in Southeast Asia, where the understanding of 'democracy' is associated with opposition to European colonial rule by 'the people'. In theory, after 1932 the king became a constitutional monarch, with no direct political power. In practice what ensued was a competition for power between the king and the royalists, and the forces that supported the new constitutional regime. Over the ensuing twenty-five years a complicated struggle developed between rival political groups which finally ended with a military coup in 1957 supported by the royalists. The coup restored the monarchy to the central position within the Thai polity for the first time since 1932, but this time under a conservative military dictatorship. This alliance between the military and the monarchy has lasted until today.

The transition from the Absolute Monarchy to a constitutional democracy after 1932 is difficult for royalists to explain in their version of Thai history. Normally, Absolute Monarchy and democracy should be seen as contradictory. The royalist solution was to represent the last absolute monarch as a democrat. King Rama VII thus has an official moniker as the 'father of Thai democracy'. According to the official history, King Rama VII had been preparing to transform Thailand into a democracy before the coup of 1932, but the king's plans were dashed by the People's Party. The People's Party's actions in overthrowing the Absolute Monarchy had had the effect of throwing the country into a period of political turmoil, which eventually led to a virtual 'dictatorship' by the parliament. In the royalist version of history politicians were the real obstacle to a true democracy. Politicians were interested only in power and money. They took advantage of the ignorance of the Thai voters, who were not sufficiently educated to choose morally upstanding representatives. The contrast between corrupt politicians and ignorant voters, and the morally righteous king who knows what is best for the people, has been a constant theme of royalist political discourse in Thailand through to the present political crisis (see Jory 2011).

Partly due to this crisis, and partly also because of the opening up of a new medium of expression that is freer from state control, the internet, the royalist narrative of Thai history is now under unprecedented challenge. Over the last decade or so a new generation of historians has attacked the official representation of the monarchy in modern Thai political history. The so-called 'father of democracy', King Rama VII, has been shown to have actively resisted the transformation to constitutional government before 1932. After 1932 the king manoeuvred to claw back the crown's powers while secretly lending his support to political movements attempting to undermine the People's Party (สมศักดิ์ 2001; ณัฐพล 2005). The political historian Somsak Jeamteerasakul has questioned the official account of the death of the king's elder brother, Rama VIII (Ananda Mahidol), in 1946 which led to the political crisis that eventually ended the political influence of Pridi and the civilian wing of the People's Party. He also showed that the royal secretary and two royal pages executed for the former king's death, who were widely believed to have been scapegoats, had been refused a royal pardon by King Bhumibol. The current king's democratic credentials were a political invention that took place after the 14 October 1973 mass student-led demonstrations to oust the leadership of the military regime – with which the monarchy was actually in political alliance. In another controversial article Somsak obliquely argued that Bhumibol had taken the leading role in drumming up anti-communist hysteria in 1975 and 1976, and consequently bears a degree of responsibility for the brutal killings of student demonstrators at Thammasat University on 6 October 1976 by royalist vigilante groups and police units linked to the Palace (สมศักดิ์ 2001).

This revisionist scholarship, limited though it is to non-official publishing outlets and constrained in what it can say by the *lèse-majesté* law, thus presents a counter-narrative to the official view of the Thai monarchy as democratic, 'above politics', and the king as representative of Buddhist virtue. Following the collapse of earlier critiques of the monarchy – a liberal version in the 1950s and the Marxist version in the 1980s – it has begun the work of resituating the monarchy in a historical narrative which plots it as the principal obstacle to the development of democracy in Thailand.

6 Conclusion

Just as today there is an intense political struggle between the royalists and the pro-parliamentary forces whose legitimacy derives from democratic elections, we are also witnessing a struggle between alternative versions of Thailand's history, which view the place of the monarchy in that history very differently. Formerly, the military had been seen as the problem for Thailand's democratization; in the new history the monarchy has taken its place. As the political conflict has become more intense, so have the attempts to silence this alternative political history, through the use of the *lèse-majesté* law, charging, arresting, and imprisoning academics and activists who attempt to disseminate this alternative history, and the belated but now much more assiduous policing of the internet, where this alternative history has flourished.

This chapter has argued that the monarchy's domination of Thailand is the major obstacle to the building of the open society. The classic features of the closed society as Popper describes it are all present in Thailand today: the state conceived of and represented as a "semi-organic unit whose members are held together by semi-biological ties – kinship, living together, sharing common efforts, common dangers, common joys and common distresses"; the "magical and irrational attitude towards the customs of social life, and the rigidity of these customs"; and the creed that "the tribe is everything and the individual nothing" (Popper 2010, 184–203): the king as the 'father' of all Thais.

But as Shearmur has noted in his chapter, for Popper the open society is a 'fatherless society'. In Thailand the closed society has been in the process of breaking down for some time, for the same reasons as Popper outlines in the case of Ancient Greece: the expansion of trade and commerce. This process leads to the development of 'abstract relations' that are characteristic of the open society, where human interaction functions on the basis of exchange and cooperation rather than on primordial ties within the tribe. For Popper (2010, 188–9), the transition to the open society is

> one of the deepest revolutions through which mankind has passed. … The breakdown of the closed society, raising as it does the problems of class and other problems of social status, must have the same effect upon the citizens as a serious family quarrel and the breaking up of the family home is liable to have on children.

What Popper (2010, 189) referred to as the "strains of civilisation" associated with the breakdown of the closed society may certainly be seen in Thailand's current crisis. They were memorably displayed in an emotional and controversial speech given by the well-known television actor Phongphat Wachirabanjong, at an awards ceremony in Bangkok in May 2010, shortly after the violent suppression of the pro-democracy Red Shirt demonstrations. The speech received much publicity in the media and the internet:

> Our Father is the pillar of our Home. Our Home is a large one. Very large. Many of us live here. When I was born this Home was very beautiful. Beautiful and warm. But it was Father's ancestors who had to sacrifice their flesh and blood and their lives to make it this way. Today our Father still tires himself looking after our Home, making sure everyone in our Home is happy.… But if there are people who hate our Father, if they no longer love our Father, I want to tell them to leave this country, because this is the Home of our Father![26]

The conservative response to the political challenge to the monarchy's place in Thai society by Thaksin, the Red Shirts, and their political allies echoes the defence of the closed society as described by Popper (2010, 196): "The reaction against these developments [in Athens] had … much on its side – tradition, the call for defending old virtue, and the old religion.… 'Back to the state of our forefathers', or 'Back to the old paternal state'". Popper (2009, 267) warned against such nostalgia: "the return to the closed society … is a return to the cage and the beasts."

If we, then, understand the conflict in Thailand today as essentially being a struggle between supporters of the closed and open society, we may appreciate the stakes involved and the depth of feeling on both sides. A prerequisite to the achievement of an open society in Thailand is a correct understanding of the nature of the obstacle to that society. Such an understanding may only be gained through an open discussion and examination of the problem of the monarchy.

Notes

1 Fukuyama's theory of the inevitable development of human society towards an end-point of economic and political freedom was based on Hegelian 'historicism', which was the target of the withering critique by Karl Popper in his book, *The Open Society and its Enemies.* Popper appears to have won the debate in Thailand, at least for now.

2 The implication was that if Thai feudalism was different from that of the West, Marx's critique of feudalism and historical materialism could not apply to it.

3 Following Sarit's coup of 1958, which was supported by the monarchy, a proclamation was issued that "The Revolutionary Council wishes to make the country a democracy … [which] … would be appropriate to the special characteristics and realities of the Thai. It will build a democracy, a Thai way of democracy" (Thak Chaloemtiarana 2007, 101).

4 Indeed, in August 2009 'Da Torpedo' (Daranee Chanchoengsilapakul), a fiery Red Shirt speaker, was convicted and jailed under the country's *lèse-majesté* law for eighteen years for making exactly this comparison; see รายงานพิเศษ – "คำพิพากษา" ดาตอร์ปิโด ในความเห็นของผู้ประกอบ วิชาชีพทางกฎหมายคนหนึ่ง (ศรัทธา หุ่นพยนต์) *ฟ้าเดียวกัน* ปีที่ 7 เล่ม 3, กันยายน 2552.

5 "Steak with Thaksin", 7 July 2006, *Wikileaks* http://wikileaks.org/cable/2006/07/06BANGKOK4041.html (accessed 21 July 2013).

6 One is reminded of Popper's summary of Plato's views of the three 'lawful' forms of government: "monarchy, aristocracy, and a conservative form of democracy" (Popper 2010, 44).

7 This scholarship is rapidly growing. See especially Paul Handley's (2006) seminal work, *The King Never Smiles: A Biography of Thailand's Bhumibol Adulyadej*; as well as McCargo (2005) and Ivarsson and Isager (2010). In Thailand scholarship is more guarded because of the *lèse-majesté* law, but one cannot study the history of the monarchy in Thailand without reading the work of Somsak Jeamteerasakul, particularly his *Prawattisat thi phueng sang: ruam bot khwam kiao kap karani 14 tula lae 6 tula* [History That Has Just Been Constructed: Collected Articles on the 14th October and 6th October Incidents] (Bangkok, 2001), as well as numerous articles published in the political science journal *Fa Dio Kan*, and his voluminous comments posted on webboards, blogs, and most recently his Facebook site where he posts regularly and which is followed by over 5000 subscribers. The journals *Fa Dio Kan* and *An* have become popular forums for articles critical of the monarchy; yet their readership is limited mainly to academics. Nevertheless, the sensitivity of the subject matter is such that the editor of *Fa Dio Kan* has faced a *lèse-majesté* charge and some bookshops refuse to stock the journal.

8 Andrew MacGregor Marshall, *Archive of Leaked U.S. Cables on Thailand*, http://thaistoryblog.wordpress.com/2011/07/05/archive-of-leaked-us-cables-on-thailand/ accessed 29 July 2013. See especially the cable of 23 November 2009, "Circles of Influence Inside the Institution of the Monarchy in King Bhumibol's Twilight".

9 As in the case of 'Da Torpedo', who is currently serving a sentence of eighteen years; see n.5 above.

10 Article 8 of the 2007 Constitution states, "The King shall be enthroned in a position of revered worship and shall not be violated. No person shall expose the King to any sort of accusation or action."

11 The Democrat Party may best be understood as the parliamentary arm of the royalists. It was founded by two aristocrat brothers, Kukrit and Seni Pramoj, in the 1940s as a political vehicle to restore the fortunes of the monarchy following the overthrow of the Absolute Monarchy in 1932.

12 See Pavin Chachavalpongpun, "Thailand's Massive Internet Censorship", *Asia Sentinel*, www.asiasentinel.com/index.php?option=com_content&task=view&id=2601&Itemid=164, accessed 21 July 2011.

13 See his version of the story of the *bodhisatta* in his incarnation as *Phra Maha Chanok [Pali: Mahajanaka]*, which is in fact a thinly veiled allegory of his own reign; ภูมิพลอดุลยเดช, พระบาทสมเด็จพระปรมินทรมหา. พระมหาชนก – *The Story of Mahajanaka*. กรุงเทพฯ: อมรินทร์พรินติงแอนด์พับลิชชิง, 2539.

14 See "Sufficiency Economy: Thailand's Answer to Globalization", UNDP Thailand, www.undp.or.th/newsandevents/2007/news_20070109.html, accessed 21 July 2011. See also the report prepared by the UNDP, *Thai Human Development Report: Sufficiency Economy and Human Development* (2007), http://hdr.undp.org/en/reports/nationalreports/asiathepacific/thailand/THAILAND_2007_en.pdf, accessed 22 July 2011. The report was published a few months after the coup and endorsed by the military-appointed prime minister Surayud Chulanont, the king's former privy councillor. Note the heavy influence of the monarchy over the report: the Acknowledgements points out that the report was 'guided by' an Advisory Panel chaired by H.E. Kasem Watanachai, Privy Councillor, and co-chaired by H.E. Dr Chirayu Israngkun Na Ayuthaya, Director General of the Bureau of the Crown Property. Contributors also include Sumet Tantivejakul, Secretary-General of the monarchy's Chaipattana Foundation and one of the leading anti-Thaksin campaigners.

15 Note again the similarity with Popper's (2010, 92) description of the economic principle of Plato's political programme:

> The state must be self sufficient. It must aim at economic autarchy, for otherwise the rulers would either be dependent on traders, or become traders themselves. The first of these alternatives would undermine their power, the second their unity and the stability of the state.

16 Most economists spend a lifetime of research and rigorous academic debate, and produce substantial, peer-reviewed publications – books and articles – to argue their theory. The smattering of speeches by Bhumibol on his 'philosophy' of the sufficiency economy consists largely of simplistic platitudes enunciated virtually entirely in Thai and therefore inaccessible to international scrutiny. Meanwhile they are protected from domestic criticism by the *lèse-majesté* law while being heavily promoted by royal foundations and state propaganda and, indeed, the state education system. For examples see "เศรษกิจพอเพียง" in มูลนิธิชัยพัฒนา, www.chaipat.or.th/chaipat/content/porpeing/porpeing.html#porpeing3, accessed 29 July 2013.

17 On the king's veiled criticism of Thaksin under the guise of promoting the sufficiency economy see his 2005 birthday speech: พระราชดำรัส พระราชทานแก่คณะบุคคลต่างๆ ทีเข้าเฝ้าฯ ถวายชัยมงคล ในโอกาสวันเฉลิมพระชนมพรรษา ณ ศาลาดุสิดาลัย สวนจิตรลดา พระราชวังดุสิตฯ วันอาทิตย์ที ๔ ธันวาคม พ.ศ. ๒๕๔๘ *The Golden Jubilee Network*, http://kanchanapisek.or.th/speeches/2005/1204.th.html, accessed 29 July 2013.

18 "Steak with Thaksin", 7 July 2006, http://wikileaks.org/cable/2006/07/06 BANGKOK 4041.html, accessed 29 July 2013. In interpreting the ambassador's account of the meeting one should bear in mind the strong sympathies of the Embassy towards the Palace and the history of close relations between the US and the current Thai monarch since the Cold War.

19 See **แผนพฒนาเศรษฐกิจและสงคมแห่งชาติ ฉบบทีสิบ พ.ศ. ๒๕๕๐ – ๒๕๕๔** www.nesdb.go.th/Default.aspx?tabid=139, accessed 29 July 2013.

20 See "Thai Junta Reiterates Elections Will Be Held This Year", www.abcmoney.co.uk/news/20200742219.htm, accessed 29 July 2013.

21 See "Amartya Sen Given UNESCAP Lifetime Achievement Award", *ESCAP Press Release, 28 March 2007,* www.unescap.org/unis/press/2007/mar/g08.asp, accessed 24 July 2011. For Surayud's speech at the award function (which, significantly, was also attended by Princess Sirindhorn), see *Statement by His Excellency General Surayud Chulanont (Ret.)*, www.unescap.org/anniversary/PM-statement.pdf, accessed 29 July 2013.

22 In 2007 the magazine had ranked Bhumibol fifth, with a net worth of $5 billion (Richest Royals, *Forbes*, 17 September 2007, www.forbes.com/forbes/2007/0917/054.html, accessed 9 January 2012), but in an apparent recalculation of the monarchy's worth in 2008 the king ranked first, with its total assets valued at $35 billion; see T. Serafin, "The World's Richest Royals", *Forbes*, 20 August 2008, www.forbes.com/2008/08/20/worlds-richest-royals-biz-richroyals08-cz_ts_0820royalintro.html, accessed 9 January 2012. Thailand's king maintains first place today.

23 Porphant Ouyyanont, "The Crown Property Bureau in Thailand and the Crisis of 1997", *Journal of Contemporary Asia* 38(1) (2008): 166.

24 It is notable that Popper and Hayek were both writing in the 1940s, and like Thais today were much more familiar with both feudalism and totalitarianism than are academics and journalists in the contemporary West.

25 For a fuller treatment, see Jory (2011).

26 Listen to the speech at **อ๊อฟ-ศีรษะนีมอบให้พระเจ้าแผ่นดิน** www.youtube.com/watch?v=qtgJMOEREMw, accessed 25 July 2013.

Bibliography

Anderson, B.R. O'G. 1978. "Studies of the Thai State, the State of Thai Studies". In Eliezer B. Ayal (ed.) *The Study of Thailand: Analyses of Knowledge, Approaches, and Prospects in Anthropology, Art History, Economics, History, and Political Science.* Ohio University, Centre for International Studies, pp. 193–257.

Chaloemtiarana, Thak. 2007. *Thailand: The Politics of Despotic Paternalism.* Chiang Mai: Silkworm Books & Cornell Southeast Asia Program.

Chachavalpongpun, Pavin. 2011. "Thailand's Massive Internet Censorship". *Asia Sentinel*, www.asiasentinel.com/index.php?option=com_content&task=view&id=2601&Itemid=164, accessed 21 July 2011.

"Amartya Sen Given UNESCAP Lifetime Achievement Award". 2007. *ESCAP Press Release, 28 March 2007*, www.unescap.org/unis/press/2007/mar/g08.asp, accessed 24 July 2011.

Fukuyama, F. 1992. *The End of History and the Last Man*. London: Penguin.

Handley, P. 2006. *The King Never Smiles: A Biography of Thailand's Bhumibol Adulyadej*. New Haven, CT: Yale University Press.

Hayek, F. 1994. *The Road to Serfdom*. Chicago, IL: University of Chicago Press.

Ivarsson, S. and L. Isager (eds). 2010. *Saying the Unsayable: Monarchy and Democracy in Thailand*. Copenhagen: NIAS Press.

Jory, P. 1998. "A History of the *Thet Maha Chat* and its Contribution to a Thai Political Culture". Ph.D. thesis. Australian National University, Canberra.

Jory, P. 2011. "Thai Historical Writing". In Schneider Axel and Daniel Woolf (eds) *The Oxford History of Historical Writing, Volume 5: Historical Writing Since 1945.* Oxford: Oxford University Press, pp. 539–58.

Jory, P. and M. Montesano. 2011. "End the Gag on Thailand's Citizens". *The Wall Street Journal*, 1 June, http://online.wsj.com/article/SB10001424052702303745304576357060336958374.html, accessed 29 July 2013.

MacGregor Marshall, A. 2011. *Archive of Leaked U.S. Cables on Thailand*, www.zenjournalist.com/2011/07/index-of-leaked-u-s-cables-on-thailand/, accessed 21 July 2011.

McCargo, D. 2005. "Network Monarchy and Legitimacy Crises in Thailand". *The Pacific Review* 18(4): 499–519.

Ouyyanont, P. 2008. "The Crown Property Bureau in Thailand and the Crisis of 1997". *Journal of Contemporary Asia* 38(1): 166–89.

Popper, K. 2010. *The Open Society and Its Enemies, Volume One: The Spell of Plato.* London: Routledge.

Popper, K. 2009. *The Open Society and Its Enemies, Volume Two: Hegel and Marx.* London: Routledge.

Reynolds, Craig J. 2006. "National Identity and Cultural Nationalism". In Craig J. Reynolds (ed.) *Seditious Histories: Contesting Thai and Southeast Asian Pasts*. Singapore: National University of Singapore Press. pp. 245–76.

Riggs, F. 1966. *Thailand: The Modernization of a Bureaucratic Polity*. Honolulu: East-West Center Press.

Serafin, T. 2008. "The World's Richest Royals". *Forbes*, 20 August, www.forbes.com/2008/08/20/worlds-richest-royals-biz-richroyals08-cz_ts_0820royalintro.html, accessed 9 January 2012.

Statement by His Excellency General Surayud Chulanont (Ret.), www.unescap.org/anniversary/PM-statement.pdf, accessed 29 July 2013.

"Steak with Thaksin". 2006. *Wikileaks*, 7 July, http://wikileaks.org/cable/2006/07/06BANGKOK4041.html, accessed 21 July 2013.

Streckfuss, D. 2011. *Truth on Trial in Thailand: Defamation, Treason and Lèse-Majesté*. Abingdon: Routledge.

"Sufficiency Economy: Thailand's Answer to Globalization". 2007. *UNDP Thailand*, www.undp.or.th/newsandevents/2007/news_20070109.html, accessed 21 July 2011.

Thai Human Development Report: Sufficiency Economy and Human Development. 2007. http://hdr.undp.org/en/reports/nationalreports/asiathepacific/thailand/THAILAND_2007_en.pdf, accessed 22 July 2011.

"Thai Junta Reiterates Elections Will Be Held This Year". 2007. www.abcmoney.co.uk/news/20200742219.htm, accessed 29 July 2013.

คึกฤทธิ์ ปราโมช. 1986. ฝรั่งศักดินา. กรุงเทพฯ สยามรัฐ.

ณัฐพล ใจจริง. 2005. "การรื้อสร้าง 2475: ฝันจริงของนักอุดมคติ 'น้ำเงินแท้' ". ศิลปวัฒนธรรม 27(2) (ธันวาคม): 79–117.

ธงชัย วินิจจะกูล. 2001. "ประวัติศาสตร์ไทยแบบราชาชาตินิยม: จากยุคอาณานิคมอำพรางสู่ราชาชาตินิยมใหม่ หรือลัทธิเสด็จพ่อของกระฎุมพีไทยในปัจจุบัน". ศิลปวัฒนธรรม 23(1) (พฤศจิกายน): 43–52.

ประมวล รุจนเสรี. 2005. พระราชอำนาจ. กรุงเทพฯ. K.K. Publishing.

แผนพฒนาเศรษฐกิจและสงคมแห่งชาติ ฉบบทีสิบ พ.ศ. ๒๕๕๐ – ๒๕๕๔www.nesdb.go.th/Default.aspx?tabid=139, accessed 29 July 2013.

พระราชดำรัส พระราชทานแก่คณะบุคคลต่างๆ ทีเข้าเฝ้าฯ ถวายชัยมงคล ในโอกาสวันเฉลิมพระชนมพรรษา ณ ศาลาดุสิดาลัย สวนจิตรลดา พระราชวังดุสิตฯ วันอาทิตย์ที ๔ ธันวาคม พ.ศ. ๒๕๔๘, *The Golden Jubilee Network*, 2005, http://kanchanapisek.or.th/speeches/2005/1204.th.html, accessed 24 July 2011.

อ๊อฬ-ศีรษะนีมอบให้พระเจ้าแผ่นดิน. www.youtube.com/watch?v=LUmO8Z9H1Ng, accessed 25 July 2013.

ภูมิพลอดุลยเดช, พระบาทสมเด็จพระปรมินทรมหา. 1996. พระมหาชนก – *The Story of Mahajanaka*. กรุงเทพฯ: อมรินทร์พรินติ้งแอนด์พับลิชชิ่ง.

สมศักดิ์ เจียมธีรสกุล. 2011. ประวัติศาสตร์ที่เพิ่งสร้าง: รวมบทความเกี่ยวกับกรณี *14* ตุลา และ *6* ตุลา. กรุงเทพฯ: สำนักพิมพ์ 6 ตุลารำลึก.

"เศรษฐกิจพอเพียง" ใน มูลนิธิชัยพัฒนา, www.chaipat.or.th/chaipat/content/porpeing/porpeing.html#porpeing3, accessed 24 July 2011.

รายงานพิเศษ – "คำพิพากษา" ดา ตอร์ปิโด ในความเห็นของผู้ประกอบ วิชาชีพทางกฎหมายคนหนึ่ง ศรัทธา หุ่นพยนต์ ฟ้าเดียวกัน ปีที่ 7 เล่ม 3, กันยายน 2552.

3 Thai populism and the middle-income trap

Peter Warr

1 Introduction

In July 2011 Thailand elected a new government, with a majority of seats won by the *Pheu Thai* ('for Thais') Party. The new government is led by Yingluck Shinawatra, the younger sister of the fugitive former prime minister Thaksin Shinawatra. It commonly said that the *Pheu Thai* Party is 'populist', while the former government, led by Abhisit Vejjajiva of the Democrat Party, is more representative of the urban, monarchist Thai establishment. Thaksin is now based in Dubai, having been convicted while abroad of conflict of interest during his 2001 to 2006 period in office. He was sentenced to two years' imprisonment but has refused to return to serve the sentence. Although Yingluck is now prime minister *in situ*, her older brother is widely considered the leader *in absentia*. Less than two months after Thaksin declared her as his choice for party leader, Yingluck became prime minister. Despite a lack of prior political experience she has a pleasant manner and an admirably explicit policy agenda, announced by her brother from Dubai. This programme was widely described as 'populism'. But what does this label mean and what does it imply for Thailand's future?

2 Populism

Wikipedia describes 'populism' as an ideology of sociopolitical thought that emphasizes the difference between 'the people' and 'the elite', and comments that in practice populist discourse typically buttresses an authoritarian, top-down process of political mobilization in which a charismatic leader addresses the masses directly, rather than through political parties or other institutions. The Cambridge dictionary adds that populism is in opposition to 'statism', which holds that a small group of professional politicians know better than the people and should therefore make decisions on their behalf. In their book *Populism in Asia* (2007), Kosuke and Phongpaichit note that populist rhetoric is typically complemented by "anti-intellectualism, anti-elitism, and often anti-foreign sentiments".

More recently, in his book on populism in Latin America, *Left Behind: Latin America and the False Promise of Populism* (2010), the UCLA economist

Sebastian Edwards describes economic populism as an emphasis on public expenditures that win political support through poorly evaluated large public projects and short-term redistributions towards targeted groups, as opposed to public investments that raise long-term productivity, all combined with large-scale corruption and a disregard for the fiscal consequences of these policies.

Do these descriptions really apply to *Pheu Thai* and its putative leader, Thaksin? I say, yes. On 23 April 2011, Thaksin announced his party's economic policies for the anticipated election, speaking to a meeting of the *Pheu Thai* faithful by video transmission from Dubai. Thaksin outlined a detailed set of economic initiatives with two components: capital intensive mega-projects and redistributive initiatives designed to attract new sources of political support.

3 Thaksin's agenda

The proposed mega-construction projects include the following:

1. A 30–60 km wall to protect Bangkok from flooding.
2. A water diversion project to bring water to twenty-five Thai river basins, diverted from Burma, Laos and Cambodia.
3. A high-speed train linking Bangkok with major cities.
4. A 'land bridge' (not a canal) linking the Gulf of Thailand with the Andaman Sea.
5. Ten new electric train lines in Bangkok.

Each of these mega-projects is popular with a significant segment of the population and, like all construction projects in Thailand, they offer the prospect of huge kick-backs for politicians and others. There is every possibility that at least some of these mega-projects, or some variant of them, would make economic sense once they were properly evaluated. But Thaksin shows no interest in waiting for that to be done. The projects are described as approved already.

The redistributive initiatives include the following:

1. A three- to five-year debt moratorium for people owing between 500,000 and one million baht.
2. A ten million baht minimum revenue guarantee for local administrative organizations.
3. A farmers' credit card project, presumably backed by the government.
4. A 15,000 baht per month minimum salary guarantee for bachelor's degree graduates.
5. A one billion baht education fund for state and private universities.
6. A tax cut for first-home buyers.
7. A tax cut for first-car buyers.
8. Free wi-fi in public areas.
9. A guaranteed price of 15,000 baht per tonne for unmilled rice.
10. An increase in the minimum wage to 300 baht per day.

The increase in the minimum wage was one initiative on which the Democrats agreed, but their proposed increase was smaller (250 baht per day). Many of the initiatives outlined above are reminiscent of Thaksin's policies during his period in office of 2001 to 2006, ended by a military coup. In addition, Thaksin recycled two promises from the 2001 election in which he won an unprecedented parliamentary majority:

1 Eliminate the drugs problem within twelve months.
2 Eliminate poverty within four years.

Following the 2001 election, 'Eliminate the drugs problem' proved to mean giving the police permission to kill anyone suspected of being a drugs dealer. The police themselves are widely said to be the most important drug dealers, so the policy was interpreted by many as a licence for the police to remove their business competitors. More than 2000 extra-judicial murders occurred, none were properly investigated and of course no one was ever charged. Although the policy was reportedly popular with Thaksin's supporters, the drug problem was not eliminated. Neither was poverty.

A feature of Thaksin's proposed policy measures is that, unlike the Democrats, they do not ignore rural people. Despite decades of rural–urban migration and the growth of Bangkok in particular, two-thirds of the Thai people still reside in rural areas, including almost all of the country's poorest people. In *Populism in Asia*, Baker and Phongpaichit point out that prior to 2000 Thaksin had shown no interest in agricultural policy and his speeches had not used the term 'the people'. Thaksin is a businessman. He knows how to sell things. His political insight was to recognize that populist rhetoric offered him the chance to win the support of Thailand's huge, relatively impoverished and disaffected rural population. He has done so with unprecedented success.

Thaksin similarly did not succeed in eliminating poverty during his earlier period in office. I have shown elsewhere that the annual rate at which poverty declined under Thaksin's government was lower than the historical average over the preceding three decades, even though global economic conditions were relatively favourable during Thakskin's period in office (Warr 2009a). In my view there was one principal reason. Thaksin's redistributive expenditures were implemented at the expense of productive investments, especially in agriculture, the economic base of most of Thailand's poor.

In a recent paper, a Thai colleague and I demonstrated that during Thaksin's period of government, expenditure on agricultural research and extension declined as a proportion of agricultural output by 77 and 60 per cent, respectively (Suphannachart and Warr 2011). Numerous studies, including our own, demonstrate that agricultural research is a powerful driver of productivity growth in agriculture and hence a driver of sustained poverty reduction (Sussankarn and Tinakorn 1998). Redistributions towards the poor can reduce poverty, but their one-off effect lasts only as long as the redistributions continue. There is no sustained effect on the productivity of the recipients.

4 Regulating the price of rice

During Thailand's 2011 election campaign, the election promises of the *Pheu Thai* Party led by Yingluck Shinawatra included the reintroduction of a rice mortgage or rice-pledging scheme for rice. It also promised that the pledging price would be 15,000 baht per tonne of paddy (approximately US$550), well in excess of the current market price of around 9000 baht. With its victory in the election of 3 July and its subsequent endorsement by the Election Commission, *Pheu Thai* is now forming a government. Although detailed policy announcements have not yet been made it seems probable that the rice mortgage policy will be implemented, roughly as promised.

The effects of the policy are likely to include an expansion of Thai rice production, an increase in domestic rice prices, a higher volume of Thai rice exports, a reduction in the average quality of Thai rice, and a reduction in regional rice export prices, all compared with what would have occurred without the reintroduction of the policy.

The first rice-pledging policy was introduced, three decades ago, during the 1981/2 growing season. The purpose was to provide cheap loans to rice farmers, enabling them to delay the sale of their crops and thereby obtain better prices by not selling immediately after the harvest. Under the scheme, farmers could use their forthcoming rice crop as collateral to borrow a fraction of its expected market value from the government-owned Bank for Agriculture and Agricultural Cooperatives.

The loans were made through the government-owned Bank for Agriculture and Agricultural Cooperatives and the interest rate was set below market rates, implying a modest subsidy. The amount the farmer could borrow was determined by the pledging price, set at around 60 per cent of the market price and the proportion of the expected crop that the farmer pledged. Relatively few farmers used the scheme and its costs were moderate. The scheme did not involve the government actually buying or selling rice unless the farmer reneged on the loan, which was rare.

In 2001/2, under the newly elected populist government of Thaksin Shinawatra, the scheme was transformed into a price support scheme, though the original name was retained. After some initial confusion the 'pledging' price was set at about 20 per cent *above* the market price. By 2005/6 this differential had expanded to about 30 per cent. Farmers were now able to sell a proportion of their crop at a price significantly above the current market price. This scheme continued until 2006, when the Thaksin government was deposed by a military coup. The new military government reverted to the old price-pledging scheme. World rice prices and market prices within Thailand were increasing at the time and the pledging price remained below the market price. A new Thaksin-aligned government under Prime Minister Samak Sundaravej reinstated the price support component in 2008 and again offered a pledging price well above the market price, although rice market prices were already at record high levels.

In late 2008 the newly installed Democrat-led government of Prime Minister Abhisit Vejjajiva modified the policy to what was called an 'income support' or 'income guarantee' policy. This new name was also misleading. It was a price guarantee system, not an income guarantee system, but it did contain limits on the amount of rice per farmer that was eligible for the price guarantee. If the market price was below a pre-established reference price, the government would pay the farmer the difference up to a maximum volume of rice per farmer – set at twenty-five tonnes. Because market prices for rice were high during the period of the Abhisit government and normally exceeded the reference prices, the scheme delivered very little subsidy to farmers.

Because the Thaksin-Samak scheme is the model for the one that will apparently be reintroduced soon by the newly elected government, it is useful to review its features. The essence is that the government becomes involved directly in rice marketing by purchasing rice from those farmers who participate in the scheme, storing and milling it, and subsequently selling it to exporters, who typically purchase approximately half of Thailand's rice crop of around twenty million tones of milled rice equivalent.

Thaksin's scheme was said to benefit small farmers. Those rice farmers who did participate received significant benefits, depending on the magnitude of their sales to the scheme. A 2008 study by Poapongsakorn and Isvilanond indicated that larger farmers, especially those in the Central Plains and lower northern regions of the country, received most of the benefits. Smaller (and hence poorer) farmers, especially those in the northeast and upper north regions, received proportionately much less. The poorest 20 per cent of farmers received only 4.5 per cent of the total benefit, measured by the value of total paddy pledged.

Large profits were also reaped by those warehouse owners and millers who were chosen by the government to store and mill the rice purchased under the scheme. The rice was eventually sold to exporters but the bidding system was non-transparent and allegedly corrupt. Huge profits were made by exporters able to purchase rice below market prices. The exporters whose bids were successful were few in number (not more than two or three) and sometimes turned out to be mysterious new participants in the industry. One such company – a new entrant to the rice export industry said to be owned by the wife of the most prominent politician at the time – was the sole successful bidder in one round of negotiations, even though its bid was well below the prevailing market price.

The scheme was unpopular with established rice exporters. Because of the non-transparent and non-competitive nature of the bidding process they were largely excluded from the economic rents enjoyed by other 'exporters' and, for reasons discussed below, their profit margins were squeezed by the scheme. Through the Thai Rice Exporters Association this group is currently campaigning against the scheme's reintroduction, presumably in anticipation of similar practices.

Calculations by Poapongsakorn of the operation of the scheme in the wet season of 2005/2006 indicate that 5.24 million tonnes of paddy were pledged, about a quarter of the total crop of twenty-two million tonnes of paddy. Total government expenditure under the scheme was around fifty billion baht and total revenue from the subsequent sale of rice was thirty-two billion baht, implying a loss of about eighteen billion baht. This loss was a transfer from general revenue (Thai taxpayers) to the beneficiaries of the scheme along with the costs of operating it. The distribution of these benefits and other costs were estimated as follows:

1 Farmers 37 per cent.
2 Millers 14 per cent.
3 Warehouse owners 4.4 per cent.
4 Recipients of export contracts 24 per cent.
5 Operating costs 15 per cent.
6 Depreciation and other costs 3.6 per cent.

In summary, farmers received a little over one-third of the benefits, most by larger farmers, and not the small farmers said to be the intended beneficiaries. A small number of 'exporters' reaped profits of not less than 4.3 billion baht (US$144 million) in the 2005/6 wet season alone.

The scheme includes some features that are similar to an export subsidy. The government buys rice domestically and sells it for export at a loss, borne by the taxpayer. It has been claimed that the scheme caused domestic market prices for paddy to be higher than they would otherwise have been because the scheme increases the domestic demand for paddy. This would mean that some indirect benefits were received by the majority of rice farmers who did not participate in the scheme. There is some scope for this claim to be correct, but the benefit from higher prices is received predominantly by those who sell the most rice. A study by Siamwalla and Jitsuchon calculated that only 10 to 13 per cent of the marketed surplus of rice is sold by the poorest 20 per cent of rice farmers.

It is significant that during the Thaksin and post-Thaksin operation of the rice mortgage scheme the commercial export industry continued to operate in coexistence with it. If domestic market prices were increased significantly, commercial exporters – who must pay market prices for their stock and then sell abroad in competition with exporters able to purchase more cheaply under the scheme – would have been bankrupted. It is possible that some market price increase occurred, squeezing the narrow profit margins of the traditional rice exporting firms, which is a further explanation for their current opposition to it. But the effect cannot have been large. The test of the future size of this domestic price effect will be whether commercial exporters remain in business after the scheme is reintroduced.

The scheme raises the volume of Thailand's rice exports and, because Thailand is such a dominant exporter, this reduces regional rice export prices to some extent, harming competitors such as Vietnam and India. There are other, reinforcing reasons why regional rice prices may soon decline. High international prices have induced a supply response from other exporters. India now has large stocks for export and has recently announced an export price below that of the

Thai product. In addition, the quality of Vietnamese rice exports has improved in recent years and this product now competes more closely with Thai rice exports.

The rice mortgage scheme reduces the quality of Thailand's rice exports because the pledging price advantage applies, regardless of the quality of the rice pledged. Farmers will offer their lowest quality of rice to the scheme and, if lower quality rice can be produced more cheaply, participating farmers will shift their operations towards these varieties. This effect has negative long-term implications for Thailand's rice exports.

Finally, the rice mortgage scheme is being reintroduced at the same time as a large minimum wage increase. The former is meant to appeal to farmers, while the latter is targeted at urban workers. Many economists fear the long-term loss of economic competitiveness and the fiscal implications of this populist approach to economic policy.

5 Thailand's middle-income trap

Thailand is caught in a self-created middle-income trap. The 'middle-income trap' is an empirical generalization based mainly on East and Southeast Asian experience: once a country reaches middle-income levels the growth rate often declines and graduation from middle-income to higher-income levels stalls. I will describe what this means, how it came about, how current policies are making it worse and what needs to be done to escape the situation.

During the decade of economic boom ending in 1997, Thailand's average annual growth rate of real GDP per person was a remarkable 8.4 per cent. Like most booms, this one ended badly. It collapsed with the Asian Financial Crisis of 1997 to 1999. Since 2000 the corresponding growth rate has been 4.1 per cent. The immediate culprit was a contraction of private investment, which declined as a proportion of GDP from an average of 30 per cent to 18 per cent over the same two periods. The effect of lower investment was twofold: it reduced aggregate demand, lowering income in the short run; and it reduced the rate of capital formation, lowering long-run growth prospects (Warr 2005, 2009b).

A decline in this investment ratio occurred in all of the crisis-affected Asian economies, including Indonesia, Malaysia, the Philippines and South Korea. The decline in Thailand was one of the largest. The contraction of investment occurred primarily among Thai-owned, rather than foreign-owned, firms. Put simply, after the crisis Thai firms became less confident about their prospects and hence less inclined to invest. An expectation of this kind is self-fulfilling. It reduces investment, which does indeed ensure that growth will be lower.

Beneath these short-term macroeconomic events lies a deeper and longer term phenomenon. Between the 1960s and 1990s Thailand achieved the transition from a poor, heavily rural backwater to a middle-income, semi-industrialized and globalized economy (Manorungsan 1989; Ingram 1971). The transition was primarily market driven and the central policy imperative was to avoid those policies that impeded absorption of low-cost labour into export-oriented labour-intensive manufacturing and services. This transition required some elementary market-supporting policy reforms: promoting a stable business environment (not necessarily meaning stable politics); open policies with respect to international trade and foreign investment; and the public provision of basic physical infrastructure, including roads, ports, reliable electricity supplies, telecommunications and policing sufficient to protect the physical assets created by business investment.

This transition has now occurred in most of East and Southeast Asia, and the pattern was similar in all countries that undertook the basic policy reforms listed above. During this transition average real incomes rose significantly, the share of the workforce employed in agriculture contracted and the incidence of absolute poverty fell. The core of this growth process is expansion of the physical capital stock, resting overwhelmingly on private investment (Krugman 1994; Vines and Warr 2003). The private financial system facilitates the link between private savings and business investment, but the process is self-limiting. As labour moves from low-productivity agriculture to more rewarding alternatives elsewhere, wages are eventually driven up. As wages rise, the profitability of labour-intensive development declines. As the return to investment in physical capital falls, the rate of private investment slackens and growth slows. The frontier for further expansion of labour-intensive export-oriented development soon moves to other, lower wage countries. The result is the dreaded 'middle-income trap'. This describes Thailand and Malaysia today and China in the very near future.

Progress from middle-income to higher income levels requires a different kind of policy reform, addressing a market failure that the private financial system cannot resolve: the under-supply of human capital. Human capital is a crucial input, created primarily by investment in education, broadly defined. But it differs from physical capital in that it does not provide the collateral that can ensure repayment of loans. Unlike physical assets, human beings can walk away. The private financial system is therefore unable to support investment in human capital. Individual families can and do invest heavily in the education of their own children, but because their resources are limited and because the recipient of the educational investment reaps only part of the returns it generates, this is insufficient to resolve the overall underinvestment in human capital.

Increasing the supply of human capital is central to overcoming the middle-income trap. It raises labour productivity directly and raises the return to physical capital, encouraging greater investment in physical capital as well. In Thailand, as in many other middle-income countries, the problem lies in the quality of education and not just the bare numbers of total school enrolments. And the problem is primarily not at the tertiary level but at the primary and secondary levels. Massive public investment and reform of the education curriculum is needed to redress these problems, requiring the raising of sufficient tax revenue to finance it and combating the backward and self-serving practices of the Ministry of Education and the teachers' unions. These are formidable obstacles.

During Thailand's boom, almost everyone gained, including the poor, though not all at the same rate. Economic expectations rose, even among groups such as lower income rural people, who had previously benefited only marginally from economic growth. But when the boom collapsed in July 1997, the new opportunities vanished and the newly expanded expectations were crushed. A sense of economic and political injustice, latent for decades, then became more acute. For large numbers of people, redistributive politics then became more appealing as a focus for their anger and as a vehicle for collective economic advancement. Opportunities then arose for political entrepreneurs who could mobilize the frustration and use it to capture power.

Enter Thaksin Shinawatra. He had made a fortune by exploiting government-granted concessions in the telecommunications industry and had been a deputy prime minister under two conservative governments in the 1990s. But around the year 2000 Thaksin saw the political opportunity created by the frustrated expectations of many low- and middle-income people, especially those in the predominantly rural north and northeast regions. He articulated the discontent felt by these people and offered hope. According to his new rhetoric, Thailand's problem was not a flawed macroeconomic strategy that had strangled growth, but injustice inflicted on 'the people' by their fellow Thais, 'the elite'. Thaksin would look after them. This was standard Latin American-style populism and it worked. Thaksin's new party won an unprecedented election victory in 2001 and repeated the achievement in 2005.

What is wrong with that? At one level, nothing. It is simply democracy in action. But a problem remains, in that Thaksin's short-term populism fails to address the underlying long-term sources of the middle-income trap and distracts attention from them. The policy platform successfully taken to the 2011 elections illustrates this point. Aside from the problem of paying for its spending initiatives, the important point is what the policy did *not* contain: anything about reforming Thailand's antiquated systems of primary and secondary education, the single greatest impediment to long-term economic progress in the country (Khoman 1993); anything else about raising the long-term productivity of Thailand's masses of unskilled and semi-skilled workers; anything about reforming the country's regressive and inadequate tax system; or anything about reducing corruption.

6 Relation to Popper's ideas

Karl Popper wrote *The Open Society and Its Enemies* during the Second World War while teaching in New Zealand, and published it in 1945. He was reacting to the threat posed at the time by the 'closed society' totalitarianisms of fascism and communism. He believed that social progress, meaning social change that reduced pain (he was a negative utilitarian), arose from the application of new ideas and the implementation of piecemeal reform, processed through critical examination. These views reflected Popper's earlier work on the philosophy of science in which he emphasized the importance of procedures that enabled scientific conjectures to be falsified by unbiased empirical testing. *The Open Society* may be thought of as the application of these ideas to the political realm. Popper thought the open society was more conducive to the process of critical examination of new ideas than a closed society, based on fixed 'tribal' ideas. It followed that freedom of the press, liberal democracy and civilized debate promoted the application of new ideas that actually worked, and thus that a society based on these principles (the open society) would outperform one based on fixed ideas (the closed society). The danger was that the transition from tribal societies to more open ones created stresses that offered political opportunities for 'strong men' to establish totalitarian states. He believed that philosophical ideas like historicism contributed to this danger.

Do these ideas help in the understanding of modern Thailand? My view is, yes, to a limited extent. There is no doubt that the transition from a traditional society to one in which economic and political relationships are changing rapidly creates stress and that this stress opens opportunities for strongman-type political opportunists. Thaksin Shinawatra is a good example. Thaksin offered a simple theory to explain the problems of the rural masses. The theory was that they were being exploited and held back by the elite. They needed a strong leader, like himself, to help them capture the political power required to establish equitable treatment. I am not sure that Thaksin really believed this crude theory, but he found it politically potent. All this sounds like Popper's account of the birth of fascism, but I do not think it had much to do with historicism. Thaksin's vision was simple and short term, without much historical overlay, and the policy measures he advocated were also short term.

Moreover, Thaksin's opponents – the elite-serving 'Yellow Shirts', as opposed to his own rural-based 'Red Shirts' – were not necessarily more supportive of critical thinking, a free press and liberal democracy than Thaksin and his followers. That is, the cleft between Thaksin's Red Shirts and the opposing Yellow Shirts did not correspond to a difference along the lines set out by Popper. Both groups supported press freedom and liberal democracy when doing so helped them politically, and opposed them when they thought otherwise. There is a continuing danger that a dictatorial outcome could emerge, but that danger is not confined to Thaksin and his followers. A repressive military coup, supporting the traditional elite against Thaksin and his followers, is a continuing possibility.

I believe that a central issue in the Thai discourse is 'respect'. The people represented by Thaksin – unskilled and semi-skilled workers, many of whom are rural residents or recent migrants from rural to urban areas – have enjoyed considerable economic progress in recent decades. But they feel that the elite still regards them and treats them like buffaloes – without respect. That hurts. They are demanding to be treated differently, and see Thaksin and his political movement as asserting their right to be taken seriously.

7 Conclusion

Thaksin's policies include some innovative ideas, and this can hardly be said of the Democrats, but his brand of populism threatens to take Thailand down the

South American dead-end described so well by Sebastian Edwards. Thailand's version of economic populism increases dependence on the state, wastes public revenue, feeds corruption, ignores the sources of long-term improvements in human productivity and diverts attention from them. It is sure to disappoint its supporters and is therefore a long-term danger to the liberal democracy that Thailand has established, at great cost, and which Karl Popper would surely have admired.

Bibliography

Edwards, S. 2010. *Left Behind: Latin America and the False Promise of Populism.* Chicago, IL: University of Chicago Press.

Ingram, J.C. 1971. *Economic Change in Thailand: 1850–1970.* Stanford, CA: Stanford University Press.

Khoman, Sirilaksana. 1993. "Education Policy". In Peter Warr (ed.) *The Thai Economy in Transition.* Cambridge: Cambridge University Press.

Kosuke, M. and Pasuk Phongpaichit. 2007. *Populism in Asia.* Kyoto Centre for Southeast Asian Studies Series in Asian Studies. Singapore: Singapore University Press.

Krugman, P. 1994. "The Myth of Asia's Miracle". *Foreign Affairs* 73(6): 62–78.

Manorungsan, Sompop. 1989. *Economic Development of Thailand, 1850–1950.* Institute of Asian Studies Monograph 42. Bangkok: Chulalongkorn University Press.

Poapongsaorn, Nipon and Somporn Isvilanond. 2008. "Key Policy Issues in the Thai Rice Industry: Myth, Misguided Policies and Critical Issues". Presented at the International Rice Research Institute Rice Policy Forum, Los Banos, Philippines, February.

Popper, K. 1971. *The Open Society and Its Enemies* (5th edn). Princeton, NJ: Princeton University Press.

Suphannachart, Waleerat and P. Warr. 2011. "Research and Productivity in Thai Agriculture". *Australian Journal of Agricultural and Resource Economics* 55(1): 35–52.

Sussankarn, Chalongphob and Pranee Tinakorn. 1998. *Productivity Growth in Thailand, 1980 to 1995.* Bangkok: Thailand Development Research Institute.

Vines, D. and P. Warr. 2003. "Thailand's Investment-driven Boom and Crisis". *Oxford Economic Papers* 55(3): 440–64.

Warr, P. 2005. "Boom, Bust and Beyond". In P. Warr (ed.) *Thailand beyond the Crisis.* London: Routledge.

——. 2009a. "The Economy under the Thaksin Government: Stalled Recovery". In J. Funston (ed.) *Divided Over Thaksin: Thailand's Coup and Problematic Transition,* Institute of Southeast Asian Studies. Singapore: Silkworm Books, Chiang Mai, pp. 150–71.

——. 2009b. "Poverty Reduction through Long-term Growth: The Thai Experience". *Asian Economic Papers* 8(2): 51–76.

4 Least free

The economic consequences of fifty years of totalitarian rule in Burma

Sean Turnell

1 Introduction

For fifty years Burma has resided at the 'wrong end' of just about every conceivable measure of economic and human development. It has also occupied the same space in international indices of human freedom. These phenomena are not unrelated, and this is, in part, because the lack of freedom in Burma is the product of what Karl Popper would call a closed rather than an open society. As discussed by other authors in more detail elsewhere in this volume, individuals in a closed economy are less likely to prosper because, by accepting (or being compelled to accept) uncritical, hierarchical and authoritarian structures that characterize traditional societies and those constructed under state socialism, existing institutions, laws and ideas are closed to scrutiny. All of this has the effect that they are less likely to change for the better, especially if change induces a relative loss of wealth or status for those who head the hierarchy.

In this chapter I explore the ways in which the lack of freedom in Burma turned the once richest country in Southeast Asia into the poorest. I will explore the historical legacy that brought the country to this sad state of affairs, and examine in more detail select manifestations of how Burma's overwhelming state undermines the economy. Highlighted are the ways in which state spending and its financing has 'crowded out' the private sector and brought monetary instability, allowed the embezzlement of Burma's export earnings, and prompted the flight of both financial and human capital. At strategic points in the narrative that follows, links to the Popperian theme of this volume will be made, but, for the most part, they will be passed over without comment, partly because they are self-evident, and partly because my main focus is less on delineating the precise nature of Burma's closed society and more on recording its economic consequences.

In March 2011 a nominal civilian government took the place of overt military rule in Burma. For the first six months or so of its existence, the new government appeared to be little more than a façade for continuing military rule. While the military remains ultimately in charge, in the latter part of 2011 this government announced various reforms that allowed some hope that Burma was at the cusp of change. By mid-2012 the reforms reached the point where Burma's principal opposition party was able to take up seats in the Parliament following a series of (more or less 'free and fair') by-elections. From there the reforms accelerated further, especially in the economic sphere. Critical in the context of greater economic freedoms were initiatives to effectively float Burma's currency, to grant greater independence to the central bank, and to encourage foreign investment. And yet, severe obstacles remain to basic economic freedoms in Burma. The most pernicious of these remain the excessive demands of the state, while new land laws have only undermined Burma's already doubtful property rights regime. Likewise, there remains a substantial gap between the rhetoric of change in Burma, and that which is manifest in practical policy-making or in concrete law. As such, while this chapter notes the reforms that have taken place, it finds that the barriers to the profound institutional reforms necessary for genuinely transformational growth in Burma are not yet in place.

2 The scorecard

International metrics of Burma's economy, and of the ability of individuals and firms to make uninhibited decisions within it, have been universally dire. According to the *Economic Freedom of the World* index (EFW), an annual publication of Canada's Fraser Institute, Burma is the second 'least free' country in the world ('bested' only by Zimbabwe).[1] The Fraser Institute's construct measures economic freedom as a composite of five attributes: the size of government in the economy; the security of property rights; access to sound money; freedom to exchange with foreigners; and the degree of regulation of credit, labour and business. In each of these attributes Burma performs not only badly, but especially poorly relative to the Asia Pacific (its attributes in so many areas have more in common with Africa than with Asia). The EFW's findings are supported by similar listings, including the Heritage Foundation/Wall Street Journal's *2013 Index of Economic Freedom* (which ranks Burma 172 out of 177 countries measured).[2]

Of course, such metrics would not matter much if they were contradictory to more traditional measures of Burma's economic circumstances. Unfortunately they are not. Once among the richest countries in Southeast Asia and, at the time of independence in 1948, widely regarded as the country 'most likely' to achieve rapid growth, Burma is now by some margin the poorest in the region. Statistics on Burma's economy are hard to come by and notoriously unreliable – nevertheless, with a per capita GDP of around US$700 per annum (around $1200 in purchasing power-parity terms), the average citizen of Burma is poorer than his or her peers in Laos ($980) and Cambodia ($815), and well short of the incomes enjoyed in Thailand ($5000).[3] That the latter country has traditionally been Burma's most important peer competitor, and was not much wealthier than Burma a scant half-century ago, is testimony to the extraordinary economic mismanagement of a succession of Burma's military rulers. It is to this issue that we now turn.

3 The legacy of the past

The current grim state of Burma's economy is the result of nearly fifty years of wilfully inept economic management under a military regime that took power in a coup in 1962, and soon after instigated a programme known as the 'Burma road to socialism'. Under this ideology most of Burma's enterprises, from the largest industries to humble village shops, were nationalized. Likewise, thereafter rational economic decision-making took a back seat to the capricious demands of the military, demands that resulted in not just the appropriation of much of Burma's output by the armed forces, but also the creation of a broader acquisitive state apparatus that resulted in gross inefficiencies, inequities, and hitherto unimagined levels of corruption. The arbitrary and erratic nature of policy-making in this era was also manifest in other destructive ways, perhaps best exemplified by the military regime's efforts to crush what they regarded as 'speculators' – by successive rounds of 'demonetizing' various denominations of the currency. These extreme and arbitrary measures did little to bring speculation to an end, but they did pauperize vast swathes of what had hitherto been Burma's middle class (Turnell 2009, 237–40). Of course, such policies are diametrically at variance with Popper's notion (discussed by Shearmur in Chapter 1, this volume) of the importance of 'institutionalized procedures' as foundational to the application of the rule of law. Policy-making in Burma on what would prove its road to pauperization was manifestly the rule of a small cadre of uniformed *men* who, in these and other ways, deliberately sought a 'closed' society.

In the face of manifest failure, Burma's socialist 'road' was abandoned in increments in subsequent years, but the fundamental nature of the regime – and of its prerogative over all important aspects of the economy – has remained constant. Burma's military apparatus throughout its rule has commandeered the largest part of the country's resources, while it has simultaneously dismantled basic market institutions. Primary among the consequently 'missing' institutions in Burma has been anything even resembling the rule of law, or of sound property rights. The greatest proportion of the population in Burma have no legal title over their property or possessions (including land), no certainty that it will not be expropriated by the state without compensation, and a circumscribed and doubtful ability to use their own labour and resources.

Instead of functioning amidst formal rights and laws, economic activity in Burma has long existed according to a set of parallel rules of the 'shadow' economy – rules determined by arbitrary procedures for dispute settlement, nepotistic patron–client relationships between the military, state and business, extra legal allocations of natural resource concessions and of licences to engage in external trade and exchange, and by a governing apparatus that is as unpredictable as it is predatory. In Burma the economic time horizon is very short and, in the absence of trust, investment in long-term capital formation, or in the acquisition of personal skills and capacities, is replaced by a short-term focus on survival.

4 Government spending

For the first time in decades, in early 2011 Burma's state budget was made public. Table 4.1 aggregates the relevant numbers (in Burma's currency, the *kyat*), the proportion of total spending allocated to each ministry and – for the purposes of comparison – the US$ equivalent for each item.

Unsurprisingly, the standout feature of Burma's state budget is the dominance of military spending. Larger than all other spending items combined, such spending consumes just over half of the budget. Yet, even as high as it is acknowledged to be, specific allocations to defence almost certainly understate its claim on Burma's financial resources. Embedded military spending in the budgets of other ministries has long been the practice in Burma, and defence likewise claims special access to foreign exchange, as well as to the earnings of a number of large military-owned corporations.

After defence, 'construction' is the next largest area of expenditure, and includes ongoing costs associated with the building of Burma's brand-new capital city of Naypyidaw ('abode of kings'). Meanwhile, shocking both for its inadequacy and the gloomy future it portends, is spending on health and education. The former, at little more than US$1.60 per capita per annum, ties with the Republic of Congo as the lowest in the world. By comparison, the equivalent numbers on per capita government health expenditure for Burma's closest ASEAN peers were Laos (US$7), Cambodia (US$11) and Vietnam (US$31). Thailand's government spent US$260 per capita on health.[4] In 2012 and again in 2013 dramatic increases in aggregate health and education expenditure were announced. Nevertheless, in both of these areas expenditure remains less than half of that made by the Government of Laos. Meanwhile, as a proportion of overall government outlays, such expenditure has actually fallen across 2012 to 2013 – health at 2.9 per cent of the budget and education 5.4 per cent (IMF 2013).

Table 4.1 State spending by ministerial category

Ministry	*2010/11 Kyat billions*	*% of total*	*US$ equivalent 2011/($m)*
Defence	1323	51	1557
Construction	296	11	348
Education	267	10	314
Agriculture	199	8	235
Electricity	78	3	92
Health	73	3	86
Other	358	14	429
TOTAL	2594	100	3052

Source: Myanmar Central Statistical Organisation (MCSO) 2011.

5 Burma's budget deficit and its financing

With total taxation revenue of only 1.2 trillion *kyat* for 2010/2011, Burma's fiscal deficit amounted to around half of government spending. Absent the earnings from state-owned enterprises that are largely held outside the public accounts (more on which later), this implies a programme of significant borrowing – from the central bank (printing money), from commercial banks and from the sale of bonds. Table 4.2 reveals the magnitudes and relativities.

As may be seen from the above, 'printing money' remains the most important way in which the Burmese state finances itself beyond taxes. Such state borrowing from the Central Bank of Myanmar rose nearly 30 per cent to K6.2 trillion in the nine months to December 2010, and accounted for just over 52 per cent of deficit financing. Government borrowing from commercial banks accounted for 38 per cent of the government's borrowing needs, while new bond sales took care of 10 per cent. The former highlights the way in which Burma's commercial banks have become an increasingly important component of the country's fiscal apparatus, and the extent to which this function has 'crowded out' their lending to the private sector. Indeed, Burma's private banks are now in the extraordinary position of lending more to the state (53per cent of the total) than they do to businesses and consumers (47 per cent).

The monetary profligacy of Burma's government has created great instability in its currency. This was manifested both in inflation (perennially the highest in Southeast Asia) and in the wide discrepancy that existed between Burma's fixed, official exchange rate (set at around K6/US$1 for nearly fifty years) and the unofficial (but predominant) market rate that over the past decade averaged around K1000/US$1. This 'parallel premium' between the official and market exchange rates (one of the largest anytime, anywhere) was something of a totem of Burma's economic decline.

In what has been one of the most significant of the early economic reforms of Burma's new quasi-civilian government, this archaic and dysfunctional exchange rate arrangement came to an end in April 2012 when it was announced that, henceforth, the value of the *kyat* would be determined according to a 'managed

Table 4.2 Financing Burma's fiscal deficit *(Kyat billions)*

Year	*Central bank lending to government*	*Commercial bank lending to government*	*Commercial bank lending to private sector*	*Government treasury bonds outstanding*
2006/07	2763	179	653	118
2007/08	3535	382	795	180
2008/09	3881	611	907	297
2009/10	4892	1103	1171	939
2010/11*	6245	2120	1886	1213

Note
* As at December (IMF 2011), (Myanmar Central Statistical Organisation (MCSO) 2011).

float'. Under the new regime, an auction is conducted each morning by the Central Bank of Myanmar at which authorized foreign exchange dealers (primarily Burma's commercial banks) place their bids for a range of foreign currencies (initially the US dollar, the euro and the Singapore dollar). Out of this a reference exchange rate is generated, around which within a small band (±0.8%) subsequent trading must take place. So far the new system seems to be working well, and the gap between formal and informal exchange rates in Burma has largely closed.

6 State embezzlement

Burma's most significant export, and the commodity whose earnings should be the source of game-changing state revenues, is the natural gas that is currently being piped through to Thailand. These exports, traded exclusively through the state-owned Myanmar Oil and Gas Enterprise (MOGE), brought in net revenues in 2010/11 of around US$1.5 billion. If the foreign exchange earnings of other state enterprise exports are added (including mining and gems of around US$1.3 billion, and of teak and other hardwood of about US$600 million), then Burma's state accumulated around US$.6 billion in net foreign exchange in 2010/11 (MCSO 2011).

Revenues of this magnitude, which are around three times domestic tax receipts, *should* have a transformative effect on Burma's budget. Indeed, if properly recorded in Burma's public accounts, the deficit discussed above would be irrelevant. In truth, Burma should have no budget deficit.

The matter of 'how' a budget deficit was thus otherwise manufactured by Burma's government was via a simple sleight of hand. Instead of recording Burma's foreign exchange earnings at the country's unofficial market exchange rate (as noted, currently at around K800/US$1, which is the true measure of the currency's purchasing power), they were recorded at the otherwise moribund official K6/US$1 exchange rate. At this rate, Burma's state enterprises contributed earnings to the budget of a mere twenty-two billion *kyat* rather than their 'true' international earnings of 2.9 *trillion kyat*. The latter amount would have removed in one stroke Burma's budget deficit if so applied. Instead, and via what were effectively 'two sets of books' in Burma's public accounts, a greatly diminished financial pie was all that was available to meet the requirements normally assumed by a state. The ample funds left over from this piece of creative bookkeeping were meanwhile credited to a so-called 'State Fund Account' administered by the central bank, but effectively controlled by Burma's most senior military officers and de facto (if perhaps not de jure) leadership.

The effective locking-up of Burma's hard currency earnings into this State Fund Account provided the military and connected parties with discretionary funds to use for purposes that might otherwise prove embarrassing if they were recorded – and then allocated – at their true purchasing power. Such uses included military materiel of various guises, and other projects of limited economic or social utility (such as the new capital city). Meanwhile, under a so-called 'Special Funds Law' promulgated just before the formation of the new government, the Commander in Chief of the Armed Forces in Burma has the right of absolute control and discretion over 'unlimited' funds for the 'perpetuation of national sovereignty', and the freedom from any 'person or organization' (including the Parliament) questioning or seeking to audit their use.[5]

The decision to effectively float the *kyat* in 2012 holds out the promise that the state appropriation noted here may soon be brought to a close (at least in its exchange rate dimension). As at mid-2013 this remains far from conclusive, however, and much will depend upon efforts to create greater transparency in underlying contracts signed with foreign energy corporations, as well as in subsequent allocations through the budget.

7 Capital flight

One of the best (and most sincere) indicators of the sentiment in which the owners of wealth in a country hold their government is the extent to which they seek to illicitly 'export' their capital to another jurisdiction. Admittedly, the proceeds of this capital are often the product of corruption, criminal activity, tax evasion, and the shadow economy more broadly, but – of great relevance to Burma – it is also often a consequence of insecurity with respect to property rights, and the search for financial safe havens against the fear of government expropriation. The typical methods for facilitating capital flight include straightforward trade mispricing (under- and over-invoicing exports and imports), and the even more basic procedure of 'carrying' money out of a country in a suitcase. But, however motivated or achieved, such illicit flows bring about a net transfer of wealth to offshore banks and financial havens. As such, and in the absence of the scrutiny allowed in an open society, they undermine both the process of capital accumulation and economic growth.

In 2011, the United Nations Development Programme (UNDP) ranked Burma as the eighth largest source of capital flight over the past twenty years (UNDP 2011, 12). According to the UNDP's estimates, which were based on World Bank data on country 'sources and uses of funds' (adjusted for trade mispricing), nearly US$9 billion flowed out of Burma between 1990 and 2008. Such capital leakage represented an average of 9 per cent of the country's GDP across the period (compared to a developing country average of around 5 per cent) (UNDP 2011, 15). It was also nearly five times the amount of foreign aid Burma received during these years. More graphically: for every dollar of aid received by Burma from 1990 to 2008, US$5 flowed right back out (UNDP 2011, 14).

8 Money and banking arrangements

As noted above, Burma's banking and financial system has become largely a subsidiary of its fiscal arrangements, as the overwhelming share of the country's financial capital is devoted to the state and its spending proclivities. This has many implications, not least that the private sector is largely denied access to finance. In 2011, a mere 15 per cent of domestic credit creation made its way into the private sector in Burma. This is in great contrast to Burma's peers and neighbours in ASEAN, for whom the private sector's portion of domestic credit mobilization is invariably above 90 per cent. The situation with respect to rural finance in Burma is even worse. The source of over half of Burma's GDP, and the home of over 70 per cent of the country's population, agriculture receives a paltry 0.4 per cent of available credit.

The insatiable demands of Burma's state apparatus have been the primary cause of dysfunction in the country's banking sector, but many ill-fitting regulations have also been a barrier to the creation of a viable financial system. Such regulations (some a hangover from the days of state socialism) include caps on interest rates, restrictions on lending and collateral, bans on certain types of deposit products and withdrawals, and an outright prohibition on commercial banks lending to farmers. The latter policy means that the vast majority of farmers and cultivators in Burma are unable to access formal finance of any kind. This forces them to go without (along with critical inputs such as fertilizer) or to rely on informal moneylenders, whose high interest rates are currently the drivers of an indebtedness cycle that has caused increasing landlessness.

Notwithstanding some of the other reforms undertaken by Burma's new government since 2011, reforms to the financial sector have made little headway under the Thein Sein administration. Foreshadowed is the opening up to foreign banks in joint-venture arrangements with local institutions, as well as a new Financial Institutions Law to allow further reforms. As at late 2013 none of this had come to pass. Similarly, as yet there have been no signs of progress in rehabilitating Burma's rural credit system.

9 Corruption and criminalization

In 2011, Transparency International listed Burma as the third most corrupt country in the world (behind North Korea and Somalia).[6] Given the unpredictable and idiosyncratic way in which Burma's informal 'rules of the game' are applied, these perceptions reflect an unsurprising reality. Such corruption, moreover, is but a component of a broader criminalization of Burma's economy. This criminalization is manifested in many ways, cultivated in an environment where powerful figures in the ruling regime (and parties with connections to it) operate independently of formal law or other checks on their actions. Of course, it is also apparent in other objectively measurable ways, including Burma's re-emerging role as a significant regional narcotics exporter. Reversing a decade of declining output, Burma's production of illicit opium has been increasing since 2007, and the country has consolidated its position as the world's second-largest producer of the narcotic (after Afghanistan). Perhaps even more significant has been Burma's growing role as a maker and trafficker of synthetic drugs (primarily amphetamine-type stimulants) to Asia and the world beyond, a development that has often been left unexamined due to the attention typically devoted to opium.[7] The US government labels Burma as one of three countries that has "failed demonstrably to meet its international narcotics obligations", and there is something of a consensus among observers of Burma that senior figures within the country's military collaborate with, and protect, leading narcotics producers. The naiveté of assuming otherwise is noted with dry understatement in the 2010 edition of the US State Department's *International Narcotics Control Strategy Report:*

> The Burmese regime monitors travel, communications and activities of its citizens to maintain tight control of the population. GOB [Government of Burma] officials are likely aware of the cultivation, production, and trafficking of illegal narcotics in areas they control.
>
> (US State Department 2010, 173)

As will be examined below, a 'privatization process' undertaken since 2010 only underlines the perception that Burma's economy has been morphing – from more or less highly centralized state control into something of a hydra of state, quasi-state, military and criminal elements.

10 A new rent-seeking oligarchy

One of the most disturbing economic developments in recent times in Burma has been the emergence of a conspicuous, and powerful, cohort of what are sometimes called 'crony capitalists' or 'oligarchs'. A new phenomenon in Burma (where wealth and influence hitherto was more or less concentrated in the military itself), these cronies are united by a few things, including something of an ostentatious braggadocio, but above all by their close connections to Burma's military rulers, past and present. From these connections, these oligarchs are able to access streams of 'economic rents' via, primarily, the concessions they win against otherwise restricted economic activity. Limited to a few individual and corporate names that have become infamous to most Burmese (the most prominent of which include Tay Za's Htoo Group, the Max Group of companies headed by Zaw Zaw, Steven Law's Asia World company, Nay Aung's IGE Group, and the Eden Group of Chit Khaing), these oligarchs enjoy government-allocated concessions that include the importation of petroleum, rights to logging extraction, jade mining, gold exploration, banking, real estate and the arms trade.

Burma's oligarchs are rarely away from the limelight, but they have been especially prominent since 2010 courtesy of their success in 'buying' a vast amount of state assets and enterprises that are being sold off by Burma's government. Altogether nearly 300 enterprises and properties have been sold (in a programme that was conducted without public tendering or any other accountable or transparent process), including ports, rice mills, cigarette and textile factories, cinemas, hotels, an airline, fish and agricultural processing plants, ruby, jade and gold mines – as well as a score of government buildings in Rangoon whose occupants have decamped to the new capital.

Carried out appropriately, at the right price and in step with other measures ensuring competition and other safeguards, the privatization of formerly state-owned assets and enterprises can yield great benefits for all, and is a policy that is more or less *de rigueur* for countries moving in genuine transition to a market economy. Unfortunately, the recent sell-offs in Burma represent what privatization programmes 'done badly' can turn into: a close to textbook example of institutional expropriation by political and economic elites. This is not without cost to the Burma even now, but the long-term damage it invites – through the resistance to necessary reforms by powerful parties whose wealth and power depend precisely on their ability to set the rules of the game in favour of their narrow interests – will likely be the real story of this unfortunate outcome.

11 (Insecure) land rights

A critical barrier to the improvement of Burma's agricultural sector is that all agricultural land is formally owned by the state. Farmers are allowed thirty-year inheritable *use* rights, with such rights determined by village-level land committees, but hitherto, land could not be legally *and* voluntarily transferred between unrelated individuals. This also held the implication that land could not be effectively used as collateral on loans. More generally, the lack of land title has long denied the Burmese cultivator the security, and the incentive, to invest in or improve their holdings.

In late 2011 a new Farmland Bill was introduced to the new Burmese Parliament, ostensibly designed to rectify some of these problems.[8] Its passage into law thereby revoking the (greatly destructive) Land Nationalization Law of 1953, the new legislation asserts a number of rights for farmers. These include:

- The right to occupy and use farmland. Such use-rights are unchanged, but their application is meant to be strengthened through the operations of the 'Farmland Management Bodies' (see below)
- The right to "ease, exchange, inherit, donate or permanently transfer" land, but not "without the consent and agreement of the legitimate (*sic*) owner".

Unfortunately, and despite its declared objective, in practice the Farmland Bill has done little to improve land tenure security for Burma's farmers. The clauses noted above are efforts in the correct direction, but their efficacy depends on both a fair starting point, and a process for resolving disputes that is transparent, just, open to public participation, and which recognizes local knowledge as the foundation of claims to land. Such a process is lacking in the Farmland Bill. Instead, a centralized process is established, under which great discretionary powers are assigned in a top-down process to 'Farmland Management Bodies', one each at the national, regional/state, district, township and village/tract levels. Authority for these bodies descends from the Central Body, which is chaired by the Minister for Agriculture and Irrigation and other senior officials in that Department, as well as the Department of Settlements and Land Records. The powers bestowed on the Farmland Management Bodies (whose internal workings are opaque) include the authority to make determinants as to who has work rights over a plot of land, to approve or not approve the transfer of such rights, to resolve any disputes over these rights (and against which there are no appeal processes), and to "revoke the right to work farmland". Should a farmer refuse to comply with an eviction order issued by the Agriculture Department or by a farmland management body, the penalty applied includes a prison term of up to six months. Anyone deemed to be obstructing any member or employee of such bodies "in the performance of … his duties" is likewise liable to six months in prison (Farmland Bill [FB], ch.12, sect. 35).

Burma's new Farmland Bill similarly does little to reform a system in which government direction to farmers of 'what, how and when' to produce (often at odds with local conditions) continues to bedevil the creation of a more rational and market-oriented agricultural sector. The Farmland Bill consolidates such directions in law, in a seemingly innocuous section which states:

> If it is deemed to be beneficial to the State or to the agriculturalists by cultivating any particular crop in any particular area or by utlilizing farmland in the prescribed manner in any particular area, the President may take or cause to be taken such measures by as he deems expedient for the cultivation of such particular crop or for the utilization of farmland.
>
> (FB, ch.10, sect. 23)

The issues above are, alas, not merely abstract or theoretical concerns. Since the passage of the Farmland Bill some 3.6 million hectares of land have allegedly been 'reassigned' from use by cultivators and in favour of local and foreign agri-businesses.[9] In essence, what the Farmland Bill (and its legislate sibling the Vacant, Fallow and Virgin Lands Bill which was passed into law at the same time) creates a more or less Burmese version of the 'eminent domain' principle under which, in most Western countries, governments can reclaim land if it can be better socially and economically employed in other ways. In the latter countries such powers, however, are moderated in practice by numerous safeguards and appeal processes, none of which yet exist in Burma. According to the Asia Legal Resource Centre, land security for Burma's farmers has "not only failed to keep pace" with land tenure improvements in neighbouring countries but, under the Laws outlined here, "have gone backwards".[10]

12 The flight of Burma's intellectual capital

The most serious of all 'capital flights' from Burma is that of human beings. We do not have exact figures of the number of people who have fled Burma since the military takeover in 1962, but clearly (given that at this moment there are over a million Burmese refugees in neighbouring countries) it must number in the several millions. Many of these, if not most, were (and are) among the best and brightest of the country's youth.

Beneath the damage wrought by the sheer magnitude of the overall numbers of people fleeing Burma are the costs to the country from the loss of individuals whose particular skills and qualities could have allowed them to contribute to nation-building. Curiously, nowhere is this more true than in economics. For reasons that are only partly explainable, Burma has (historically) provided unusually fertile soil for the nurturing of economists. The roll-call of just some of the more internationally famous of these include Hla Myint (University of Rangoon, then London School of Economics), Tun Wai (University of Rangoon, then Yale University), R.M. Sundrum (University of Rangoon, then the World Bank and Australian National University), Khin Maung Gyi (University of Rangoon, then National University of Singapore), Mya Maung (University of Rangoon, then Boston College), as well as the keynote writer in this volume, Ronald Findlay (University of Rangoon, then Columbia University). Of course, contained in the word 'then' in the parenthesis here, separating the University of Rangoon from these other eminent places of learning, is a most succinct summary of just one aspect of Burma's human tragedy.

13 2011/12 political reforms

In March 2011, a nominally civilian government came into office in Burma. Created out of the deeply flawed elections held in 2010, it was headed by a new president, Thein Sein, who had been prime minister in the previous military regime. All leading figures in the government had likewise been members of the previous regime and members of its proxy political party, the USDP (Union Solidarity Development Party). Burma's 2008 Constitution allocated the military 25 per cent of seats in the national Parliament, reserved critical cabinet ministries for military representatives, and granted the commander-in-chief of the armed forces extraordinary, self-activated reserve powers. With constitutional amendments requiring a greater than 75 per cent majority vote in the Parliament, the structural barriers to reform in Burma were, and are, formidable.

In the light of these obstacles, it was perhaps not surprising that expectations with regard to the reformist credentials of Burma's new government were not high, and in its initial months it did little to contradict them. During the first sitting of the new Parliament, members were restricted in terms of their movement – where they could stay in the new capital, Naypyidaw; the visitors they could receive; what they could carry into the parliamentary building – and the questions they could ask. No debate was allowed over government appointments, while local and foreign journalists were banned. According to the instructions issued by the speaker of the National Assembly (the upper house), "Parliament representatives ... are to discuss any matters in unison. It is important not to have a sense of contradiction.... The Parliament should not be in a debate-like situation."[11] Meanwhile, across the country in 2011, ethnic tensions rose, press censorship increased, and questionable dealings with North Korea raised international concerns.

The emergence of a more optimistic political narrative coincided with the second sitting of the new Parliament in August 2011, and increased activity by Aung San Suu Kyi (effectively Burma's opposition leader, and Nobel Peace

Prize laureate), who in the same month commenced her first political trip outside Rangoon since her release from house arrest the previous November. In August her first meeting with President Thein Sein took place, amid what became a series of meetings between the opposition leader and government ministers and officials. There followed a sequence of pronouncements that created a turnaround in sentiment towards the new government. In September, long-standing bans on news websites were lifted, including those of human rights and exile media, and the government invited the International Monetary Fund (IMF) to send a team to advise them on exchange rate reform. Meanwhile, new laws were crafted allowing the formation of labour unions and the right to strike, and for the re-registration of Aung San Suu Kyi's National League for Democracy (NLD) as a political party that was both legal and able to contest future elections.

The most striking of the events suggesting possible change in Burma occurred with the announcement by President Thein Sein (in September 2011) that work on the Myitsone Dam would be suspended. This announcement came in the wake of what had become a groundswell of opposition to the dam. Situated at the convergence of two smaller rivers flowing into the Irrawaddy in Burma's Kachin State, the dam was a joint venture between a Chinese state-owned electricity enterprise and various Burma contractors. Over 90 per cent of the hydroelectricity it produced was bound for China's Yunnan Province. This latter aspect, plus the fact that the dam would flood a vast area and displace tens of thousands of people, became a focal point of criticism from environmental and civil society groups all over the world, including within Burma itself.

Having become something of a symbol of the increasing anxiety in Burma about China's growing dominance over the economy (an anxiety that extends to the senior ranks of the military), Thein Sein's decision to suspend construction of the Myitsone Dam was a popular one. To the extent that it seemed to represent a rebuff to Beijing, it was also a clever playing of the 'China card' with respect to the president's efforts to sell the government as something demonstrably 'new' to the international community. In this he largely succeeded, a fact no better demonstrated than by the subsequent visit to Burma in December 2011 of US Secretary of State Hilary Clinton. The first such high-level visit in over fifty years, the visit concluded with the announcement of an array of measures designed to *partially* normalize relations between the US and Burma. These came to include the 'suspension' (but not the repeal) of the economic sanctions the US had long applied to new investment in Burma, as well as on various trade and financial contacts. Other countries and entities, including the United Kingdom, the EU and Australia, soon followed suit. The final repeal of such sanctions will require further political reform, but especially the release of political prisoners (Burma continues to incarcerate over 1000 of such prisoners) and the cessation of military aggression in ethnic minority areas. On both of these issues progress has, as yet, been less than complete.

In April 2012 Burma's reform narrative reached a critical milestone in the form of a series of by-elections for forty-six vacant seats in the Parliament. The lead-up to these elections was not without irregularities, but in the end the polls themselves were conducted more or less freely and fairly. For the NLD the elections were an unmitigated success. The party won forty-three of the forty-four seats it contested (a disqualified candidate in one seat was the only setback), including one gained by Aung San Suu Kyi herself. A few weeks later, finally confident that she would be allowed to return, Aung San Suu Kyi at last made the journey to Norway to receive in person the Nobel Peace Prize she had been awarded twenty-two years earlier.

14 Economic reforms

The first meeting between Aung San Suu Kyi and Thein Sein in August 2011 took place at the 'National Workshop on Reforms for Economic Development in Myanmar', convened by U Myint, the President's chief economic adviser. An internationally renowned economist respected on all sides of the political divide, U Myint has used these workshops (the one attended by Suu Kyi was the second in the series) to build momentum on economic reform and to expand the possibilities of allowable discussion. The latter aspect was perhaps best exemplified by U Myint's own presentation at the workshop, which focused on the hitherto taboo topic of corruption.

Concrete policy actions to match the ambitious rhetoric of economic reform in Burma have been uneven and slow in coming, and in late 2013 many fundamental obstacles continue to frustrate the hopes of those looking for genuinely transformational change. Nevertheless, a limited number of meaningful reforms have now been put in place. One of these was the changes to Burma's exchange rate arrangements noted above. Two others were, first, to grant greater independence to the central bank and, second, to encourage foreign direct investment. It is to these that we now turn.

Central bank independence

In July 2013 a new Central Bank of Myanmar Law (CBML) came into effect. The objective of this new law (which replaces one of the same name promulgated in 1990) was to grant greater independence to Burma's central bank. Hitherto, and as already noted above, the Central Bank of Myanmar (CBM) had been little more than a money-printing outfit whose remit was more or less confined to the funding of Burma's chronic budget deficits. The CBML ostensibly grants Burma's central bank greater independence via a number of measures. The most important of these measures include the following:

- Elevating the position of CBM Governor to the equivalent of a Minister of Cabinet (and thus relocating it outside the Ministry of Finance, within which it had been simply a division).
- Creating a nine-member decision-making board of directors that includes four representatives from the CBM itself (the Governor and three newly

created Deputy Governors) and five external 'experts'. Such directors, as well as the Governor and Deputies, cannot be removed in the absence of malfeasance of some sort, or a presidential determination that they are "incapable of discharging their duties" (CBML, ch.3, sect. 9).

- The CBM will no longer be able to buy primary issues of government bonds, or to otherwise lend to the government, in the absence of the approval of the Parliament. Government bonds may be purchased from other banks, and from the general public, but without the nod of the Parliament this can only be done through (at present non-existent) secondary securities markets.
- In modern central banking practice, transparency and accountability is meant to be the natural accompaniment of independence. Under the new CBML, Burma's central bank is compelled to submit reports on monetary conditions to the Parliament at least twice a year, and to publish quarterly reports on monetary developments.

All of this is to the good, but it is not yet enough to pronounce that Burma now has a truly independent central bank. As noted above, the CBM is no longer able to directly fund Burma's budget deficits without the Parliament, but it is still able to purchase government securities from other state-owned banks. At present these banks are large purchasers of government debt. Of course, ultimately all will depend on the ability of future governments to be able to finance their spending by selling bonds to the public, borrowing from offshore and from private banks, and (most important of all) creating the fiscal circumstances (spending restraint and adequate taxation) that do not offer the incentives for 'money printing'.

A new foreign investment law

For much of the past fifty years, foreign investment in Burma has been both unwelcome and restricted. In November 2012, however, a new Foreign Investment Law (FIL) was promulgated. Its purpose is to make Burma a more attractive destination to investors abroad, while at the same time protecting certain sensitive sectors. Crafted accordingly is a law that contains several seemingly contradictory themes, which are meant to blend, however, in a way "to support businesses that cannot yet be run by the State and citizens, or businesses that have insufficient funds and technology" (FIL, ch. III, sect. 8a). Among the inducements to attract foreign investors include a range of tax incentives, the most prominent of which is a 'tax holiday' on any profits that foreign investors might make in their first five consecutive years of their business. Other tax breaks cover exemptions for goods produced for export, accelerated depreciation allowances, and the removal of customs duties on imported inputs. Beyond the tax concessions are other enticements, including a (sadly) necessary guarantee to foreign investors that their businesses will "not be nationalized within the term of contract" (FIL, ch. XIII, sect. 28).

The FIL continues to contain various restrictions on foreign investment in Burma, however. These include outright prohibitions in some areas, notably including small business operations in retail and agriculture, as well as a range of activities in which foreign investment can only take place in a joint venture (with up to 80 per cent foreign equity) with a local Burmese partner. Included among the joint-venture-*only* activities is the production and distribution of most food and beverages, infrastructure development and construction, large-scale mining, private hospitals and health care, and most tourism businesses. Among the activities in which foreigners can play no role at all include local language media and small-scale mining and energy projects. Finally, allowable only with special approval include foreign investment in banking and other financial services, foreign language media and telecommunications.

15 Conclusion

What is sometimes regarded as *China's* economic miracle owes its impetus to the expansion of economic freedom granted to its people and enterprises. Equally, most of China's current and looming problems come largely from the tight grip that the country's state apparatus *continues* to hold over the same.

The lack of understanding of what accounts for the success of China and other countries (that contain critical elements of openness in the *economic* sphere if not the political – see Chapters 6 and 8 by Tyers and Coleman, this volume) matches closely the lack of understanding held by successive military regimes in Burma over what constitute the necessary foundations for truly transformative economic growth and development. Such foundations include, at their centre, economic freedom. The freedom to exchange, to enter into contract, to have those contracts protected by law, to do all of this in a reliable monetary unit of account provides the institutions that in turn drive the incentives to produce, create, and to deliver growth. Economic freedom is not yet in place in Burma. Until it arrives, the people of this country of almost boundless potential will continue to suffer and stagnate, and be less than what they could be.

Notes

1 For the EFW Report, rankings and methodologies, see "Economic Freedom of the World 2012 Annual Report", www.freetheworld.com/reports.html (accessed 16 August 2013).

2 For the Heritage Foundation/Wall Street Journal's rankings and methodology, see www.heritage.org/index/ranking, (accessed 15 August 2013).

3 Per capita GDP data sourced from the IMF's *World Economic Outlook Database*, April 2011, www.imf.org/external/ns/cs.aspx?id=28 (accessed 11 August 2013).

4 Health expenditure data sourced from the World Health Organization, www.who.int/research/en/ (accessed 13 July 2013).

5 The Special Funds Law was promulgated on 17 January 2011. See Wai Moe, "Than Shwe grants himself power to access 'Special Funds'", *The Irrawaddy*, 4 March 2011, http://irrawaddy.org/article.php?art_id=20878 (accessed 13 August 2013).

6 Transparency International's latest Corruption Perceptions Index may be found at http://cpi.transparency.org/cpi2011/results/ (accessed 19 August 2013).

7 For more on Burma's prominent role in the production and trafficking of narcotics, see UN Office on Drugs and Crime (UNODC) (2009); US State Department (2010).

8 For English translations of the Farmland Bill and the Vacant, Fallow and Virgin Lands Bills, see www.burmalibrary.org/docs12/2011_Farmland_Bill(en).pdf and www.burmalibrary.org/docs13/VFVLM_Law-en.pdf. For a taste of the discussion around these laws, see "Burma: Draft Land Law Denies Basic Rights to Farmers", *Asia Human Rights Commission*, 1 November 2011, www.humanrights.asia/news/ahrc-news/AHRC-STM-163–2011 (accessed 19 August 2013), and Thomas Keane, "Expert Cautions on 'Land Grab' Model", *The Myanmar Times*, 27 February to 4 March 2012, http://mmtimes.com/2012/news/616/news61612.html (accessed 19 August 2013).

9 "Land Confiscation Issue a Major Concern for Burma Rights Groups", *Mizzima*, 23 October 2012, www.mizzima.com/news/inside-burma/8271-land-confiscation-issue-major-concern-burmas-rights-groups.html (accessed 20 December 2012). See also Kyaw Kyaw, "Land Reform is Key to Burma's Future", *The Diplomat*, 25 August 2012, http://thediplomat.com/2012/08/25/land-reform-key-to-burmas-future/ (accessed 22 August 2013).

10 Stung by rising incidences of farmer protests, and other high-profile disputes over land, the Thein Sein administration belatedly recognized some of the shortcomings of its new agricultural land bills. Promises were made throughout 2012 that the land bills would return to the Parliament for modification, but by the second sitting of the Parliament in 2013 little progress on this front was apparent. In September 2012 a Land Investigation Committee was formed by the Parliament to investigate 'land grabs'. The Committee reported over 300 especially egregious examples to the Parliament to be taken up for the January 2013 sitting. Noe Noe Aung, "Commission will Report over 300 Land Grabs to Myanmar MPs", *The Myanmar Times*, 17 December 2012, www.mmtimes.com/index.php/national-news/3591-commission-will-report-over-300-land-grabs-to-hluttaw.html (accessed 22 August 2013).

11 Wai Moe, "Burma's 15 Minute Parliament", *The Irrawaddy*, 22 February 2011, www.irrawaddy.org/article.php?art_id=20803 (accessed 2 November 2011).

Bibliography

International Monetary Fund (IMF). 2011. *International Financial Statistics, June 2011.* Washington, DC: IMF.

——. 2013. *Myanmar: Staff Monitored Programme, IMF Country Report No. 13/13.* Washington, DC: IMF.

Myanmar Central Statistical Office MCSO. 2011. Available at: www.mnped.gov.mm/index.php?option=com_content&view=article&id=95&Itemid=112&lang=en.

Republic of the Union of Myanmar. 2011. *Foreign Investment Law (Pyidaungsu Hluttaw Law No. 21/2012).* Naypyitaw.

——. 2013. *Central Bank of Myanmar Law (Pyidaungsu Hluttaw Law No. 16/2013).* Naypyitaw.

Turnell, S. 2009. *Fiery Dragons: Banks, Moneylenders and Microfinance in Burma.* Copenhagen: NIAS Press.

United Nations Development Programme (UNDP). 2011. *Illicit Financial Flows from the Least Developed Countries: 1990–2008.* New York: UNDP.

United Nations Office on Drugs and Crime (UNODC). 2010. *Opium Poppy Cultivation in South-East Asia; Lao PDR, Burma.* Bangkok: UNODC.

United States State Department. 2010. *International Narcotics Control Strategy Report 2010.* Washington, DC: Bureau of International Narcotics and Law Enforcement Affairs. US State Department.

5 Development and freedom in Burma

Ronald E. Findlay

I interpret my task in this chapter as being the challenging one of not only examining the possible relevance of Karl Popper's *The Open Society and Its Enemies* (OSE) to political and economic events in Burma, but also the reciprocal one of assessing what light the Burmese experience might cast on the applicability of Popper's analysis, based as we know almost exclusively on European conditions and concerns, to a part of the world entirely outside his scholarly interests. As I hope to convince the reader, we can all learn much more from looking at Popper and Burma together than would at first sight have seemed plausible.

The OSE is a very strange and utterly idiosyncratic work of genius that does not fall into any of the standard categories of academic discourse. It is undoubtedly intellectual history, with the first volume devoted to Plato and the second to Hegel and Marx, but it ignores almost every other political thinker in between, and the objective is not the usual scholarly one of dispassionate exegesis and commentary but a fiercely polemical attack on all three as mortal enemies of human freedom, inspirers of the monstrous twentieth-century totalitarian horrors of fascism and communism. Very little is in fact said about the character, institutional structure and other relevant features of the 'open society' itself, with most of the space devoted to the sustained excoriation of the three great 'enemies'. Plato and Marx are both given their due as deep and original thinkers, with the former designated as the greatest philosopher of all time, but Hegel is contemptuously dismissed as a 'charlatan'. The crucial transition from the traditional 'closed society' to the original and paradigmatic 'open society' is taken as occurring in Athens in the sixth and fifth centuries BCE. The earlier 'organic' tribal society of the ancient Greeks, like that of the Maoris at the time of the British colonization of New Zealand, was based on custom and kinship relations that assigned fixed roles and values to all individuals within it, with no scope for personal choice or responsibility other than to act in accordance with tradition.

Change was brought about first by the growth of population, which led to attempts to alleviate the pressure on resources by sending out settlers to found 'daughter cities' all over the Mediterranean, but the cultural contacts formed in this way only stimulated the growth of seafaring and commerce, particularly in Athens with her favourable location and natural resource endowments of olive trees and the silver mines of Laureum. As Popper (1971, i, 177) states, "Perhaps the most powerful cause of the breakdown of the closed society was the development of sea-communications and commerce", and further on the same page, "These two, seafaring and commerce, became the main characteristics of Athenian imperialism as it developed in the fifth century BC". This growing prosperity from trade led to a shift in power from established landowning elites to a class of poorer citizens, who rowed and manned the fleet of triremes that were financed by this windfall, resulting in the democratic reforms associated with the names of Solon in 594 and Cleisthenes in 508/507 (see Cartledge 2011, ch. 8). The expansion of Athenian wealth and power led not only to these internal political changes but to the establishment of a maritime 'empire' over other allied Greek city-states and the efflorescence of cultural achievements that made Athens, in the words of Pericles, the "education of Hellas". It is this fifth-century Athenian society of Pericles and Socrates that Popper identified and revered as his model of the open society, despite the admitted presence of large-scale slavery, and the exclusion of women and immigrants from citizenship. The strains and tensions of these changes associated with seafaring and commerce led to conflict and opposition, not only with Sparta and other rival Greek city-states, but internally as well in the anti-democratic reaction of the Thirty Tyrants, including the most able and ruthless of them, Critias, a kinsman of Plato. Popper sees all the works of Plato, including the *Republic* and the *Laws*, as inspired by the desire to restore the closed society of the past and to arrest any further prospect of change, so as to relieve the Athenians of what a later writer would call the "fear of freedom" and the stress and *stasis* which that entailed. If fifth-century BCE Athens was the ideal of the open society, its contemporary great rival Sparta was the ideal of the closed society, with the long and bitterly fought Peloponnesian Wars "between Athenian democracy and the arrested oligarchic tribalism of Sparta", as Popper (1971, i, 178) phrases it, presaging in his mind the twentieth-century clash of the Western democracies with fascism and communism.

What relevance could all these events in ancient Greece possibly have for contemporary Burma? Could pre-colonial Burma be described as a 'closed society' as defined by Popper, and could colonial Burma under British rule possibly qualify as an 'open society', or perhaps as the forerunner of a later one? To begin to answer these questions we will need at least a very brief historical excursus to provide the necessary background. The traditional Burmese society that British imperialism encountered in the early nineteenth century had long passed out of the tribal stage and could be looked upon as formed by a succession of irrigation-based agrarian empires somewhat akin to the Persian and Egyptian examples with which Herodotus and the Greeks were familiar. The mass of the society were taxpaying peasants, supporting the court and administrative system of a despotic ruler as well as a Buddhist religious establishment that interpreted the cosmic order and sustained the moral foundations of the system. The first of these agrarian empires was that of the Pagan Dynasty, established by King Anawrahta (r. 1044–77) at the same time as the Norman Conquest and that lasted until the late thirteenth century. Its main achievements were the first unification of most of the country, the introduction of Theravada

Buddhism from Ceylon, and the construction of the vast number of splendid temples visible to this day. Two great kings of the later Toungoo Dynasty, Tabinshwehti (1531–51) and especially Bayinnaung (1551–81), extended Burmese dominion into Siam and Laos, sacking the capital Ayuthia with armies that employed significant numbers of Portuguese mercenaries as musketeers and artillerymen, after subduing the Mon kingdom of Pegu in Lower Burma. A Mon revival and invasion of Upper Burma in the middle of the eighteenth century was repelled and crushed by Alaungpaya (r. 1752–60), founder of the Konbaung Dynasty that was overthrown by the British in 1886 after the three Anglo-Burmese Wars of 1824–6, 1852 and 1885–6. Despite some trade and crucial cultural influences coming from overseas, such as Buddhism from Ceylon during the Pagan period and the introduction of firearms by the Portuguese in the sixteenth century, the society could be described in a sense as 'closed' until contact with the expanding commercial empire of the British in the early nineteenth century, not unlike China, Japan and Korea during the same period, even though this adjective might be disputed by most contemporary historians of Asia as a Eurocentric 'Orientalist' prejudice. There were ongoing trading contacts with the Dutch, French and British East India Companies but it was not until the three Anglo-Burmese Wars that territory and political independence were lost, while the country was at the same time opened up to the influence of the now rapidly growing world economy, albeit mediated through the control of the colonial powers. Rapid change did undoubtedly occur thereafter, especially following the occupation of all of Lower Burma and the establishment of Rangoon as a major harbour in the 1850s, soon followed by the opening of the Suez Canal in 1869 and the stimulus this gave to the expansion of trade in rice and teak. This led to an influx of population from the surviving Konbaung kingdom of Mindon (r. 1853–78) in Upper Burma to cultivate the potentially fertile lands of the Irrawaddy Delta after the swamps and mangrove forests were cleared. Commercial disputes between the two regimes, trumped-up pretexts in the opinion of nationalist historians (see Htin Aung 1967), led to the eventual complete annexation of the entire country in 1886 and the exile to India of Thibaw (r. 1878–85), the last Burmese king, ironically matching the earlier exile to Burma of the last Mughal emperor Bahadur Shah Zafar II, buried anonymously in Rangoon in 1862 (see Dalrymple 2006).

From a military standpoint the three wars were increasingly one-sided affairs, reflecting the rapid progress of European military technology relative to that of a traditional non-European state, as was so common in the course of the nineteenth century. Alaungpaya, the founder of the Konbaung dynasty, had beheaded officers of the French East India Company with impunity and offered service to many whom he had captured in his artillery train. Their expertise was used to good effect by his successors to defeat substantial incursions by Chinese and Manchu troops in the 1760s. His fourth son Bodawpaya (r. 1782–1819) ruled over more territory than any other previous king of Burma and his forces clashed repeatedly with East India Company and allied troops in Assam and Bengal on the frontiers of the two domains. When the first war provoked by these border disputes broke out during the reign of the succeeding king Bagyidaw (1819–37) the legendary Burmese general Maha Bandula provided spirited and effective resistance to the British forces, despite the antiquated muskets and cannon and defective ammunition of his troops, before falling himself in action. The coastal provinces of Arakan in the west and Tenasserim in the east were ceded as a result of this victory by the British in 1826, providing a convenient addition of Southeast Asian coastline to add to Singapore and Penang, recently acquired by Stamford Raffles. There was still a gap in the Bay of Bengal coastline, however, filled with the prize of Rangoon at the mouth of the Irrawaddy which Governor-General Lord Dalhousie was very glad to obtain in 1852 as a consequence of the Second Anglo-Burmese War, itself provoked by some high-handed naval activities of his subordinate Commodore Lambert. The entire stretch of the great river up to the Yunnan border with China fell into British hands after disputes over teak forests led to the third and last of the wars in 1885, which ended in the capture of the royal capital of Mandalay, the sack of the palace and the overthrow of the Konbaung Dynasty. The Opium Wars of the 1840s had secured the front door to the coveted China trade to Britain and now the back door was secured too.

From about the 1850s onward under British rule Burma developed into what J.S. Furnivall (1948) famously called a "plural society", with different ethnic communities occupying their own special niches within the overall administrative framework of the colonial regime. The Burmese themselves were the rice cultivators, the foundation of the entire economic system, but dependent on credit provided by the Chettiar moneylenders from South India with their land as collateral, while wholesale and retail trade was largely in the hands of Chinese and Indian merchants. The small Eurasian community was employed mainly in the middle echelons of the public services such as railways, police and customs. The very small British elite occupied the top rungs of the economic and social ladder in the administration and the mostly resource-extractive commercial enterprises. The ethnic Burmese elite, many of whom were descendants of the previous royal bureaucracy, for the most part entered law and medicine as well as the lower tiers of the civil service that were open to them. The relative abundance of land and natural resources, and the expanding world economy from the 1850s to the late 1920s, ensured a relatively rapid rate of export-led economic growth until this was abruptly reversed by the onset of the Great Depression, which hit the export-dependent economies of Southeast Asia particularly hard. The collapse of rice prices led to wholesale alienation of the land used as collateral to the Chettiars, and also to race riots and a major agrarian uprising, the Saya San Rebellion, in the early 1930s, ruthlessly suppressed by the use of machine-guns and even aeroplanes (see Adas 1979). These disturbances were followed later in the decade by a strike of university students in 1936 and a major strike of oilfield workers in Yenangyaung in 1938. Most importantly, all these events sparked a strong nationalist reaction on the part of the less privileged members of the Burmese elite, particularly the students of Rangoon University. They formed a party known as the 'Thakins', or masters, to show their

British overlords that they intended soon to rule in their own house. The independence movements in India, and even Ireland, provided inspiring models for them to emulate, while Japan was not slow to seize the opportunity to take advantage of the situation to further her own imperial ambitions. Their leader and most charismatic personality was Aung San, born in 1915 in the small town of Natmauk in Central Burma to a respectable family of relatively modest circumstances that however had a history of resistance to the British.

At this point we need to enquire into what Popper thought about imperialism, or colonialism, on the one hand, and nationalism on the other, in relation to his ideal of the open society. With regard to modern imperialism, Popper in the OSE discusses it mainly in relation to the theories of Marx, Engels and Lenin. He notes that Marx himself saw imperialism in India and China as ultimately a progressive force, liberating them from the stagnation of the "Asiatic Mode of Production" in which they had allegedly been trapped for millennia. Engels is criticized for the specious claim that the Marxian predictions of the increasing misery of the European proletariats would have come true, had it not been for the fact that colonial exploitation enabled their "bourgeoisification" at the expense of their counterparts in the colonies. Popper refutes this by saying that the position of workers in the Scandinavian countries without any colonies, and in the United States, was no worse than that of workers in Belgium or Holland with their vast colonial possessions, making it untenable to defend the increasing misery prediction on this ground. Popper (1971, ii, 189) goes on to say:

> although the misery imposed upon the natives through colonization is one of the darkest chapters in the history of civilization, it cannot be asserted that their misery has increased since the time of Marx. The exact opposite is the case; things have greatly improved.

No evidence is provided for this almost certainly false claim of a significant improvement in the standard of living of workers and peasants in the colonies from the 1880s to the 1930s. It was certainly not the case in Burma. Lenin is cited for the idea that since colonial investment raises the overall rate of profit and boosts wages at home in the imperial centres, revolutionary activity in the colonies would reverse this tendency and hence hasten the revolution within the metropolitan powers themselves. Thus Popper's attitude to modern imperialism, while certainly not entirely approving, is definitely not very critical either, and may perhaps even be construed as favourable. We know as well that he was very attached to an idealized version of the multiethnic, multilingual Austro-Hungarian Empire into which he was born.

In fact, as noted above, the fifth-century Athens that was Popper's paradigmatic model of the open society was itself also an empire, though not a territorial one such as Rome or Britain. Athens was the leader of a league of city-states known as the Delian League, extracting contributions for financing the opposition to Sparta from its often reluctant allies by the threat of military force. The poorer citizens who were the rowers of the triremes in its war fleets formed what may be called the 'democratic base' of the Athenian empire, with women, slaves and immigrants excluded from citizenship. Popper (1971, i, 181) was rather uneasy about these undemocratic features of his ideal society, but he argued that "tribalist exclusiveness and self-sufficiency", i.e. as in Sparta, "could be superseded only by some form of imperialism. And it must be said that certain of the imperialist measures introduced by Athens were rather liberal." The moral condemnation by Thucydides of the Athenian attack on Syracuse during the Peloponnesian War is countered by the charge that he was an unpatriotic anti-democrat anyway, despite his being "the greatest historian, perhaps, who ever lived", just like Plato. The extraction of taxes or tribute from the allies was defended as what we would now call, in connection with NATO, 'burden-sharing'. Against the charge that Athens enriched herself at the expense of her allies through trade, he says that it was better than the Roman policy of simply looting her smaller allies and that "A Plutocracy is better than a Lootocracy" (Popper 1971, i, 298).

I make these points not to accuse Popper of being an "enemy of the open society" himself, as some of his LSE students and colleagues used to joke, but rather to emphasize that his concept of the open society is not an idealistic utopian fantasy but a sternly realistic and unsentimental one. The open society is always going to have enemies, and resisting them always requires sacrifice and sometimes compromise of one's principles, so much could apparently be forgiven so long as the values of critical rationality and the free play of ideas continue to be adhered to. Most people today, or at least most people on the Upper West Side of Manhattan where I live, would probably think that an open society and an empire are necessarily incompatible concepts, but they should just think of the United States, under presidents of both parties, before condemning Popper and the ancient Athenians.

Yet, however enlightened and liberal any empire may be, it always provokes resistance and opposition on the part of those under its sway, despite whatever benefits they may enjoy from its existence. Popper discusses this issue in most detail with reference to Hegel. The Napoleonic invasion of Germany inevitably created an "instinctive and revolutionary nationalism" that was "one of those typical tribal reactions against the expansion of a supra-national empire" (Popper, 1971, ii, 55). This nationalism was directed not only against the French invaders but against the Prussian crown as well. According to Popper (1971, ii, 64), Hegel, as an adviser to the Prussian king Frederick William, saw that "nationalism answers a need – the desire of men to find and to know their definite place in the world, and to belong to a powerful collective body", and was able to cleverly exploit this natural human sentiment by "transforming it into a well-disciplined Prussian authoritarianism", and he thus "brought back a powerful weapon into the camp of the closed society, where it fundamentally belonged". Thus Popper's considered view of nationalism is that while the initial impulse is itself a revolutionary and humanitarian one, it can always be perverted into a reactionary force that is a mortal enemy of any possibility of an open society. This intense dislike of nationalism is perhaps most strongly and unconditionally expressed in the statement in his autobiography that "All nationalism or racialism is evil, and Jewish nationalism is no exception" (Popper 1976, 105).

Having thus gained some insight into Popper's views on imperialism and nationalism, we can now relate them to the Burmese experience during the period of British rule. Could we say, for example, that colonial Burma was, in Popper's admittedly rather qualified sense, an 'open society'? Perhaps the best argument for this counter-intuitive proposition is that there was a substantial influx of population from the territory of the surviving Burmese kingdom following the Second Anglo-Burmese War into Lower Burma under colonial rule, stimulated by the opportunity to clear fertile arable land from the swamps and forests of the Irrawaddy Delta and to gain access for rice exports to the world market, not permitted by the Burmese kings who always wanted to ensure an adequate supply for domestic consumption (see Adas 1974). The interest rates that had to be paid to the Chettiars for seasonal credit between planting and harvesting, the reduced fraction of the world price of rice received by the Burmese peasants after the rice millers and traders took their monopsonistic shares, and the land revenue that had to be paid to the colonial administration, could all be regarded as the costs of participating in a competitive market process that they were prepared to put up with, as compared to the less attractive prospect of simply remaining in the royal domains and paying taxes on their subsistence cultivation. In other words, could one say that they "voted with their feet" to enjoy the economic opportunities provided by a colonial state in preference to whatever was available to them in their own still independent kingdom? The counter-argument would be that had they known the eventual outcome of this process, when rice prices collapsed and they lost their lands in the 1930s, they may have decided it was a mistake to have made their original move. Popper could argue, however, that the open society as he sees it does not provide any guarantee of economic security, though he would not have been against measures to relieve economic distress. The rule of law and civil liberties may also have been regarded as more stable and predictable for the peasant farmers in the colonial zone than if they had remained under the rule of the traditional monarchy. In any case, the option to remain in the closed society was itself no longer open after 1886.

The intense nationalist reaction on the part of the Burmese in the 1930s could not be criticized by Popper or any fair-minded observer, since no people in the world can be expected to meekly submit to alien rule, no matter what benefits it may have provided for them before the onset of the Great Depression. A student strike at Rangoon University in 1936 led by Aung San gained widespread support. He eventually left the country in disguise to escape arrest and to contact Japanese agents for assistance against the British. A group of young Burmese revolutionaries, the 'Thirty Comrades' led by Aung San with Ne Win as one of the members, were given military training by the Japanese and returned with the invading force in 1942 as the Burma Independence Army. Although denounced for this as a traitor by the British, his actions could clearly be justified on the grounds that an oppressed people has no obligation of loyalty to its uninvited rulers. The about-face after the Burmese found that they had exchanged one alien ruler for a worse one, leading them to collaborate with General Slim and the Fourteenth Army to retake Burma, is also perfectly understandable. The withdrawal of Britain and the handover of power to the AFPFL government in 1948, after the tragic assassination of Aung San in July 1947 at the instigation of U Saw, a disgruntled pre-war politician, did credit to both the Burmese side, led until his death by Aung San, and the British, led by Lord Mountbatten, Sir Hubert Rance and Clement Attlee as prime minister. The adoption of the democratic federal constitution by the newly independent state, especially after the conference at Panglong in the Shan States in February 1947 where Aung San secured the consent to it of all the national minorities, gave hope for the establishment of a genuinely open society in the fullest sense of the term.

Despite the outbreak of the communist and various ethnic insurgencies, the decade of the 1950s was on the whole a prosperous and highly progressive one for Burma, with free parliamentary elections, general respect for civil liberties, including a very free press in both Burmese and the English-language dailies *Nation* edited by Edward Law Yone and the *Guardian* edited by U Sein Win, as well as significant strides in education and infrastructure. The Indian mercantile community to a large extent continued to operate in the import and domestic wholesale trade in the major urban areas, and the role of the Chettiars in agricultural credit was taken over by the state. Even the split of the ruling AFPFL into two opposed factions, while ominous for the political future, did not in itself imply a breach of parliamentary democracy, since the two factions could operate as competing political parties within the framework of the Constitution.

All of this very favourable development was of course brought to an abrupt end by the military coup of March 1962 led by General Ne Win which jailed the entire political class and abolished the democratic Constitution. The incentive for the coup was provided by a general atmosphere of malaise in the country resulting from the continued quarrels of the two civilian political factions, economic mismanagement by Prime Minister U Nu's government, and rumblings of further discontent by the national minorities. These circumstances permitted the military to proclaim that it was acting as the true guardian of the national interest by preventing a slide into general disorder and the dissolution of the federal union. An early protest by the Rangoon University students on 7 July 1962 was suppressed with a large number of casualties, and the Student Union building, which occupied a hallowed place in the history of the Burmese independence movement as the site of the 1936 strike, was blown up on Ne Win's order. The military has subsequently been continuously in power, in one way or another, for the past fifty years and there is no definite end in sight, despite the release from house arrest of Daw Aung San Suu Kyi and the considerable liberalization that has taken place in the last three years under President Thein Sein.

On the surface at least it would seem that the many enemies of the open society in Burma have all conspired, jointly and severally, to not just killing, or even strangling it at birth, but preventing it from ever being born in the first place. The story that I have outlined above seems to go in a straight line from the traditional closed society of the Burmese dynasties that fell into the clutches of British imperialism, leading to a nationalist backlash that in turn was perverted, under the influence of the Japanese invasion, into an authoritarian militarism which has held the country in a relentless grip ever since the national experiment with parliamentary democracy that began with the declaration of independence on 4 January 1948 came to an end with the coup of 2 March 1962. This pattern is indeed reminiscent of the one noted by Popper in connection with the diversion of the justifiable upsurge of national feeling in the German lands against the Napoleonic invasion into the militaristic authoritarianism of the Prussian state under the nefarious influence of Hegel and Fichte.

In their admirable and informative book on the end of Britain's Asian empire, the historians Christopher Bayly and Tim Harper (2007, 548) state:

> In Burma it was a combination of unending internal conflict and foreign intervention which led to the rise and seemingly endless rule of the military in a country which had once been one of the brightest hopes for Asian prosperity. Burma had all but become one of the world's first 'failed states', as piously categorized by western political scientists.

Most of their book is concerned with the events from the outbreak of the Second World War to the granting of independence, so it would be useful in the present context to address the role of the military and the 'failed state' issue in the subsequent periods of democratic civilian rule under the AFPFL, both before and after the split, and the military regimes that followed the 1962 coup. Bayly and Harper (2007, 549) rightly note that:

> Independence had given a huge moral boost to the peoples of India, Pakistan and Burma. The sense of relief from the grip of European colonialism was palpable, perhaps not least because it had shown some of its worst sides just before and during the early stages of the Second World War.

Despite enormous difficulties encountered both during the war and in its immediate aftermath with the communist and ethnic insurgencies, and the incalculable loss of Aung San, the democratic government of the thoroughly decent and sincere U Nu, devout Buddhist and ardent social democrat, had prevailed to restore more than a semblance of normalcy to the nation as a whole and made an important start on the long-term task of economic development.

On the economic front the government launched an eight-year plan that was to run from 1952 to 1960 with ambitious but not unrealistic goals. The projected world price of rice, however, on which the foreign exchange earnings estimates were based, fell sharply following the Korean War boom, necessitating a scaling back of the growth targets, but considerable progress across most sectors was still achieved. American consultants devised the plan and participated in its implementation, but Burmese ministers, civil servants, economists and technical experts were also fully involved. The extent of nationalization was limited and controlled, and there was an active private sector with Western firms, local Chinese and Indian merchants and entrepreneurs, and a rapidly growing native Burmese business community. Internationally the country was actively involved in the 'non-aligned' movement and the United Nations. Education and health care made great progress and Rangoon University, which had been staffed almost entirely by expatriates from its establishment in 1920 to 1942, had Burmese faculty with British and American Ph.Ds in charge of most departments by the early 1960s, including the Medical and Engineering schools. The insurgencies still dragged on, but there was a reasonable degree of law and order in most parts of the country.

The ruling party at independence, the Anti-Fascist People's Freedom League (AFPFL), like the Congress Party in India, was initially a coalition of communist, socialist and various other nationalist parties. The communists were the first to break away, even before independence, since they wanted a closer alignment with the Soviet bloc rather than what they thought was too much dependence on the British. They themselves were split into a 'Red Flag' faction led by Thakin Soe and a 'White Flag' faction led by Thakin Than Tun, both of which 'went underground' and continued to engage in limited hostilities with the government, while another group called the Burma Workers and Peasants Party (BWPP) remained within the legal fold. The remaining non-communist component parties of the AFPFL ruled the country, winning free elections in 1952 and 1956 before splitting into two bitterly contending factions in February 1958, one consisting of the Socialist Party led by U Ba Swe and U Kyaw Nyein, known as the 'stable' faction, and the other a 'clean' faction led by U Nu himself and Thakin Tin. All of these splits were due more to personal differences between the leaders rather than to any real ideological or policy conflicts. The division was so bitter and dysfunctional for the body politic that U Nu decided, with the concurrence of the other faction, to ask General Ne Win, head of the armed forces, to form a caretaker government until the next election could be held, leaving the choice of which faction would rule up to the people. Although General Ne Win maintained a posture of strict neutrality, two very senior officers, Brigadiers Maung Maung and Aung Gyi, were regarded as being close to the 'stable' faction. The election was held in May 1960 and gave U Nu's faction an unexpectedly sweeping victory.

During the caretaker regime the two brigadiers were very prominent. Aung Gyi, who came from a Sino-Burmese family in the small town of Paungde, displayed impressive entrepreneurial qualities in forming the Burma Economic Development Corporation (BEDC) as a private-public enterprise connected to the military, which undertook a number of largely successful infrastructure, industrial and agricultural projects. Maung Maung was instrumental in inviting Dr Hla Myint, Burma's best-known economist, to return from Oxford to become Rector of Rangoon University and raise the standards for admission and graduation. Squatters were forcibly removed and relocated to give Rangoon a cleaner and more orderly appearance. These, and other measures intended to promote development and efficiency, were not popular with either the students or the masses, resulting in the defeat of the stable Swe-Nyein faction with which they were associated in the public mind in the May 1960 elections. Unfortunately, U Nu's regime had no effective team in charge of economic policy, which became increasingly irresponsible and populist. Dr Hla Myint's attempts to raise examination standards at the University were overturned and he resigned in disgust to return to England, where he soon took up a chair at the London School of Economics, from which he had obtained a Ph.D with a brilliant dissertation on *Theories of Welfare Economics*, under the great Friedrich Hayek, in the 1940s. U Nu himself became increasingly concerned with Buddhism instead of politics, further adding to a general sense of malaise and drift in the country as a whole.

It was in these circumstances that General Ne Win struck with a perfectly executed coup that transformed the political future of the country literally overnight before dawn broke on 2 March 1962. Most members of the professional and business middle class, even if they did not exactly welcome the coup, were not too unhappy either, owing to the disillusionment created by the failure of U Nu's return to power. There was also an expectation that the caretaker regime policies would be continued, including the mixed-economy approach favoured by Aung Gyi and the BEDC, and that this would give the country a welcome sense of discipline and direction. No one had expected the drastic turn to the Left that Ne Win was to take with the launching of his "Burmese Way to Socialism" programme, with the creation of an authoritarian one-party state of the so-called Burma Socialist Programme Party (BSPP), and an almost completely nationalized command economy. How is this to be explained?

My own sense is that Ne Win had become increasingly concerned with what he thought were American attempts to subvert Burmese sovereignty in the interest of resisting both Soviet and Chinese communism and propping up the Kuomintang regime in Taiwan, some of whose forces were setting themselves up within Burmese territory on the Thai and Yunnan borders, financing their operations with drug smuggling. Although he had displayed no particular enthusiasm for Soviet Russia, Mao Zedong or Marxism, there is no doubt that the model of central planning appealed to his military mind, combined with his suspicion that free-market capitalism in Burma would create unreliable business interests that would welcome American support and be open to subversion. He also seems to have believed that most academics and civil servants were time-serving opportunists and not true patriots like his fellow military officers. He probably acquired this notion that only the noble warrior caste could be the true defenders of the nation from his Japanese training during the war, which was then inculcated to subsequent new recruits to the officer corps. Brigadier Maung Maung, extremely prominent during the caretaker regime, had been quietly retired from the military and given a diplomatic post before the coup, while Aung Gyi was sidelined and later removed, leaving Ne Win with no remaining subordinates of comparable stature who could possibly challenge him.

Not trusting academics and civil servants for economic advice, he turned to two communist intellectuals, U Ba Nyein and *Yebaw* 'Comrade' Chan Aye, asking each of them separately to present an outline of the economic policy they thought the country should follow. U Ba Nyein was one of a remarkable group of pre-war economics Honours students taught at Rangoon University by Dr Harro Bernardelli, a distinguished Austrian economist recommended for the position of Professor of Economics by Lionel Robbins. This group included, in addition to the aforementioned Dr Hla Myint, my own teacher and mentor Dr Tun Thin, who won the David A. Wells Prize for the best Ph.D dissertation written at Harvard in 1952, supervised by Wassily Leontief, and Ezra Solomon from the small community of Burmese Jews, who got his Ph.D at Chicago under Milton Friedman. Dr Tun Thin went on to become director of the Asian Department at the IMF and Solomon was a leading member of the Council of Economic Advisers under Richard Nixon. Unlike the others, U Ba Nyein did not go abroad for further study, but passed the civil service examination with flying colours and, subsequently, either resigned or was dismissed from the civil service for his strong Marxist convictions and communist sympathies. Chan Aye was an economics Honours student at Rangoon University in the late 1940s, but then went underground to join Thakin Soe. He later surrendered and accepted amnesty, earning a living from economic journalism.

This was the time when the Soviet Union itself was undergoing an intense re-examination of its own approach of the best economic path to follow after the death of Stalin. The old detailed Gosplan method of centralized planning was being criticized by Kantorovich, Nemchinov, Lieberman and others as not giving due regard to scarcity, making it necessary to reform the price system and introduce more flexible methods of economic planning and management. Yebaw Chan Aye was very interested in these developments and would come over to the Economics Department at the university to discuss them with us. Two other very well-known senior communist intellectuals, the famous writer and politician U Thein Pe Myint and the bookseller Thakin Kyaw Sein of the People's Literature House, also joined some of our discussions, and agreed with Chan Aye that the old Stalinist approach was completely outmoded and in any case completely inapplicable to Burma, which they believed needed to go through a 'bourgeois' phase of development before attempting to achieve socialism. When asked by Ne Win to prepare his plan, Chan Aye turned to our university group at the Institute of Economics led by the Rector Dr Aye Hlaing, a cousin of Brigadier Aung Gyi who had by then already fallen from power, together with Dr Khin Maung Kyi and myself, and to U Thet Tun of the government's Central Statistical and Economics Department (CSED), and his deputy U Kaung Tin, for help in drawing it up. U Ba Nyein, who was still deeply attached to the unreconstructed Stalinist model, was simultaneously drawing up his alternative plan, assisted by U Chit Maung, an Oxford graduate who was deputy secretary of the Ministry of Finance and Revenue.

The Chan Aye plan that we proposed called for a strong export-oriented approach, revising the existing pricing system for paddy purchase to give more incentive to farmers, and in general for Burma to follow its evolving comparative advantage in the world economy as the best path towards progress and prosperity, with both the public and private sectors playing an active and complementary role (see Thet Tun (2011) for a brief description). U Ba Nyein's plan was to greatly extend nationalization and economic control along old-style Stalinist lines, much to the chagrin of even the Soviet and Eastern bloc embassies in Rangoon, which were of course sure that any policy along these lines would be doomed to failure. Ne Win met both Chan Aye and Ba Nyein on the same morning to listen to their plans. We waited tensely at the University for Chan Aye's return, which did not take long. He said that Ne Win had told him that our plan, if adopted, would deliver Burma into the hands of the CIA, and that he was therefore going with the Ba Nyein alternative. Ba Nyein's approach was warmly endorsed by the quartermaster General Brigadier Tin Pe, to whom Ne Win delegated responsibility for all economic matters, and he then proceeded to implement it with the disastrous results over the next two decades that led to the great uprising of workers and students in 1988. This protest was crushed with extreme violence, completely discrediting Ne Win and his associates, and bringing about the abandonment of the entire approach associated with the Burmese Way to socialism. The most destructive legacy of communism as an enemy of the open society in the Burmese context was not so much the insurgencies of Thakin Than Tun and Thakin Soe as the pernicious inspiration its misguided economic doctrines gave to U Ba Nyein and Brigadier Tin Pe.

After a brief period of confusion the military formed a State Law and Order Restoration Council (SLORC) under General Saw Maung. The defunct BSPP was replaced by the National Union Party (NUP), and in May 1990 free multiparty elections were held. Aung San's daughter Aung San Suu Kyi, now too well known to require any further information to be provided about her here (but see Popham (2011) for a timely biography), formed a National League for Democracy (NLD) with a group of retired army officers and other sympathizers and contested the election, winning about 90 per cent of the seats and completely frustrating the regime's attempt to gain the appearance of legitimacy by an NUP victory. The results of the election were not recognized, and Aung San Suu Kyi and several senior colleagues were placed under arrest, while many other leaders and supporters went into exile.

The military regime, now led by General Than Shwe, modified its economic strategy to give more scope to the private sector, but any positive aspects of this shift were counterbalanced by a massive upsurge of corruption, which had generally not been widely prevalent under the previous system, despite its many other faults. With the exchange rate still ridiculously overvalued, illegal overland trade across the Thai and Yunnan borders continued to be the main outlet for economic initiative. Natural gas discoveries offshore and Chinese economic assistance provided the main sources of official foreign exchange for the government. During all this time Burma was, of course, falling further and further behind Thailand and the rest of Southeast Asia in economic development and social progress and into increasing dependence on China, while sanctions restricted access to the United States and Europe for trade and foreign investment. Public dissatisfaction erupted again with the 'Saffron Revolution' of the monks in 2007, followed the next year by the devastation of Cyclone Nargis. It was becoming increasingly clear to all observers, and perhaps most importantly to the military leaders themselves, that their monopolistic stranglehold on power over the country could only be sustained at the cost of increasingly becoming a de facto vassal state of China. This appears to me to be the main reason that the decision was taken to draw up a new constitution and to hold elections in 2010, with a 'civilian' government led by a cadre of senior military personnel who took off their uniforms and assumed presidential and ministerial office, and a parliament in which 25 per cent of the seats were reserved to the military. The NLD did not participate in the election, but Aung San Suu Kyi was released from arrest and soon after held talks with the new president Thein Sein.

The regime seem finally to have realized that they would have to tolerate what is to them her exasperating presence in the public limelight as the necessary price to be paid for any hope of admission to the international community and thus reducing dependence on China. She and other members of the NLD won most of the contested seats in April 2012 by-elections, confirming the continuing charismatic authority of the Aung San name and legend. Sanctions are being lifted, conditional on further political liberalization, and Burma now appears to be ready to return to full engagement with the world economy for which it has been waiting for so long. The acid test for the achievement of genuine democracy will be what happens in 2015, the year of the next full elections. The Constitution reserves 25 per cent of the seats for the military but it is obvious to all that any fair contest will result in the NLD getting most of the remaining 75 per cent. It may also be noted that 2015 will be the centenary of Aung San's birth.

As Popper stated, the force that brought about the first transition from the closed to the open society in ancient Athens was "the growth of seafaring and commerce", and the social, cultural and political impact of this force, which we now call 'globalization', seems to be impinging ever more strongly not only on Burma but throughout the non-Western world in these first two decades of the twenty-first century.

Bibliography

Adas, M. 1974. *The Burma Delta: Economic Development and Social Change on an Asian Rice Frontier, 1852–1941*. Madison: University of Wisconsin Press.

——. 1979. *Prophets of Rebellion: Millenarial Protest Movements against the European Colonial Order*. Cambridge: Cambridge University Press.

Bayly, C. and T. Harper. 2007. *Forgotten Wars: The End of Britain's Asian Empire*. London: Penguin.

Cartledge, P. 2011. *Ancient Greece: A Very Short Introduction*. Oxford: Oxford University Press.

Dalrymple, W. 2006. *The Last Mughal*. London: Bloomsbury.

Furnivall, J.S. 1948. *Colonial Policy and Practice*. Cambridge: Cambridge University Press.

Htin Aung, Maung. 1967. *A History of Burma*. New York: Columbia University Press.

Popham, P. 2011. *The Lady and the Peacock*. London: Rider Books.

Popper, K. 1971. *The Open Society and Its Enemies*, vols 1 and 2. Princeton, NJ: Princeton University Press.

——. 1976. *Unended Quest: An Intellectual Autobiography.* London: Fontana Paperbacks.

Thet Tun, U. 2011. *Waves of Influence.* Yangon: Thin Sapay.

6 The rise and robustness of economic freedom in China[1]

Rod Tyers

1 Introduction

Central to Karl Popper's (1945) thesis is the idea that liberal democracy is the only form of government allowing institutional evolution that raises welfare without destructive transitions involving violence or bloodshed. The wider East Asian experience may be seen as offering support to this idea, since the emergence of economic prosperity in many Asian economies has been accompanied by the evolution of their political systems towards liberal democracy. The same cannot be said for the totalitarian Asian states, however, of which China is the most significant. In those a distinction is made between economic and political freedoms, with great advances in liberalism towards the former accompanying spectacular economic gains.

This distinction between economic and political freedoms is encouraged by the rhetoric of the modern Chinese Communist Party (CCP) and, indeed, by China's recent history.[2] While it is not correct to deny any post-Mao evolution of Mainland China's political system in favour of individual freedoms,[3] the expansion in economic freedoms accorded the Chinese people during this period has been immense by any measure. The economic policy reforms introduced by Deng Xiaoping's administration centred on such dicta as "economic development is the centre of party work" and "it always stands to reason to develop the economy faster". Projecting these views, he transformed the CCP from one centred on class struggle to a vehicle for economic growth. Seeing the latter as the desired end, his philosophy was pragmatic, as suggested by many of his oft-cited quotes, including: "It doesn't matter if a cat is black or white, so long as it catches mice" and, in response to criticism that a key consequence was the more rapid enrichment of some than of others, "poverty is not socialism; to be rich is glorious" and "let some people get rich first".[4]

This transformation of the role of the CCP from an instrument for class struggle into a vehicle for economic growth was cemented into party and national policy by Jiang Zemin, whose theory of the "three represents", outlined below, were written into China's state Constitution in 2003.[5] The resulting change made the delivery of growth and development central to the party's ideology. The resulting dispensation of Chinese economic freedoms, including private ownership and production, freedom to trade and move, and freedom to borrow and lend, have transformed the Chinese economy from a highly populated but isolated poor country in the Maoist era to one of the most important drivers of global economic performance today. Since the CCP takeover in 1949, real per capita income in China has grown ten-fold, with the great majority being achieved since the Deng Xiaoping reforms.[6] But this has not been merely a gain for China and its people. The rest of the world economy has also benefited from an associated improvement in its terms of trade and cheaper credit that has, in turn, fostered investment and growth (Harris *et al.* 2011; Robertson and Xu 2010; Tyers 2013b).

Yet these gains, both in China and in the rest of the world, are fragile, and the Chinese regime that has produced them faces potentially destabilizing threats from within and without. For this reason, there looms a "middle-income trap" (World Bank 2010) of the type that appears to have restrained numerous countries from taking the final steps towards Western real per capita income levels. The road-blocks that could cause this are many. Within China there are high environmental costs which will require substantial public investment to rectify. There is also increased income inequality, associated with considerable rents in the state-owned sector, which will be politically difficult to unwind (Tyers 2012). This inequality also coincides with ethnic socioeconomic stratification in China's periphery, which has precipitated increased class, ethnic and regional conflicts. Outside China, threats include the global financial crisis and its aftermath, engendering slower export growth. Equally, if not more important, and of more durable significance, is political xenophobia towards the Chinese in the Western democracies. China's political system is seen as denying basic human rights by some, its large government and defence forces are seen as a strategic threat by others, and still others see its economic policies as antithetical to Western interests.[7] Such voices ignore the immense benefits enjoyed by the average Chinese on the one hand and by the West on the other. For the West these benefits include the substantial lowering of the cost of manufactured consumption and intermediate goods and the reduced cost of credit, both of which tend increasingly to be taken for granted.[8]

This chapter examines the role of economic freedoms in China in the creation and dissemination of these global benefits and the robustness of the system that delivers them. The following section discusses the economic freedoms themselves and the institutions on which they rely. Section 3 offers a short history of the evolution of economic policy in China and its reliance to date on export-led growth, while Section 4 discusses the challenges to continued export-led growth and the case for a change in China's growth strategy. The associated risks to continued economic freedom in China are discussed in Section 5. Finally, Section 6 suggests some possible "soft landings" via which economic freedoms and their associated benefits may be sustained.

2 Economic freedoms and their exercise

The key economic freedoms offer only a component of the broad principles of 'liberty' defined by John Stuart Mill (1848, 1859), but these particular freedoms are more prominent in his subsequent (and posthumously published) reconsideration of this issue (Mill 1907). Clearly the Chinese have shown that these economic freedoms have the power to unleash great improvements in private economic welfare. They embody: (1) the ownership of the fruits of production; (2) control over the disposition of their labour by individual workers; (3) ownership of physical capital; (4) freedom to trade products and to supply or rent factors of production (own labour and physical capital), which implies private choice of job or place of work; and (5) freedom to borrow and lend, and hence to accumulate private wealth. These freedoms are not simply dispensed by the enactment of laws, however. They require active maintenance by the state and this necessitates that resources be committed to the defence of assigned property rights, implying secure national borders and reliable domestic policing. But even this is not sufficient. Property rights are of little purpose unless they, or products that stem from them, can be freely traded. This requires that the state also enforce (1) commercial laws that support contract, corporate governance, patent rights and competition rules, and (2) product and service standards that maintain quality and thereby reduce risks associated with trading. In addition, no product, service or primary factor markets can function without a maintained infrastructure. Telecommunications ensure that product and trading information can be exchanged and that products, financial assets and factors of production can be transported. Finally, since the exploitation of private property rights is risky, it is facilitated by bankruptcy laws that protect individual investors and a social safety net that ensures access to survival income and health services when ventures fail.[9]

Of course, the source of all these factors essential to the underwriting of economic freedoms is economic development. All are weakened by widespread poverty. Critically, economic development requires a securely integrated state supporting integrated markets for its goods and services. There is little doubt that tribalism, and divided polities in general, including the extreme of civil wars, lead to poor and ineffective governance, and in particular poor economic policy. These lead to politically destabilizing policy bias and therefore interference in economic freedoms, and to non-facilitating corruption, thus preventing or retarding development (North 1990; Haber *et al.* 2008). More than this, however, is the more basic idea of John Locke ([1689]1821), that a successfully liberal society requires that citizens share fundamental beliefs and philosophy. This, in turn, requires shared commitments to common public goods, such as the handshake as an implicit contract, courtesy in transport and public places, and, in general, the widespread acceptance of and commitment to the "do unto others" rule.[10]

3 China looking back

The historical trajectory by which China arrived at the Rostovian lift-off point described in the previous section is well known to China watchers and students of Chinese history. Yet it is nonetheless important at this point to retrace and enrich our understanding of this historical path in the context of recent economic literature. Moreover, the evolution of China's political economy since the Maoist era provides a foundation for its subsequent transformation under Deng Xiaoping and the eventual adoption of certain characteristics of an open society.

The last successful China-wide regime was in the eighteenth century, during the heyday of the Qing Dynasty. For the time, China's product and service markets were integrated and the state conferred considerable economic freedoms (Gelber 2007). During the nineteenth century, however, this integration diminished under colonial influence, with regional warlords buttressed by concessions to different colonial powers. This segmentation continued until the Second World War, notwithstanding the formation of the Republic of China in 1912 with Sun Yatsen as its first president. Following the Second World War a civil war ensued that was won by the communist forces led by Mao Zedong in 1949. Thus commenced twenty-seven years of totalitarian rule under a regime motivated by "Marxist Leninist Mao Zedong thought", implying a political regime oriented to class struggle and favouring China's numerically dominant rural peasantry, as distinct from Marx's industrial proletariat.

The totalitarian regime of 1949 to 1978

The focus of Mao's CCP was continuing revolution and class struggle. All production, including farming, was collectivized and no private ownership of the means of production was permitted. This, and the security paranoia common to such totalitarian states, suppressed entrepreneurial initiative. Frequent purges were seen as necessary to the maintenance of the power hierarchy and the ideological focus, but these were economically disruptive, causing loss of experienced managerial leadership at all levels. A lack of free debate over economic policy made possible the national implementation of a number of ultimately destructive ideas, including the disastrous 'great leap forward' – a failed attempt at rural-centred industrialization. The subsequent 'cultural revolution' saw a frenzied nationwide purging of Chinese society's intellectuals and professionals, again weakening human capital growth and economic management, further setting back China's overall economic growth.

China's economy did grow during this period, however, though the extent of this growth is both difficult to measure and controversial (Robertson 2011). The mechanisms were two-fold. First, Mao's preoccupation with the power of the state, and hence its precedence over individual welfare, led to his view that population expansion should be encouraged. Of course, while this expanded China's real GDP, it slowed real per capita income growth (Golley and Tyers 2011). Second, China's totalitarian state, like that of the Soviet Union, was able to save and accumulate physical capital collectively, though it did this with less success than in the Soviet case during the same period.

To return more explicitly to the theme of this book, the Maoist regime was a classic exemplar of a closed society, and those who controlled it were clearly enemies of the *open* society in the Popperian sense. Specifically, historicism – the Marxist inevitability of the passing of economic control from capital owners with the Maoist peasant revolutionary twist – was used to justify totalitarianism as inevitable. Political and economic freedoms were curtailed; and individuals were prevented from publicly scrutinizing the institutions, laws and ideas that were the fabric of the state. Even those in the party hierarchy had little opportunity to avoid Maoist dictates for fear of fatal recrimination. Vast numbers died or suffered bitterly from food shortages following forced collectivization, the folly of the great leap forward and the collapse of the civil and economic society under the Cultural Revolution.[11] The Chinese state did become stronger, but at great cost. The depth of the control maintained by the totalitarian state, and its associated social and economic momentum, highlights the conundrum that arises from the spectacular transformation in the 1980s.

Deng Xiaoping, Jiang Zemin and the rise of economic freedom

Following the death of Mao there was a weak political transition, while purges took place of the 'gang of four' which had dominated policy during his final years. By 1978, the new regime of the pragmatist Deng Xiaoping had emerged. He was a survivor of the 'Long March, a victim of the Cultural Revolution and a prisoner of the gang of four, but nonetheless irrepressible (Vogel 2011). He saw the inefficiencies of state capitalism constraining collective progress and he decided that development and growth should be the primary mission of the CCP. To this end he sought to harness individual initiative and opportunity. This led, for example, to the rural 'responsibility system' that transformed Chinese agriculture by returning some economic freedoms to individual farmers and to the establishment of 'special economic zones' that boosted private manufacturing investment and employment. In association, there was a general opening of domestic merchandize markets to private enterprise, foreign investment and international trade.

At the same time, Deng rejected Mao's view that population growth was beneficial and so the policy of encouraging large families was replaced by the draconian 'one-child policy'. While this denied one fundamental freedom (the choice of one's family size) it greatly slowed China's population growth and contributed to the resurgence of growth in real per capita income. The mechanisms were two-fold. First and most important was the raising of the capital-to-labour ratio and hence labour productivity. Second, and much discussed, was the subsequent decline in the number of dependent young people and hence the rise in China's labour force relative to its dependent population. This is referred to as the "demographic dividend" (Bloom and Williamson 1998; Golley and Tyers 2011).

Deng Xiaoping was followed as Chinese leader by Jiang Zemin, a pragmatist of similar philosophy. His theory of the 'three represents' sees the CCP as the guardian of, first, "the requirements in the development of advanced productive forces in China", second, "the orientation of the advanced culture in China", and third, "the fundamental interests of the broadest masses of the people in China".[12] The 'Represents' were adopted at the sixteenth Party Congress in November 2002 and written into the Party Constitution. In March 2003, the National People's Congress decided to include them in the State Constitution. With this, the transformation of China's political approach to economic policy, from one stressing inequality and the power of the peasantry to one fostering overall growth, was complete.

The upshot of this transformation is the wide adoption of elements of Popper's open society. This may be seen as a turn from Mao's idealism and a return to pragmatism, a very old tradition in Chinese governance by which is meant the adoption of open society elements when it is advantageous to do so, even if it is against the totalitarian CCP principles. This links closely to one of Popper's key themes, namely to accept institutions and existing relationships as only provisionally valuable, and then expose them to scrutiny so as to change them for the better (Popper's idea of *fallibalism*). Thus, the Chinese leadership is pragmatic in relation to what exists, embracing change and doing so in a piecemeal Popperian fashion: seeing what works and what does not. This characterization is further exemplified by the modern regime's experimentation at the provincial level with alternative policy responses to perceived problems; including experimentation with fertility policy as well as public health, retirement insurance and financial deregulation.

The new regime of Shi Jinping and Li Keqiang represents a political departure from that of Hu Jintao and Wen Jiabao. For one thing, since Shi is a member of the 'princelings' coalition (as distinct from the 'Youth League' coalition of Hu Jintao and Wen Jiabao), it is aligned more towards the traditions of Jiang Zemin, which reinforces the orientation towards private wealth. At the same time, there remains in the party considerable support for Maoist approaches, the conflict with which rose to the surface during the Bo Xilai episode of 2012 to 2013 (Wishik 2012). This had an ideological component in that Bo was linked with the party's New Left, exemplified by his Mao-style campaigns, such as the 'smash the black' anti-organized crime campaign and his advocacy of an ultra-egalitarian and ultra-nationalist development model for China, known as the 'Chongqing model'. In the end, the rise of Bo's power in the CCP was terminated, not by overwhelming ideological resistance to his approaches but by the actions of an associate who fled to the US embassy for personal protection. Bo's enemies in the CCP included liberal intellectuals for whom he was seen as too totalitarian, lawyers and legal professionals who were concerned that he had flouted due process in Chongqing and Dalian, the military elites who feared Bo's orientation towards the concentration of power, and entrepreneurs who were alarmed at Bo's anti-market tendencies exhibited by his treatment of Wal-Mart stores in Chongqing. It will never be known whether a raw ideological struggle between the New Left and these opposing forces would have emerged with similar results. The exposure of the New Left, however, confirms that the worsening income and wealth inequality will exacerbate internal party conflicts if growth slows and opportunities for the poor and working class diminish.

Key economic policy junctures

Of particular importance at the outset was the responsibility system in Chinese agriculture, at the time the dominant sector of its economy. It gave farmers ownership of their product and the right to sell at the best attainable prices. To achieve this it was necessary to legalize private markets for agricultural produce. Farmers were required to yield to the state a proportion of their output at state prices but were then permitted to sell any remainder on the private markets. The result was a very considerable increase in output and overall productivity which was the more important for the overall economy because of the comparative size of its agricultural sector. Then, in 1979, there emerged the 'special economic zones', constructed around China's most crowded southern cities. This began the accommodation of surplus urban and, most importantly, rural labour in foreign invested private and semi-private manufacturing. A further boost to productivity resulted and the zones were so successful that the policies which made them special were eventually broadened to the coastal provinces and thence to the country as a whole.

In 1994, China's exchange rate was unified and the policy of maintaining a fixed de facto US dollar peg initiated. This greatly reduced financial uncertainty and fostered foreign investment, initiating China's modern growth surge. At the same time, Chinese law was being reformed, among other things to protect property rights over physical and financial capital, and a new tax system was implemented that included income and consumption taxation. Soon after, stock markets were opened in Shanghai and Shenzen, broadening the array of options available to China's ardent savers, albeit initially with heavily regulated share ownership as between domestic and foreign residents and tight restrictions on the issue of equity by state-owned corporations.

Most important in China's recent past was its accession to membership of the World Trade Organisation (WTO), which was concluded in 2001. The Chinese state thereby conceded some sovereignty over trade and related policies, further boosting investor confidence and thereby raising China's overall, and foreign direct, investment. This ushered in a period of truly extraordinary economic growth with annual real expansions in GDP exceeding 10 per cent for several years. This acceleration in China's growth since the 1990s is illustrated in Figure 6.1. A complicating factor during this period, however, was a substantial rise in China's current account surplus, to about one-tenth of its GDP.[13] This is explained by the fact that China's total domestic saving exceeds its investment by this proportion, and this is due to several factors that act in concert.

First, China's very large saving rate sees more than half of its GDP set aside each year. This is not merely because rapid recent expansions leave households

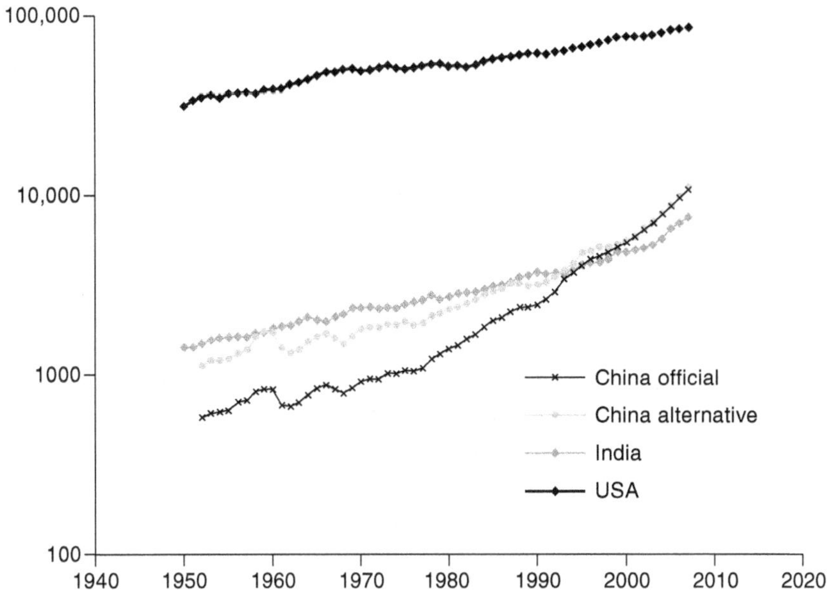

Figure 6.1 Fruits of economic freedoms—China's relative growth real GDP per worker (PPP $, log scale).

seeing their 'permanent incomes' surpassed, remembering poorer times and fearing a return to them once the boom passes. It is also because the state-owned enterprises, which were unprofitable in the 1990s, have since become very profitable and their earnings are not repatriated to the public but rather passed directly to financial markets as investment. Second, and almost as extraordinary, 45 per cent of GDP is invested and it is unlikely that many high-returning projects remain to justify an increase in this proportion. Public investment has increased since the global financial crisis but this is not a sustainable solution to the problem which, ultimately, requires further industrial reforms (Azziz and Cui 2007; Tyers and Lu 2008; Kuijs 2006; Kuijs and He 2007).[14]

Recent events

Since the 1990s the rise in China's current account surplus has raised bilateral imbalances as political issues in the US and Europe. As firms based in those countries have relocated their labour-intensive manufacturing to China, their levels of manufacturing employment have declined. Even though the resulting trade has benefited both regions, it has raised structural unemployment, at least temporarily. Since the Chinese don't vote in European or US elections, they are ready political scapegoats. Much of the blame has centred on China's exchange rate policy, whereby it is suggested that China is artificially cheapening its products so as to raise exports and reduce imports. This confuses the true origin of China's current account surplus, which, as shown above, depends on its saving relative to its investment. In the end, the issue is China's high saving rate, but even this serves to cheapen credit in the rest of the world and, more directly, to pay for the US national debt. In any case, pressure from abroad for China to appreciate heightened in the 2000s and has remained strong ever since.

In 2005 some flexibility was introduced into the nominal exchange rate regime. This aided a real appreciation upward of 30 per cent to 2008, though the underlying force behind this appears to have been increasing Chinese labour costs (Tyers and Zhang 2010; Jacob 2011). Although this flexibility was temporarily suspended in 2008, the appreciating trend has continued ever since. The global financial crisis of 2008 buffeted the Chinese economy, on which the main effect was to reduce demand for its exports by almost one-third. For two years China was faced with a structural unemployment problem of its own, which was solved by the return of some workers to agriculture and the diversion of government spending to additional public infrastructure projects. More recently, under pressure from Europe, the US and international institutions, but also to accommodate domestic pressures over income distribution, the Chinese government has decided to "look inward for growth" and so rely less on exports. This policy stance has become a new CCP orthodoxy (Jia and Liu 2009; Wen 2011; Yi 2011).

4 The challenge to export-led growth

Economic development is primarily about raising the proportion of the population in the middle class. For countries that start out poor and primarily rural, this requires rural–urban migration and, at least initially, basic (mainly primary) education and training. These conditions supply a workforce suitable for light manufacturing. If the protection of property rights and the export infrastructure facilities are sufficient, this then attracts capital that is supplied from domestic saving and foreign direct investment (FDI).[15] Some of the migration to urban areas goes into construction and other services, which expand, but the transition to very high real per capita income is part of a second stage that then requires further education and training suited to the growth of sophisticated services (Lucas 2002).

This development strategy requires relatively free trade, since the growth in the local supply of light manufactures that occurs in the early stage is more than can meet local demand. Such developing countries realize their comparative advantage in light manufacturing and so transform their home labour forces by exporting. As it turns out, this transformation of developing countries is also beneficial to those that are already industrialized. This is because the resulting change in the international terms of trade is positive for them – light manufactured imports are cheaper, and skill-intensive durable (consumer and capital) goods, which they export, are in higher demand. Moreover, since the opening of such developing economies in this way supplies additional low-skilled labour to the integrated global economy, foreign direct investment opportunities are abundant and savers in industrialized countries earn higher returns. Idiosyncratically, Asian development has seen very rapid growth, surpassing for the middle class at least their 'permanent' incomes, and so it has also offered high savings to households and firms (Modigliani and Cao 2004) which has resulted in excess saving to the global economy.This has financed investment and government expenditures in the industrialized economies in ways that have enhanced their growth.[16]

This convenient and successful pattern of expanded interdependence has been the basis for catch-up by poorer countries and regions for more than a century (Dooley *et al.* 2004). Then why should the Chinese choose to 'look inward' now? The reasons are many. First, it is inevitable that Mainland China will graduate to industrialized status and therefore cease to depend on labour-intensive exports in the manner of Japan, the Republic of Korea, Taiwan and Hong Kong before it. This generally coincides with a slowdown in the rate of rural to urban migration and an acceleration in the rate of rise in real wages – the "turning point" of Lewis (1955). The proximity of this transition in the Chinese case is the subject of ardent debate (Garnaut 2010; Golley and Meng 2011), though it is approaching rapidly. It is nonetheless true that demographic changes associated with China's one-child policy will accelerate it, and labour costs have indeed grown more sharply in recent years (Tyers and Zhang 2011). The transition to slower growth can be abrupt and destructive, as in the case of Japan (Tyers 2012), and so the Chinese may be wisely planning their transition early.

A second important reason is that growth has slowed in the regions to which China's exports are directed. This raises the prospect that the terms of trade may shift more rapidly against it if exports continue to be pushed out at the current rate, and so a smaller proportion of the benefits from export-led growth would accrue to China.[17] Third is the political pressure from destination regions against China's current account surplus and its effects on manufacturing employment abroad. Associated political attacks on Chinese exports, and anti-Chinese xenophobia in general, are the more likely when the movement of vast numbers of Chinese workers into the modern sector is perceived as being associated with the unemployment of one-tenth of workers in Western Europe and the US. This association has high-level backing in policy debates, particularly in the US (Bernanke 2006; Bergsten *et al.* 2008; Lardy 2006; Krugman 2010a, 2010b).[18] That this unemployment has more to do with domestic policy misjudgements plays poorly in the West.

The Western backlash is essentially mercantilist and much of it, including Paul Krugman's many published comments, is directed at China's exchange rate policy. The perception in the US that countries like China use exchange rate protection stems from the role of the US dollar as the reserve currency and the difficulty it faces when a lack of competitiveness would justify a depreciation against others. In the 1980s, this anger had been directed against Japan, leading to the Plaza Accord and a large and destructive appreciation of the Yen (Goyal and McKinnon 2003; Hamada and Okada 2009; Obstfeld 2008), and ultimately to the US Exchange Rates and International Economic Policy Coordination Act of 1988, which formalized the US 'defence' against currency manipulators. Poverty, and its associated low wages, has been seen in US policy debates as an unfair trade advantage rather than a problem that is solved by expanded trade. The fact that the underlying real exchange rate of China against the US has appreciated substantially since 2004 and continues to appreciate seems to have been missed (Tyers and Zhang 2011). Thus, the combination of high-level brow-beating on macroeconomic policy and threats of retaliation must surely have had an impact on Chinese policy choice.[19]

Finally, China is constantly criticized for its lack of political rights and for its treatment of minorities such as the Tibetans and the *Hui zu*. This criticism is sometimes justified but it often stems from fear of China as a potential strategic opponent and a sense that the advocacy of additional political and religious rights might weaken it in such a competition.[20] These external criticisms of the Chinese state and its policies, while occasionally well intentioned, are too often xenophobic and made in ignorance of or disregard for the considerable benefits of Chinese growth for the West.[21]

These challenges to the export-led growth model in China may also turn into challenges to the support of the CCP for economic freedoms, since it was this model that provided prompt economic rewards of unprecedented scale in return for each wave of granted freedoms. As these economic rewards diminish in relative size the political support for China's open economic society could falter. It is to this vulnerability that we now turn.

5 The risks to economic freedom in China

Economic freedoms and the development they have fostered are precarious in China because they are the gift of a totalitarian political regime that has supported them while they have been advantageous to the CCP. The regime could, more readily than a liberal democracy, shift its strategy again, as abruptly as it did in 1978. It could foster a shift towards a more liberal democracy, as appears to be occurring at the village level (Wang 2012), but a slowing of growth and the rising inequality anticipated by Deng Xiaoping's opponents could also cause a shift in the opposite direction – towards a new class struggle. The circumstances under which it would consider this therefore warrant consideration and it is argued here that the slower growth due to stem from the choice to 'look inward' could be an early trigger.

The middle-income trap and slowdown literature

There is increasing interest in middle income slowdowns by developing countries that have heretofore grown strongly out of poverty (World Bank 2010; Eichengreen *et al.* 2011). This literature is concerned with distinguishing the natural slowdown in the convergence process as poorer countries approach full industrialization – which is due to diminishing returns to physical and human capital and hence diminished catch-up investment incentives (Lucas 2009) – from the retardation of growth due to political vested interests opposing the economic policy reforms needed for the final catch-up phase (Riedel 2011). The sense in which the slowdown is considered a 'trap' derives from a divergence of collective interests from those of the leadership group, with the latter associated with rent extraction (corruption) that peaks at middle levels of real per capita income. If the final phase of convergence is seen as requiring more dispersion of power to control the corruption and release the rents, then there are important implications for China.

So where are the rents and the vested interests that could retard China's future growth? The financial sector is one location. Very high saving challenges this sector to allocate that saving across investment opportunities efficiently. The many weaknesses in this process, stemming in part from the protection of state-owned financial institutions, have already received considerable attention (Riedel 2007; Walter and Howie 2011). Yet the potential gains from further industrial reform that reduces rents in protected corners of the economy extend well beyond the financial sector. To quantify this, in a separate study I have used a mathematical model of the Chinese economy to examine the sources of future Chinese growth (Tyers 2013a).

Numerical simulations on looking inward for growth

The simulations are comparatively static and indicative, though they derive from a database representative of the Chinese economy in 2005, at the peak of China's recent growth spurt. They employ a mathematical model which captures the oligopolistic structure of the Chinese economy during that period, as summarized in Table 6.1, and it incorporates oligopolistic pricing behaviour throughout the economy. What is clear from China's economic structure is that

Table 6.1 Structure of the Chinese economy*

Per cent	*Value-added share of GDP*	*Share of total production employment*	*Share of total exports*	*Pure profit share of gross revenue*
Agriculture	13	24	2	0
Petroleum, coal, metals	16	11	10	20
Light manufacturing	29	33	82	5
Services	42	32	6	20
Total	100	100	100	12

Source: Model database, derived from Dimaranan and McDougall (2002), and an update of the national data to 2005, as described in Tyers (2013a).

Note

* Pure profits are calculated from national statistics estimates of accounting profits, deducting required returns to service industry specific prime rates. Here they are presented gross of tax and corporate saving, and as shares of total revenue.

the agricultural and export light manufacturing sectors are relatively competitive, with little economic rent accruing to physical capital owners. The more protected heavy manufacturing and services sectors, on the other hand, have high rents, half the nation's value added and almost half of total employment.

Continued export-led growth is simulated by a further rise in agricultural labour productivity and, via foreign direct investment (FDI), in total factor productivity in the light manufacturing export sector, combined with an arbitrarily low increase in an exogenous real production wage. Workers continue to be released by agriculture and expansion is substantial, as expected. The results are given in Table 6.2, which also includes a simulation of the same shocks, except that the Lewis turning point is past and the supply of production labour has begun to contract. Growth then stems from the productivity

Table 6.2 Simulated export-led growth and government expansion effects[a]

Per cent	*Continued export-led growth*[b]	*Export-led growth beyond the Lewis turning point*[c]	*Post-turning point with 3% foreign demand contraction*[d]	*Government expansion 30% consumption tax financed*[e]
Real GDP	9.5	2.2	0.0	3.8
Real GNP	14.9	6.8	5.4	−13.1
Real exchange rate	5.6	6.3	6.7	0.1
Exports/GDP	−1.5	−4.6	−7.9	−0.5
Consumption/GDP	2.3	2.3	3.5	−10.2
CA surplus/GDP	24.4	−7.5	−15.7	−19.3
Production employment	4.9	−4.7	−6.3	0.0
Real production wage	5.0	10.0	10.0	−2.3
Real skilled wage	6.2	−1.1	−3.4	−0.5
Physical capital stock	4.3	−0.4	−2.0	−0.6

Source: Simulation results detailed in Tyers (2013a).

Notes

a These simulations are all made in long-run mode— endogenous capital stock with exogenous external rate of return on excess saving and perfect mobility of workers between agriculture and the other sectors.

b This simulation retains the existing policy regime and applies 4% labour productivity in agriculture, to continue to release workers, and 4% productivity in light manufacturing (the export sector) due to continued FDI, combined with an exogenous rise in the real production wage of just 2%. Modern sector labour demand rises substantially.

c Here the exogenous real production wage is increased 10%, reflecting scarcity, consistent with the decline in labour supply shown.

d This simulation establishes that, if there is a labour supply slowdown sufficient to raise the real production wage by 10%, all that is needed to kill off growth completely is a contraction in overall export demand by 3%.

e This simulates a consumption tax financed fiscal expansion which raises the government spending share of GDP by a quarter with fixed production employment and an endogenous real production wage.

changes alone and is much reduced. The real production wage rises faster, however, and there is a reduction in the current account surplus due to a decline in pure profits in the protected sectors (in effect, a gain by workers at the expense of capital) and hence a decline in corporate saving. Table 6.2 also shows the effects of one of the proposed mechanisms for new growth – further expansion of government activity. Consumption tax financing causes overall economic activity to rise modestly but the protected heavy manufacturing and services sectors, and hence capital income, are the principal beneficiaries, with households and workers worse off. Although the results for other sources of tax revenue are not shown, if the government expansion is financed from company tax, the net effects on overall economic activity are still small. Expanded government activity, by itself, is therefore not a significant source of future Chinese growth.

The greatest potential for inwardly generated growth rests with industrial reform, which applies to both heavy manufacturing and services, including financial services. This has numerous dimensions. One is pure privatization, which ensures that all after-tax company income accrues to households and so may be allocated by them to saving or consumption (Tyers and Lu 2008). By itself, as indicated in the first column of Table 6.3, this reduces national saving and the current account surplus. Other than this, however, the simulation suggests that privatization generates no substantial growth.[22] Another popular industrial policy reform is to retain the proportion of state ownership but to force price competition by fragmenting state-owned enterprises (SOEs). The problem with this approach is that, while it does induce more competitive pricing, it raises fixed costs substantially, and the simulations show that the latter effect dominates the former, yielding no positive growth.

Substantial growth is available, however, from directly attacking the rents accruing to SOEs by regulating their pricing with a view to forcing them to price at average cost. This has been considerably successful in the industrial countries and the simulations show that the effect is to reduce costs in industries whose products are used throughout the economy and hence to expand economic activity substantially. The export sector is a substantial beneficiary from this, and, aside from the overall expansion it offers, the associated redistribution is away from capital owners towards workers. Yet this desirable result requires the redistribution of very considerable rents currently accruing to China's industrial elite. It is politically difficult, for the reasons made clear by Riedel (2011). The final simulation offered in Table 6.3 shows the effect of encouraging FDI in China's services sector, and the associated productivity growth, on overall performance. Not only is the growth effect considerable, but it also offers a step towards the convergence of the Chinese economy with the industrialized West. As Table 6.3 indicates, the simulation yields substantially higher real wages, the result of which is a redistribution of industrial output and exports in favour of heavier manufacturing. The Chinese economy continues to open upbut it is much more reliant than before on intra-industry trade with the West, in the manner of the US and Western Europe.

Table 6.3 Simulated industrial reforms and expansion potential[a]

Per cent	*Pure privatization of SOEs*[b]	*Pure splitting of SOEs—three-fold fragmentation*	*Price caps on SOE oligopolies*[c]	*FDI-driven services growth: 4% productivity*
Real GDP	1.4	–19.8	28.9	17.9
Real GNP	–2.6	–29.3	27.1	20.0
Real exchange rate	0.2	2.5	–7.6	–5.4
Exports/GDP	–5.1	–14.2	22.3	6.3
Consumption/GDP	10.3	21.8	5.0	5.4
CA surplus/GDP	–83.0	–297	132	94.3
Real production wage	1.3	37.2	30.5	17.6
Real skilled wage	2.2	–0.7	42.8	22.7
Physical capital stock	1.1	45.2	26.1	13.3

Source: Simulation results detailed in Tyers (2013a).

Notes

a These simulations are all made in long-run mode —endogenous capital stock with exogenous external rate of return on excess saving, exogenous labour supply with endogenous real wage, and perfect mobility of workers between agriculture and the other sectors.

b Pure privatization requires that all corporate income after tax should accrue to the collective private household and be split between consumption and saving at private rates.

c Price caps alter the pricing formulae of oligopolistic firms, forcing them to halve their mark-ups over their average costs.

The difficult politics of internally generated growth

To gain substantial further growth by looking inward, China will need to combine other elements of industrial reform with a more ardent regulatory attack on oligopoly rents. This will be difficult politically, as will the other key element of further growth, namely substantial productivity growth in the primarily state-owned services sector. Achieving this will require levels of FDI in services that parallel those in Chinese manufacturing. Heretofore, the CCP has opposed foreign ownership in key services and heavy manufacturing industries. Allowing such FDI will also be very difficult politically.

The inward search for continued growth is therefore a key threat to economic performance and hence to the attitude towards economic freedoms of the CCP. At the same time, the rise of domestic inequality and its associated class and ethnic conflict will keep the CCP under pressure. Indeed, ironically, the distributional stress is also a source of domestic pressure to look inward in the sense that larger public investments, and larger government in general, do redistribute resources even if they inhibit their growth; hence the frequent reference at the highest levels to looking inward as "rebalancing" (Wen 2007, 2011). These pressures to look inward will continue to be reinforced by the Western clamour for human rights in general and Western public sympathies with minority opponents of the CCP. Should these pressures cause the CCP to choose yet another refocus, this time a return to class struggle, economic freedoms in China will be restricted and economic stagnation will manifest. Such developments will clearly oppose the interests of the average Chinese and the whole of the global economy.

6 Soft resolutions

One natural force that may resolve the potential conflicts – especially those that relate to rising domestic inequality and comparatively low consumption growth – is the impending Lewis turning point. Its arrival will see accelerated real wage growth and hence the fruits of further growth will be less concentrated and, since this will raise the share of total income available to households and hence consumption expenditure, the corporate share of saving and the overall saving rate should fall. It will, of course, bring with it the need for costly adjustments since, as shown in the previous section, growth will slow and the supply of labour to the heretofore efficient and relatively competitive light manufacturing sector will gradually dry up. Moreover, the net benefits from China's growth that accrue to the global economy will also decline. Yet if, as some believe (Garnaut 2010), this transition is imminent, the silver lining it brings will be reduced political pressure on the CCP from at home and abroad and hence less incentive to abandon economic freedoms as a means of advancing both the party and the nation.

Even if the Lewis transition is imminent, there remains the matter of an orderly economic transition. Both the Republic of Korea and Taiwan made orderly economic transitions away from dependence on the transformation of their labour forces and labour-intensive exports. Political transformations towards liberal democracy also occurred in both, commencing as their urban middle classes assumed numerical majorities. Of course, they were helped in this by the stimulus associated with China's own growth surge. Japan's initial transition was orderly, surviving the oil and commodity crises of the 1970s, but it was subsequently disrupted by policy errors during the 1980s and early 1990s. Japan's comparatively liberal democracy could not chart those waters effectively, even with the growth of China on its doorstep. Now China must do so, but without the external stimulus associated with a growth surge in a large near neighbour.

To find further substantial growth, the CCP must dig deep and produce industrial reforms that reduce the rents that currently concentrate economic gains while at the same time welcoming FDI into its hitherto protected services sectors. This will be a tall order politically. Yet China's governments since the early 1980s have faced constant political and economic challenges and they have thus far muddled through effectively. There is reason to expect that the next Chinese government will fare similarly.[23] The fundamentals behind Chinese growth to date seem sound, and the obstacles to continued transformation are known to the government and its branches (*The Economist* 2011). Yet there has never been a full year recession in three decades and the political response to a significant slowdown of the type the Western democracies have weathered frequently remains uncharted.

As Riedel (2007) indicates, the main challenges take the form of the need for improved governance, a stronger social safety net and improved environmental protection, but most of all it needs financial reform to facilitate the flow of its considerable saving into productive domestic investment. The external clamour for policies to stimulate faster consumption growth, however, is essentially xenophobic, and is tantamount to demands that the Chinese should invest less and have their economy perform more poorly. A strong Chinese economy and a smooth economic transition are in the global collective interest and hence Western political pressure needs to be restrained. At the same time, the Chinese are in a better position to learn from the Japanese experience and resist external pressure for economic policy changes that are not beneficial domestically. With a modicum of good fortune the CCP will hang on to Deng Xiaoping's and Jiang Zemin's theory for long enough to allow its smooth economic transition and the establishment of a dominant middle class. Thereafter, the stage is set for an associated political transition that will confer on the Chinese people the remainder of the freedoms required for something closer to a Popperian open society.

Notes

1 Funding for the research described in this chapter is from Australian Research Council Discovery Grant No. DP0557885. Thanks for valuable discussions on this topic are due to Jane Golley, Peter Robertson and Wu Yanrui, and for research assistance to Tsun Se Cheong.
2 Indeed, the distinction has a longer history in Asia as is readily discerned from an inspection of the politics and economic performance of Hong Kong. See Li (2012).
3 Since the Deng Xiaoping era there have been numerous political reforms, among which are the relaxation of media controls, the broadening of party membership criteria, the expansion of intra-party democracy and minority representation, the transformation of the justice system from military to civil administration with massive military demobilization and budget cuts, the tolerance of 'two systems' with the establishment of the Hong Kong Special Administrative Region, and reduced restrictions on inter-provincial and international travel and migration. In addition, very recent pressures for political reform at the village level appear to have borne fruit (Wang 2012).
4 See Deng Xiaoping (2000); Vogel (2011).
5 For some explanation of the three represents, see Section 2.
6 This result is clear from PPP adjusted Penn World Tables data, to be discussed in Section 3.
7 For a summary, focusing in particular on China's macroeconomic policy, see Tyers and Zhang (2010). A typical US perspective is offered in Bergsten *et al.* (2008) and Lardy (2012).
8 The very cheap short-term credit that helped precipitate the US financial collapse in 2008 was not directly due to Chinese long-term lending but rather to US Federal Reserve monetary policy after 2001, which led to very low short rates and negative short real rates.
9 This addresses the concern of Rawls (1971) that the performance of the poorest in a community is of concern to all because of the "veil of ignorance".
10 Common philosophies can emerge from historical politico-religious tyrannies or from cultural isolation, but they can also be a consequence of encouragement by the modern state as in Singapore's campaigns against littering, spitting and other antisocial behaviours. Government campaigns of this type are common in China also.

11 Dikotter (2010) estimates over fifty million premature deaths due to the great leap forward alone, due primarily to Mao's acquisition of heavy industrial technology from the Soviets and his determination to honour its repayment in kind by shipping grain to Russia.

12 Ye (2000) offers the formal detail, and Lawrence (2000), Bao Tong (2002), Fewsmith (2003) and Gilley (1998) provide English-language interpretations. Bao critiques the three represents. He was the closest aide to former Communist Party Secretary General Zhao Ziyang in the 1980s. He served seven years in prison for opposing the 1989 crackdown on student protesters in Tiananmen Square and lived thereafter in Beijing under police surveillance.

13 The current account is $CA=X-M+N=SD-I$, where N is net factor income from abroad, SD is the sum of private and government saving and I is investment. The right-hand side of this identity stems from the combination of aggregate expenditure on GDP, $Y=C+I+G+X+M$; the fact that GNP is $YN=Y+N$; the GNP disposal identity, $YN=C+T+S$, and the balance of payments, $BoP=0=KA+CA$, where KA is the capital (and financial) account.

14 Another perspective on China's current account surplus is that it is due to the intra-Asian trade in manufacturing components (Athukorala 2005). Since the Chinese economy carries out a lot of final assembly of components supplied in other Asian states, China's current account surplus is in some way representative of the whole of Asia, being much enhanced by the diversion of exports from other Asian economies that once went to the US and Europe but now go to China for some value adding before leaving China for the same destinations.

15 For more on the central role of investment, see Riedel *et al.* (2007).

16 While it is true that cheaper credit has not always led to growth-enhancing expenditures in these countries, their errors in public and private expenditure patterns have not been the fault of the Asian high savers.

17 Krugman (2010b) even declares that "China is making all of us poorer".

18 This raises the prospect of "immiserising growth", which is already hotly debated as a consequence of Chinese export expansion, at least for smaller, poorer exporters that compete with China (Bhagwati 1958).

19 As of 2012, the intensity with which China's exchange rate is debated in the US has abated slightly, to be replaced in serious forums by the next area of real economic conflict between them, namely the protection of intellectual property rights held by US firms.

20 This has a parallel in the complaints in the US that Chinese Americans are disproportionately successful in secondary schools and top university admissions. Doonsbury once quipped that "Chinese Americans should let their children watch more television".

21 It might further be argued that Chinese growth has also been good for the minorities about which complaints arise. Unrest appears to stem not so much from concern over their standard of living but, rather, from the submergence of their cultures by the regional influx of Han Chinese.

22 Had it been assumed that privatization might eliminate x-inefficiency and hence raise productivity, some growth might be expected from this change, though it would be a one-off change.

23 The Bo Xilai incident and its thus far careful resolution is seen by many as a sign of the steadying of the CCP's political ship in the face of conflicts between the new super-rich and the larger Chinese public, represented by the CCP's two main factions (Wishik 2012).

Bibliography

Athukorala, P.C. 2005. "Components Trade and Implications for Asian Structural Adjustment". In R. Garnaut and L. Song (eds) *The China Boom and its Discontents.* Canberra: Asia-Pacific Press, ch. 12.

Azziz, J. and L. Cui. 2007. "Explaining China's Low Consumption: The Neglected Role of Household Income". *International Monetary Fund Working Paper WP 07/181.* Washington, DC.

Bao Tong. 2002. "Three Represents: Marking the End of an Era". *Far Eastern Economic Review* (5 September). This journal has now closed, but the article is also available from its archives and those of *The Asian Wall Street Journal.*

Bardhan, P. 2010. *Awakening Giants, Feet of Clay: Assessing the Economic Rise of China and India.* Princeton, NJ: Princeton University Press.

Bergsten, C.F., C. Freeman, N.R. Lardy and D.J. Mitchell. 2008. *China's Rise: Challenges and Opportunities.* Washington, DC: Peterson Institute for International Economics.

Bernanke, B. 2006. "Speech to the Chinese Academy of Social Sciences". Beijing, 15 December. www.federalreserve.gov/BoardDocs/Speeches/2006/20061215.

Bhagwati, J.N. 1958. "Immiserizing Growth: a Geometrical Note". Review of Economic Studies 25(3): 201–5.

Bloom, D.E. and J.G. Williamson. 1998. "Demographic Transitions and Economic Miracles in Emerging Asia". World Bank Economic Review 12(3): 419–55.

Cai, F. 2010. "Demographic Transition, Demographic Dividend And Lewis Turning Point In China". *China Economic Journal* 3(2): 107–19.

Corden, W.M. 1994. *Economic Policy, Exchange Rates and the International System.* Oxford: Oxford University Press.

Deer, L. and L. Song, 2012. "China's Approach to Rebalancing: A Conceptual and Policy Framework". *China and the World Economy* 20(1): 1–26.

Deng Xiaoping. 2000. *Selected Works.* Information Network of the Guangdong Provincial Research Center for Deng Xiaoping Theory [in Chinese].

Dikotter, F. 2010. *Mao's Great Famine*. London: Bloomsbury.

Dimaranan, B.V. and R.A. McDougall. 2002. *Global Trade, Assistance and Production: The GTAP 5 Data Base*, May. Purdue University, Lafayette: Center for Global Trade Analysis.

Dooley, M.P., D. Folkerts-Landau and P. Garber. 2004. "Direct Investment, Rising Real Wages and the Absorption of Excess Labor in the Periphery". *NBER Working Paper 10626* (July). Cambridge, MA: National Bureau of Economic Research.

Easterly, W. 2001. "The Lost Decades: Developing Countries' Stagnation in Spite of Policy Reform 1980–1998". *Mimeo*, February. Washington, DC: World Bank.

Economist. 2011. "How Real is China's Growth?" 1 June: economist.com/blogs/freeexchange/2011/05/chinas_economy.

Eichengreen, B., D. Park and K. Shin. 2011. "When Fast Growing Economies Slow Down: International Evidence and Implications for China". *NBER Working Paper*, 16919. Cambridge, MA: National Bureau of Economic Research.

Fewsmith, J. 2003. "Studying the Three Represents". *China Leadership Monitor* 8(fall): 1-11. Available at: www.hoover.org/publications/china-leadership-monitor/article/7961.

Garnaut, R. 2010. "Macroeconomic Implications of the Turning Point". *China Economic Journal* 3(2): 181–90.

Gelber, H.G. 2007. *The Dragon and the Foreign Devils: China and the World, 1100 BC to the Present*. New York: Walker and Company.

Gilley, B. 1998. *Tiger on the Brink – Jiang Zemin and China's New Elite*. Berkeley: University of California Press.

Golley, J. and X. Meng. 2011. "Has China Run Out of Surplus Labour?" *Chinese Economic Review* 22(4): 555–72.

Golley, J. and R. Tyers. 2011. "Contrasting Giants: Demographic Change and Economic Performance in China and India". *SSRN Labor: Demographics and Economics of the Family e-Journal* 3(67).

Goyal, R. and R.I. McKinnon. 2003. "Japan's Negative Risk Premium in Interest Rates: The Liquidity Trap and the Fall in Bank Lending". *The World Economy* 26(March): 339–63.

Haber, S.H., D.C. North and B.R. Weingast. 2008. "Introduction". In S.H. Haber, D.C. North and B.R. Weingast (eds) *Political Institutions and Financial Development*. Stanford, CA: Stanford University Press, pp. 1–9.

Hamada, K. and Y. Okada. 2009. "Monetary and International Factors Behind Japan's Lost Decade". *Journal of the Japanese and International Economies* 23(2): 200–19.

Harris, R.G.P., E. Robertson and J. Xu. 2011. "The International Effects of China's Trade and Education Booms". *The World Economy* 34(10): 1703–25.

Jacob, R. 2011. "China Labour Unrest Flares as Orders Fall". *Financial Times*, 23 November.

Jia, K. and W. Liu. 2009. *China's Fiscal Policies During the Post-Crisis Era*. Beijing: Research Institute for Fiscal Science, Ministry of Finance.

Krugman, P. 2010a. "Taking on China". *New York Times*, 30 September.

——. 2010b. "Capital Export, Elasticity Pessimism and the *Renminbi* (Wonkish)". *New York Times* (blog), 16 March.

Kuijs, L. 2006. "How Will China's Saving–Investment Balance Evolve?" *World Bank Policy Research Working Paper 3958*, July. Beijing.

Kuijs, L. and J. He. 2007. "Rebalancing China's Economy – Modelling a Policy Package". *World Bank China Working Paper No. 7*, September. Beijing.

Lam, W.W.L. 2000. "Jiang Still Thinking it Through". *South China Morning Post*, 5 January.

Lardy, N. 2006. 'Toward a Consumption-driven Growth Path". *Policy Brief* 06–6. Washington, DC: Peterson Institute for International Economics.

——. 2011. "An Economic Slowdown in China". *The World in 2012 Festival. The Economist*, 1–3 December. New York: www.worldin2012.economist.com.

——. 2012. *Sustaining China's Growth after the Global Financial Crisis*. Washington, DC: Peterson Institute for International Economics.

Lawrence, S.V. 2000. "Three Cheers for the Party". *Far Eastern Economic Review* 26 (October): 32–35.

Lewis, W.A. 1955. *The Theory of Economic Growth*. London: Taylor and Francis.

Li, K.W. 2012. *Economic Freedom: Lessons of Hong Kong*. World Scientific Press and Imperial College Press, May.

Little, I., R. Cooper, M. Corden and R. Rajapatirana. 1993. *Boom, Crisis and Adjustment: The Macroeconomic Experience of Developing Countries*. Washington, DC: Oxford University Press for the World Bank.

Locke, J. [1689]1821. *Two Treatises on Government*. London: Whitmore and Fenn, and C. Brown.

Lucas, R.E. Jr. 2002. "A Million Mutinies: The Key to Economic Development". In R.E. Lucas Jr. *Lectures on Economic Growth*. Cambridge, MA: Harvard University Press.

——. 2009. “Trade and the Diffusion of the Industrial Revolution”. *American Economic Journal: Macroeconomics* 1(1): 1–25.

Mill, J.S. 1848. *The Principles of Political Economy*. London: Hackett Publishing.

——. 1859. *On Liberty*. London: Longman, Roberts and Green.

——. 1907. “On Social Freedom, or the Necessary Limits of Individual Freedom Arising From Social Life”. *Oxford and Cambridge Review* June: 57–83.

Modigliani, F. and S. Cao 2004. “The Chinese Saving Puzzle and the Life-cycle Hypothesis”. *Journal of Economic Literature* 42(1): 145–70.

North, D.C. 1990. *Institutions, Institutional Change and Economic Performance*. Cambridge: Cambridge University Press.

Obstfeld, M. 2008. “Time of Troubles: The Yen and Japan’s Economy, 1985–2008”. Presented at the ESRI-Chicago GSB-Columbia Business School Conference on “Japan’s Bubble, Deflation and Long Term Stagnation”. Federal Reserve Bank of San Francisco, December: 11–12.

Popper, K.R. 1945. *The Open Society and its Enemies*, 2 vols. London: Routledge.

Rawls, J. 1971. *A Theory of Justice*. Cambridge, MA: Harvard University Press.

Riedel, J. 2006. *Seeing But Not Believing: Technological Progress and Structural Change in China*. Johns Hopkins University: School of Advanced International Studies.

——. 2007. “China Needs Many Things But Not a New Growth Engine”. *Financial Times*, 21 February, Asia edn.

——. 2011. *The Slowing Down Of Long Term Growth in Asia: Natural Causes, the Middle Income Trap and Politics*. Johns Hopkins University: School of Advanced International Studies.

Riedel, J., J. Jin and J. Gao. 2007. *How China Grows: Investment, Finance and Reform*. Princeton, NJ: Princeton University Press, and Beijing: Peking University Press.

Robertson, P. E. 2011. “Clash of the Titans: Comparing India And China”. In J. Golley and L. Song (eds) *Rising China: Global Challenges and Opportunities*. Canberra: ANU Press, ch. 14.

Robertson, P. E. and J.Y. Xu. 2010. “In China’s Wake: Has Asia Gained from China’s Growth?” *Economics Discussion Paper 10.15*. Perth: UWA Business School, June.

Tyers, R. 2012. “Japanese Economic Stagnation: Causes and Global Implications”. *The Economic Record* 88(283): 517–36.

——. 2013a. “Looking Inward for Transformative Growth in China”. *CAMA Working Paper No. 48/2013*. Australian National University, Canberra: Centre for Applied Macroeconomics, March.

——. 2013b. “International Effects of China’s Rise and Transition: Neoclassical and Keynesian Perspectives”. *CAMA Working Paper No. 44–2013*. Australian National University, Canberra: Centre for Applied Macroeconomics, July.

Tyers, R. and I. Bain. 2008. “American and European Financial Shocks: Implications for China’s Economic Performance”. In L. Song and W.T. Woo (eds) *China’s Dilemma: Economic Growth, the Environment and Climate Change*. Canberra: Asia Pacific Press, the Brookings Institution Press, and Social Sciences Academic Press, Beijing, July, pp. 59–89.

Tyers, R. and F. Lu. 2008. “Competition Policy, Corporate Saving and China’s Current Account Surplus”. *Working Papers in Economics and Econometrics No. 496*. Australian National University, Canberra: College of Business and Economics, July.

Tyers, R. and Y. Zhang. 2011. “Appreciating the *Renminbi*”. *The World Economy* 34(2): 265–97.

Tyers, R., J. Golley, Y. Bu and I. Bain. 2008. “China’s Economic Growth and Its Real Exchange Rate”. *China Economic Journal* 1(2): 123–45.

Vogel, E. 2011. *Deng Xiaoping and the Transformation of China*. Cambridge, MA: Belknap Press/Harvard University Press.

Walter, C.E. and F.J.T. Howie. 2011. *Red Capitalism: The Fragile Financial Foundation of China's Extraordinary Rise*. Singapore: John Wiley and Sons.

Wang Zhanyang. 2012. "Wukan and Village Autonomy". *China Digital Times*, Chinadigitaltimes.net, 10 January.

Wen Jiabao. 2007. *The Conditions for China to be Able to Continue to Guarantee Stable and Rapid Economic Development*, www.npc.gov.cn, 16 March (accessed 28 October 2011).

——. 2011. *Report on Work of the Government*, www.npc.gov.cn, 5 March (accessed 24 March 2011).

Williamson, J. 2012. "Is the Beijing Consensus now Dominant?" *Special Essay on Asia Policy No. 13.* Washington, DC: Peterson Institute for International Economics. January.

Wishik, A. 2012. "The Bo Xilai Crisis: A Curse or a Blessing for China? An Interview with Cheng Li". *National Bureau of Asian Research*. Posted 18 April.

World Bank, 2010. "Escaping the Middle-income Trap". In *East Asia and Pacific Economic Update 2010 Volume 2: Robust Recovery, Rising Risks*. November, ch. 2.

Yi, Gang. 2011. "How China Plans To Strike An Economic Balance". *CaiXin Online* English, 4 February.

7 Singapore

Plato's other republic?

Jeremy Shearmur

1 Introduction

Singapore is a small – but remarkably successful – East Asian country. It is of interest in the context of the present study not only in itself, but for three other reasons. First, because it offers a model of a society which is modern but is not, historically, a Western-style open society. Further, it offers a striking model of how such a society can operate with a high degree of engagement with Western commercial companies. Not only is this of interest in itself, but it is also striking as an alternative model of development, not least for countries with a Chinese ethnic population – and perhaps even China itself.

Second, in Karl Popper's *Open Society and Its Enemies* (Popper [1945] 1963), one of the targets of his critical discussion was Plato. In part, as he subsequently explained, this was because there seemed to him to be striking parallels between Plato – for whom he had the greatest admiration – and Hitler, for whom he had no time at all, when each was seen as offering a reaction to a social transition towards an open society.[1] In addition to this theme, however, Popper also took issue with Plato's *Republic* when seen as a model for a particular kind of ideal society. This ideal had certain commonalities with the ideas of some of Popper's contemporaries – both conservatives, and also certain socialist planners, notably some of those in the Fabian tradition. (It is here striking that not only were the Webbs sympathizers with aspects of the Soviet Union,[2] when seen as an exercise in rational planning, but H.G. Wells' *A Modern Utopia* (1905) is clearly in the tradition of Plato's *Republic*.) Singapore is in some ways striking as a creation of modern top-down planning, albeit conducted in a manner that opens it up to, rather than closing it off from, commercial activity. Not only does Singapore in this sense exemplify some of the very features of Plato's *Republic* of which Popper was critical. It is also interesting that, in his study of Lee Kuan Yew, Michael D. Barr (2000, 56, 58) noted the influence upon him of Fabian legal theorists under whom he studied at Cambridge.

Third, I have already noted that modern Singapore was, in a sense, created as somewhere that would be open to commercial activity. The visitor to Singapore is immediately struck not just by its commercial activities, but also by its social openness to commercial influences. The young citizens of Singapore will shop in stores which bring together a striking range of opportunities from not just the Western world but also Japan. But they operate in an open and high-tech environment (the openness of the internet itself having served to short-circuit certain of the controls that had operated with regard to assembly, and the censorship of the press). In addition, many young people from Singapore study overseas in Western countries. This poses an interesting problem. Plato had viewed commerce as an enemy of his *Republic* (cf. Popper [1945]1963, ch. 10). One might ask: Is the distinctive kind of political order that has been created in Singapore likely to be stable in the longer term, given that its citizens would appear increasingly open to influences from societies which are not under the kind of paternalistic control that there has been in Singapore in the past? In asking this, I do not mean: Will Singapore collapse? Rather, my question is: Can one expect Singapore, over time, to lose some of its distinctiveness, and to start to look like other modern societies? I will suggest that some recent developments – and certain underlying tendencies in Singapore – are suggestive of this. Should I be correct, this – in line with my first point – is of wider significance than for Singapore itself. For it might suggest that, in the longer term, the kind of idea of a non-Western modern society exemplified by Singapore may not be open to others, either.[3]

2 From Popper to Singapore

Karl Popper's book about the open society was entitled *The Open Society and Its Enemies*. While in that book Popper set out positive ideas concerning the character of an open society – which I have reviewed in the first chapter in this volume – much of his writing was directed towards the critical analysis of enemies of the open society. His concern, in that volume, was not with those who were totally opposed to the idea of an open society. Rather, his particular concern was with the way in which people whom he considered to be humanitarian and liberal in their underlying views had been led astray by intellectual influences which turned them into opponents of democracy, and believers in the need for anti-humanitarian approaches. Popper, in his book, engaged critically in this context with the work of Plato and of Marx.

At the time at which he was writing, the need to address Marxism was obvious enough. Popper himself had had considerable experience of Marxism. He had, as a young man, worked in the office of the Austrian Communist Party. Popper, as he has often described, became disillusioned about the claims of Marxism. However, for a while he remained a socialist, and played an active role in teaching in a socialist youth organization – which he was later to describe as totalitarian in its tendencies. In the subsequent period, it was the socialist party in Austria which offered the only resistance to national socialism and conservative reaction, but Popper felt that its Marxist ideas undermined fatally its effectiveness as an opposition.[4] He believed, however, that Marxist ideas would continue to be significant: there was a great deal of interest in Marxism among, for example, some British intellectuals. The Soviet Union stood as a source of inspiration for some people, too. Popper considered that Marxist ideas would be likely to be of continuing significance after the Second World War – and that, for this reason, it was important to engage with them critically.

Plato may have seemed a less obvious choice. Popper felt, however, that his elitism and his critique of democracy were influential in leading some on the Right away from the ideals of the open society. (It is striking that the idea that Plato's *Republic* offered a model for developments in Germany was shared by someone to whom Popper was in other respects in strong disagreement: Otto Neurath; see Neurath and Lawerys 1945.) In addition, as I mentioned in Chapter 1 (this volume), in a striking paper which he gave as a talk following the publication of *The Open Society*, and which has only been published recently, Popper discussed the way in which it seemed to him that there were some odd parallels between the concerns of Plato and of Hitler – in particular, in terms of their experiencing destructive social change, and feeling in the face of this that it was necessary to try to rebuild the kind of organic community which was being lost.

There was, however, a much more direct link between Popper and the criticism of Plato's ideas, since one of Popper's friends in Vienna was the philosopher Julius Kraft, and he was a follower of the unorthodox Kantian, Leonard Nelson (who had revived the little-known ideas of the nineteenth-century writer, J.J. Fries). Nelson wrote extensively on issues in philosophy, but also, in the aftermath of the First World War, wrote on political themes. Here, he was engaged in a self-conscious revival of Platonic ideas as an alternative to democracy. (He favoured the idea of a political movement dedicated to an ideal, within which promotion would occur on the basis of dedication to the development and furthering of the ideal – as occurred, say, in the Catholic Church or the army; see Nelson 1928.)

Popper took Nelson's ideas seriously: his *Logic of Scientific Discovery* (Popper 1959) contains a discussion of 'Fries' trilemma', while his first book on the theory of knowledge (only recently available in English; see Popper 2009) contains quite extensive discussions of the ideas of Fries and of Nelson. Nelson, however, was not just a theorist: there was also an actual political organization set up based on the model of his ideas. A formal attempt was made to recruit Popper into it by Kraft and one of Nelson's associates. (It was, in fact, socialist in its character;[5] those involved were in opposition to Hitler, and the organization, shorn of its elitism, became one of the components which eventually went into the formation of the post-Second World War German Social Democrats.) Popper rejected the invitation, and it turns out that some of his first critical writing about Plato – the discussion which became his treatment of Plato's ideas about leadership, which appears in ch. 7 of his *Open Society* – was originally written as a critique of Nelson.

The result of all this is that Popper's *Open Society* contains some quite full discussion of Plato's political ideas – notably from the *Republic*, but also from his *Laws*. All this leads Popper to take issue with an approach to politics which would see political power as properly, exclusively in the hands of an educated elite, who would be selected and specially trained from an early age. He was critical, also, of the view that it was only such an elite who should, properly, be concerned with political issues, and that they should exercise paternalistic control for the well-being of the society (and, through that, of ordinary citizens). Popper took issue with many of the details of Plato's account; but he was particularly opposed to his claim that the guardians should rule, supported by a military-cum-police force of 'auxiliaries', and that they were entitled to rule by virtue of their knowledge and expertise.

It is worth noting that while Plato's ideas were in many respects distinctive to the period at which he was writing, and, in their idealization of arrangements to be found at the time in Sparta, were concerned to explicate and defend an ideal of a static community in which commerce and change were seen as sources of problems, there is, as I mentioned in section 1, a sense in which some of his ideas lived on in part of the political Left. One might, for example, note the way in which, following the French Revolution, the Saint-Simonians and Auguste Comte espoused ideas of a society ruled by an educated elite. There is obviously a further parallel in terms of the ideas of some of the Fabians – compare, in this context especially, some of H.G. Wells' novels which are designed explicitly as offering propaganda for such a viewpoint.

The *point* of all this, in our present context, is that many of the things to which Popper took exception in Plato may in fact be found in Singapore. Singapore is striking in offering an alternative to the kinds of arrangements that may be found in Western liberal democracies, and one which exhibits some odd echoes of Platonic themes.[6] It is, however, interesting because – as distinct from Plato – this is combined with a strong embrace of the ideal of a commercial society. That is to say, while Plato's ideas are in many respects archaic, and the ideas of the Fabians were tied to ideas about economic organization which today do not have much appeal, Singapore may surely be judged not only to be successful in itself, but also to offer a model of a prosperous commercial society of a kind that contrasts with that of 'Western' countries.

3 A first experience of Singapore

The initial impressions of a visitor to Singapore from a Western country are likely to be immensely positive. The airport is clean, spacious and well organized. Public transportation or reasonably priced cabs are readily available. The MRT system is clean, and very well organized.[7] And, if one takes a cab from the airport one drives through wide boulevards, by the side of which there is a striking display of tropical flowers. If one explores, there is the interest of an Asian city – but in a setting which is well regulated, and without the squalor and deprivation which is to be seen elsewhere. In some of the shopping malls, one finds a kind of savvy consumerism directed towards and enjoyed by young people that is probably unmatched anywhere. Older or remote locations, while poorer, compare well with what may be found in many of the cities of Western Europe. In addition, the degree of diversity and catering to life in a multicultural society is also impressive: Hindu temples may be found virtually next door to Chinese temples, while there is both a striking Hindu temple – with ornate statuary – and a South Indian Mosque on the edge of Chinatown. Public notices (e.g. in the Metro system) may be found in English, Chinese, Tamil and Malay. The population itself seems to exhibit a remarkable degree of affluence and good health.[8]

It is, however, worth bearing in mind that it is no accident that Singapore makes such an impression on the Western visitor – just because, in a sense, it has been designed to do so. The ruling party sought a path to modernization by way of making Singapore attractive to those running Western companies. Not only was Singapore remodelled physically on such a basis, but one might also see Singapore itself – and its population – as a kind of artefact. The population of Singapore has been the subject of a more extensive form of social engineering than almost anywhere outside of Russia or China. But – and this is what is striking – the social engineering seems in many respects to have been spectacularly successful, even though (as we will see below) it has also given rise to certain problems.

Singapore, to the visitor, looks almost like a Disney interpretation of Asia: it is clean, harmonious, nice to be in, and also safe. It is striking, however, that – as was my own experience – even the casual Western visitor may find that there are odd notes. A taxi driver's stray remark: "This is not a free society." A comment from a friend that, if more than about four people are talking at one of the tables in the outdoor food courts, they may find the police keeping an eye on them as to what they are talking about. And if they dip into things further, they may find interesting – but striking – discussions by bloggers as to the character of censorship, or discover that the distinguished Singapore novelist and poet Catherine Lim was publicly taken to task by the Prime Minister for crossing informal 'OB' (out of bounds) markers about what kind of social criticism was allowed in the press. (What she said was not only mild, but expressed in a manner that was, in its intention, clearly friendly to the government.[9])

It all reminded me of a striking, but perhaps apocryphal, story that I was told about one of the Disney theme parks. A student apparently took into the park, in a bag, the uniform of a decidedly non-Disney cartoon figure, a Smurf, into which he changed in a lavatory. No sooner, however, had the Smurf gone out into the park than out of nowhere he was descended on by security people, who took him off for questioning, and I believe expelled him from paradise. Clearly, if one is maintaining a theme park with a family-friendly atmosphere to which the general public have access, then one probably needs to make use of people who will nip undesirable or otherwise problematic behaviour in the bud. One might also wonder, however, to what extent the remarkable kind of social order in Singapore is simply a product of habit and tradition, to what extent a product of deliberate socialization and policing. To look at this, we need to consider something of Singapore's history.

4 The making of Singapore

Singapore developed as a British colony, dependent upon the hinterland of Malaya. Two key aspects in its subsequent development were, on the one side, the defeat of Britain by Japan. (Lee Kuan Yew's account of the psychological impact of this upon him is here very revealing; see Lee 1998.) This also eventually had the important consequence of leading to the withdrawal of British activities and resources from Singapore; something that had played an important role in its economy. On the other side, there was the failure of the project of a wider Malaysia, including Singapore. The result of this was that Singapore was left on its own, without the colonial or the economic role it had occupied earlier.

It was also faced with a range of problems. There were tensions between the different racial groups in its population – leading to race riots. This, further, was set against a background in which Malaya was left with some hostility towards Singapore, which itself was dependent upon Malaya for its water supply. In addition, among the Chinese population, communist ideas – and the early achievements of communist China – were making an impact, and those who were influenced by these ideas were not constrained by the formal rules of democratic politics.

Lee Kuan Yew and his associates showed striking abilities – and ruthlessness – in gaining political power. They learned from the political organization of the Chinese communists. In addition, they inherited the laws of a British colony, which gave them powers of a kind that, for example, a government in Britain would not itself possess. They also faced a crisis: How was Singapore to make a living? How were racial tensions to be avoided? One might see the measures that the People's Action Party took as necessitated by the circumstances they faced. But it has been aptly commented that there has developed a tradition of depicting Singapore as facing crises to cope with for which the only alternative was the PAP and its leadership.

It would not be sensible, here, to attempt to offer a fuller account of the making of Singapore through time. Let me, rather, highlight just a few of the features of the country as they currently stand.[10]

Most obvious is the fact that Singapore is a meritocracy. In a manner that oddly parallels Plato's *Republic*, people are selected to potentially play a role in the running of Singapore from an early age. There is considerable pressure on all children to perform well,[11] while there is special selection of those who may, in time, form part of the educated elite. For those who deliver on their initial promise, there is, typically, a path involving overseas study at elite foreign universities, ending with well-paid positions in the administration. For those who join and move to positions of leadership in the PAP, there is the prospect of political power and considerable financial reward – something that may be seen as offering an alternative solution to Plato's to the problem of the potential corruption of the elite.

Plato, it may be recalled, was concerned about the way in which his guardians might be led astray by the possibilities of material wealth or nepotism. His response to this was to insist that his guardians should not handle money – and that they should live in communal facilities, rather like an officers' mess in the army. In addition, while they were free to have sexual relations,[12] they would not know who their children are – the kids being brought up by other people. In

Singapore, problems of corruption are dealt with by, on the one side, those in senior political or administrative positions being well rewarded. There is also, in the PAP, a cult of anti-corruption (cf. Bellows 2009), symbolized by leading members sometimes dressing in white,[13] and people have been removed from positions of power if there was any sign of personal problems that might undermine their effectiveness in government (e.g. problems with alcohol). Nepotism, however, is not something for which a comparable resolution has been offered, and there is potentially a problem – at least for the future – about the way in which, in Singapore, positions of power have gone to people who are relatives of Lee Kuan Yew, when power is also supposed to be associated with the very highest individual merit.

Second, there is the issue of democracy. Singapore is, formally speaking, democratic; and recently political opposition has been expressed to the PAP via the ballot-box. In fact, there has been long-standing opposition – part of the Chinese population was never reconciled to the rule of the PAP and from time to time voted for various opposition parties. However, things have been made difficult for the opposition, including the development of multi-member constituencies in which it was more difficult for an opposition to win. It is also worth noting that Lee Kuan Yew explicitly stated that if constituencies voted for the opposition, they would face consequences such as the loss of government-provided services.[14] In addition, prominent members of the opposition have regularly faced legal actions for libel if they expressed criticism in an intemperate manner or called into question the probity of the political leadership. There has been some controversy about the role, in the support of the regime, of the judiciary;[15] but suffice it to say that the kinds of laws on the basis of which action has been taken – and which have led to stiff fines, and personal bankruptcy – would not be available in other democratic countries.

A few additional points are worth noting here. First, while there is a non-state voluntary sector in Singapore, legal arrangements there make sure that it does not venture into politics: the making of overt critical points about government policy, or de facto engagement in political actions of various kinds, which is a commonplace on the part of 'civil society' organizations in Western countries, is illegal in Singapore, and any organization which gets close to the mark is liable to find itself reminded strongly that if it wishes to engage in politics it has to be a political and not a civil body. Second, there is extensive censorship as to what may be voiced in public, and what may be published. Comments made even in overseas publications by Singapore residents may lead to legal action being taken against them in Singapore. (Here, the example of Christopher Lingle is interesting: he held a visiting appointment at the National University in Singapore, voiced a critical comment in the international press which – while it did not refer to them directly – was interpreted in Singapore as questioning the political objectivity of the Singapore judiciary, and found that legal action was taken against him, such that he judged it politic to flee the country.[16]) At the same time, there is remarkable freedom in respect of the publication of material in an academic as contrasted with a public sphere setting, such that a great deal of what could be interpreted as highly critical material is published in a strictly academic context. Academic material which is deemed politically critical, however, may not be publicly available in Singapore. For example, the book which Lingle wrote about Singapore after his rapid exit, *Singapore's Authoritarian Capitalism* (Lingle 1996), while available in the National University of Singapore, is not held by the National Library (although they hold another book of his). In addition, there is the issue of the internet where the situation is complex, and may be said to allow for considerable freedom.[17] However, there are particular sensitivities about issues to do with race[18] and religion, the integrity of the judiciary, and politics more generally.

Race and religion merit separate discussion. As I have mentioned above, Singapore suffered race riots in its initial years of independence. The situation is also sensitive because its population has an ethnic Chinese majority, but it is surrounded by large countries such as Malaysia and Indonesia, which have minority ethnic Chinese populations, but where the populations are predominantly ethnically Malay, and Muslim. In Singapore, the ethnic Chinese have been particularly successful in terms of education and business, and the relatively disadvantaged position of the Malay population has been a continuing object of concern. All this has led to complicated policies for the management of ethnicity and religion, of a kind that as far as I know are not to be found elsewhere.

First, there has been an ongoing project of the management of Singapore identity.[19] Lee Kuan Yew noted that Singapore initially faced problems with regard to the modernization of a society which included peasant farmers, commenting that initially, some people wished to take their pigs with them when they moved into new, high-rise accommodation. Over time, there has been a strong concern for the education of the population and the inculcation of values based on the PAP's interpretation of Confucian themes (cf. Bauer and Bell 1999). The citizens of Singapore are disciplined for the workplace, and are also subjected to a barrage of clearly expressed information and instructions about how to live, from disease prevention to guidance against falling into the gaps between the MRT trains and the platforms. There have also been programmes to encourage social integration among the different ethnic communities. While there are well-known areas of ethnic concentration, such as China Town and Little India, these date back to the colonial period. Now, publicly supported housing is racially integrated by way of the use of a quota system, such that proportions of people of different racial backgrounds have to be maintained even in respect of private sales of publicly subsidized housing.

All this pales, however, in relation to what has happened in respect of the Chinese population. The Chinese in Singapore are historically drawn from different areas in Southern China, and spoke a variety of southern Chinese dialects. This was reflected in education up to university level, where schools offering instruction in a variety of dialects were supported by the Chinese community. All this, however, was rationalized by the government in a striking way. Each ethnic community is now provided with schooling in English, and also in its own 'native' language (Malay, Tamil – historically, the bulk of the Singapore Indian population came from southern India – and Chinese). But what is provided for the Chinese population is Mandarin – the northern Chinese dialect which has been adopted by the Chinese mainland, and which was not spoken as a native first language by any significant proportion of the Singapore population. This has been effective – the Chinese population who have grown up since this reform speaking predominantly English[20] or Mandarin. But it has led to problems for those older Chinese who spoke only southern dialects, who, it has been reported, find that they don't share a common language with their grandchildren. Given the way in which language has been taken as a marker for ethnic identity and has played such a role in nationalism, for such social engineering to have taken place for pragmatic reasons (due to the advantages of having a common language with the Mainland) is quite remarkable (cf. Newman 1986).

There have been further ramifications to this with regard to religion. The Singapore government has, as I noted above, favoured its interpretation of the Confucian tradition as offering a general ethos for the whole population.[21] The transmission of this, however, seems to have been something that was interrelated with Chinese traditional religious practises, which tend in Singapore to be bundled in with Taoism. The shift to English and Mandarin, and the rationalistic caste of mind that has been encouraged in Singapore, has had striking consequences in the area of religion in terms of a marked shift on the part of the Chinese population from Taoism towards (often evangelical) Christianity, and Buddhism (cf. Vaish 2008). (The relation to rationalism comes about in the sense that popular Taoist and traditional religions seem to have been largely rooted in religious customs and practices passed on within the family, as opposed to being something for which a strong – or, indeed, any – clear theoretical rationale may be offered.) Once people come to expect that religious ideas should offer a strong rationale for their practices, Buddhism and Christianity have an advantage because they possess intellectual resources which do not seem to be on offer within the other traditions. This is not clear-cut, religious arrangements in Singapore being strikingly eclectic;[22] but there certainly seem to be signs of marked decline in, say, the patronage and financial support of traditional, clan-based Taoist temples. If the transmission of filial piety of the kind that the government favours is, sociologically, tied up with the older practices, the situation here may become interesting.

It is also striking that in Singapore, religion is managed as part of the wider issue of multicultural relations. Both Islam and Christianity exist in Singapore; and each of them is, intrinsically, universalistic and proselytizing, and this is certainly the case for evangelical Christianity of the kind found in Singapore.[23] However, it is clear that in Singapore there are OB limits with respect to who may be proselytized – so that while Christians are free to address the Chinese and also European expatriates, the Malays are off limits. There are, though, public celebrations of religious festivals which could presumably give rise to interest across ethnic divides (e.g. the Hindu Festival of Lights; I have a vivid memory of part of Orchard Road being shut off briefly at Christmas in connection with Christmas festivities – which included Chinese gentlemen dressed as Roman centurions).

5 Success – and the future

Singapore must surely be judged a success. Its economic growth has been spectacular (although issues may be raised about the distribution of its benefits), and various of its programmes directed at public policy problems are looked at as possible models for adoption elsewhere (cf. Miller 2010). In addition, Singapore has a well-educated, and in my experience delightful, population. At the same time, it is important to recall the comment from the taxi driver to which I referred earlier: his whispered remark that Singapore is not a free country. The old joke, 'Singapore is a fine city' – followed by examples of all the kinds of things for which one may be fined for misbehaviour – is also important to bear in mind. Beyond that, one may ask: Just what does it feel like to be the object of heavy-handed, ongoing government paternalism, however well intentioned and conducted?

What to make of this is clearly an issue for the ongoing consideration of the population of Singapore – for while the style of government is authoritarian, Singapore is a democracy. And while, in the past, a combination of censorship, limitations on free speech and assembly, and discouragement from voting for the opposition have given the PAP overwhelming power, there are indications that things are changing.

In part – and this goes back to my initial question about the stability of Singapore – this would appear to be a product of social change. As the country has grown more affluent, the massive improvements in the economy which transformed the country since it left Malaysia are increasingly likely to be taken for granted by people who have grown up with them. However, if one can so put it, the highly educated and technology-savvy population which has been created by the Singapore government is surely not as likely to be as deferential towards it as people were willing to be in the past. The development of the internet has brought into existence something which cannot be easily controlled in the same way that government controlled communication in the past. Foreign travel, increased overseas higher education, and the increasing role of Singapore as a destination for overseas students (cf. Sanderson (2002) for useful background information) will also increase the number of people who have had experience of life under regimes of a different kind from that in Singapore.

It would seem plausible to take such factors as playing an important role in the background to the recent relatively strong showing of the opposition in the most recent elections.[24] In the face of this, the government commissioned an enquiry, in the light of which government salaries were cut. Since then, there have been more signs on the part of the population of a willingness to engage in decorous protests (albeit within a heavily regulated setting[25]) and a voicing of concern at what are perceived as problems posed by high rates of immigration into Singapore (itself relating to underlying economic issues facing the country).[26] All this, in turn, has given rise to indications that the Singapore government is becoming more responsive to the views of its citizens, and less self-confident than it has been in the past that it knows the right way in which everything should be run.[27]

How things unfold in Singapore will surely be a matter of interest – in which one can only wish everyone well. However, the issues here would appear significant not only for Singapore and the flourishing of its citizens, but also because of their wider significance. For they are also of interest in terms of what we are to make of the longer term sociological viability of a model of government and social organization which stands in marked contrast to that of 'Western' countries, and in certain respects also to the ideals of Popper's open society. It will surely prove interesting as to whether Singapore's citizens choose to maintain the existing system in place. And the problems that have been encountered by what in many respects seems to have been a *successful* alternative to an open society may give others pause should they find it attractive as a possible model for how they might organize themselves.

Notes

1 See, on this, Popper's "A Theory of Totalitarianism", now in Popper (2008).
2 See Sydney and Beatrice Webb (1935).
3 I should stress that this is neither a prediction, nor an exercise in historicism of the kind that Popper condemned. It relates, rather, to issues about the stability of certain kinds of social structures. Whatever the outcome, choice is always possible.
4 See, on this, examples discussed in Popper's ([1945]1963) and, more generally, Malachi Hacohen's remarkable 2002 study of the early Popper, *Karl Popper: The Formative Years*.
5 See, for a brief discussion and references, István Deák, *Weimer Germany's Left-Wing Intellectuals* (1969, 158).
6 These are, surely, more plausibly seen in the context of, in part, a carry-over of British colonial arrangements, and, as Michael Barr has suggested (Barr 2000), as possibly a product of Fabian influences upon Lee Kuan Yew during his legal training in Cambridge after the Second World War, than as a result of the influence of Plato.
7 Despite some recent problems. Cf. "Singapore MRT Breaks Down for Third Day in a Row", *Jakarta Globe*, 18 April 2012, www.thejakartaglobe.com/home/singapore-mrt-breaks-down-for-third-day-in-a-row/512271; this and all other urls last consulted 2 September 2012.
8 Cf. http://data.worldbank.org/country/singapore#cp_fin. There has been recent concern, in Singapore, about the 'income gap', and some attempts have been made to address it by way of public policy measures. Cf. http://sg.finance.yahoo.com/news/income-gap-singapore-narrows-2011–082900645.html. However, it should be noted that there are a significant number of migrant workers without permanent residential status: www.abc.net.au/news/2011–03–02/migrant-workers-reveal-hidden-side-to-singapore/1963716.
9 See, on this, the discussion on p. 162 in Laurence Wei-Teng Leong's "The 'Straight' Times: New Media and Sexual Citizenship in Singapore" (2005), and the way in which he brings out how the informality of the guidelines as to what is acceptable leads to self-censorship.
10 It may well be said that what I am depicting is Singapore up until recent times, and that, currently, some important changes are taking place (witness the recent political performance of the PAP, and the plans, announced in January 2012, for the reduction of the salaries of those holding top governmental positions in the face of popular pressure). I will say a little about recent changes, and their possible significance, at the end of this chapter.
11 See, for an amusing take on this, the 2002 Singapore film *I not Stupid*: cf. http://en.wikipedia.org/wiki/I_Not_Stupid.

12 There were, though, eugenic and numerological restrictions on mating, on which see Popper's (hostile) account in his *The Open Society* (Popper [1945]1963).
13 Something otherwise associated with death, ghosts, etc. – cf. the 2007 Singapore movie, *Men in White* – a term that is also sometimes used for PAP members!
14 As late as 2011, Lee Kuan Yew was quoted in the press as saying: "We accept the verdict of the people, but they must also accept the consequences of their actions. You must expect the PAP to look after PAP constituencies first." See http://sg.news.yahoo.com/blogs/singaporescene/pap-loses-aljunied-voters-5-years-repent-mm-155825423.html.
15 For some of the controversy about which, see Seow (2006).
16 See, for a brief account, Garry Rodan, *Transparency and Authoritarian Rule in Southeast Asia* (Rodan 2004, 32).
17 For a useful brief survey of Singapore censorship generally, from 2003, by a particularly perceptive Singapore blogger who is also a gay activist, see www.yawningbread.org/arch_2003/yax-308.htm. The Wikipedia entry http://en.wikipedia.org/wiki/Censorship_in_Singapore gives an up-to-the minute picture, with plenty of useful links. The US State Department survey www.state.gov/g/drl/rls/hrrpt/2005/61626.htm offers an interesting account both of some of the relevant legislation, and of actions which were taken under it in 2005.
18 Some people were jailed in 2005 for making racially provocative comments on the internet. (See the final reference in n. 17.)
19 See, for a useful account, Ben-Huat Chua (1995, ch. 5).
20 Or, in informal settings, Singlish: what is colloquially spoken – despite government disapproval – is a lively version of English common to Singapore and Malaysia. See, for information and entertainment, the *Coxford Singlish Dictionary*, Singapore: Angsana, 2002, also available online at: www.talkingcock.com/html/lexec.php?lexicon=lexicon&op=LexPKL.
21 How this is to be squared with its multiculturalism is a problem that I am happy to leave to the Singapore government!
22 I have been struck, for example, by the way in which religious statues in certain stores selling religious artefacts have themselves become locations at which people worship, and by the way in which figures of the Hindu god Ganesh turn up among what are otherwise exclusively Buddhist artefacts.
23 There is a certain tension here, just because in some places Christianity may in effect serve as a marker of an ethnic population.
24 On which the U.S. Department of State's "2011 Human Rights Reports: Singapore" reported that they "were generally free and fair; however, the PAP continued to benefit from procedural obstacles in the path of political opponents". See: www.state.gov/j/drl/rls/hrrpt/2011/eap/186306.htm.
25 Cf. "Protest-scared Singapore Allows 'SlutWalk'", *Jakarta Globe*, 30 November 2011, www.thejakartaglobe.com/international/protest-scared-singapore-allows-slutwalk/481753, which is interesting because it is a local example of what had been a series of international protests.
26 Cf. 'Singapore Leader Urges Tolerance of Foreigners', *Wall Street Journal Asia*, 26 August 2012, http://online.wsj.com/article/SB10000872396390444506004577613311934830648.html?mod=googlenews_wsj.
27 Cf. "Quelling the Rising Discontent", *The Star Online*, 18 August 2012, http://thestar.com.my/columnists/story.asp?file=/2012/8/18/columnists/insightdownsouth/11874587&sec=insightdownsouth.

Bibliography

Barr, M. 2000. Lee Kuan Yew: The Beliefs Behind the Man. Washington, DC: Georgetown University Press.

Bauer, J. and D. Bell (eds). 1999. The East Asian Challenge for Human Rights. Cambridge: Cambridge University Press.

Bellows, T. 2009. "Meritocracy and the Singapore Political System". Asian Journal of Political Science 17(1): 24–44.

Chua, B. 1995. Communitarian Ideology and Democracy in Singapore. London and New York: Routledge.

Deák, I. 1969. Weimer Germany's Left-Wing Intellectuals. Berkeley and Los Angeles: University of California Press.

Hacohen, M. 2002. Karl Popper: The Formative Years. Cambridge: Cambridge University Press.

Lee, K. 1998. The Singapore Story. Singapore and London: Prentice Hall.

Lingle, C. 1996. Singapore's Authoritarian Capitalism. Barcelona: Edicions Sirocco, and Fairfax, VA: The Locke Institute.

Miller, M. 2010. "What We Can Learn from Singapore's Health Model". Washington Post, 3 March 2010, www.washingtonpost.com/wp-dyn/content/article/2010/03/03/AR2010030301396.html (accessed 2 September 2012).

Nelson, L. 1928. Politics and Education. London: Allen & Unwin.

Neurath, O. and J. Lawerys, 1945. "Plato's Republic and German Education". Journal of Education 77 (February): 57–59.

Newman, J. 1986. "Singapore's Speak Mandarin Campaign: The Educational Argument". Southeast Asian Journal of Social Science 14(2): 52–67.

Popper, K. [1945]1963. The Open Society and Its Enemies. London: Routledge.

——. 1959. The Logic of Scientific Discovery. London: Hutchinson.

——. 2008. *After the Open Society*, ed. J. Shearmur and P. Turner. London: Routledge.

——. 2009. *The Two Fundamental Problems of the Theory of Knowledge*, ed. T.E. Hansen. Abingdon: Routledge.

Rodan, G. 2004. *Transparency and Authoritarian Rule in Southeast Asia*. London: Routledge Curzon.

Sanderson, G. 2002. "International Education Developments in Singapore". *International Education Journal* 3(2): 85–103. Available at: http://ehlt.flinders.edu.au/education/iej/articles/v3n2/sandersn/paper.pdf.

Seow, F. 2006. *Beyond Suspicion? The Singapore Judiciary*. Monograph 55. New Haven, CT: Yale Southeast Asia Studies.

Vaish, V. 2008. "Mother Tongues, English, and Religion in Singapore". *World Englishes* 27(3/4): 450–64.

Webb, S. and B. Webb. 1935. *Soviet Communism: A New Civilization?* London: Longman.

Wei-Teng Leong, L. 2005. "The 'Straight' Times: New Media and Sexual Citizenship in Singapore". In A. Romano and M. Bromley (eds) *Journalism and Democracy in Asia*. London: Routledge, pp. 159–71.

Wells, H.G. 1905. *A Modern Utopia*. London: Chapman & Hall.

8 Popular despotism

An economist's explanation

William Coleman

1 Introduction

The shadow of the totalitarian state looms long in *The Open Society and Its Enemies*, and Popper's work may be taken as an attempt to account for this twentieth-century nightmare. But his explanation has a particular one-sidedness that is probably inevitable from a philosopher of science: for all its digressions, it is at bottom epistemological. The inescapable implication of Popper's work is that the fundamental affliction of 'closed societies' is a deep epistemological error: a dogmatic mindset. In tandem, the vital and defining grace of a liberal society in Popper's estimate is its healthily critical attitude. The vigour of these implications is barely circumscribed by Popper's adherence to 'situational logic' or even his statement that, if he had to choose, he would side with materialism over idealism (Popper 1945, ii, 110). To Popper, Stalin's state was a 'practical consequence' of Marx's philosophy of prophecy (Popper 1945, ii, 144–5).

The point of this chapter is to press that rational choice theory provides an alternative to Popper's philosophical accounting for the roots of the unfree society. It explores how one might attempt to rationalize such a society in terms rational choice logic rather than epistemological dysfunction. This exploration may be dubbed an 'economist's theory of despotism', as the application of rational choice logic to despotism – with barely recourse to 'culture', 'history' or vertical and horizontal ties – has been most pursued by economists (Olson 2000; Wintrobe 1998).

Rather than address the totalitarian state, this chapter analyses a form of despotism that is of greater current significance: 'popular despotism'. In this species of unfree society – well exemplified by twenty-first-century China and Russia – the population has little 'in principle' objection to this monopolization of power by one-party states (either de facto or *de jure*). Indeed, the populace appears to give the ruling party its genuine support; and the authenticity of this support is only underlined by the absence in these societies of mass coercion, and a degree of civil freedom which (however compromised by Western standards) was quite unknown to twentieth-century totalitarian states.[1] This phenomenon of 'popular despotism' is kindred with 'illiberal democracy' (explored by political sociologists of Asia, such as Bell *et al.* 1995), in which the absence of a real contest by rival political parties for power is so widely favoured by the population that it is endorsed through genuinely democratic processes. The exemplar would be Singapore, and Japan may constitute another, more diluted, case.[2] In both popular despotism and illiberal democracy the population willingly endorses a state in which a genuine competition for power by rival political parties is unknown.

The philosopher will have no difficulty in advancing an 'epistemological failure' diagnosis of the 'popular despotism', by invoking indoctrination, ignorance, delusion, superstition, or even stupidity. In keeping with its rational actor remit, this chapter's analysis will contend that popular despotism rests instead upon the existence of some sweeping, collective project that each member of the population believes will serve his or her own interests. The analysis further maintains that this collective project amounts to only a precarious and ephemeral basis for popular despotism, and therefore popular despotism will become *either* less popular *or* less despotic as time passes.

2 Order based on power versus order based on legitimacy

Any rationalization of popular despotism must touch upon the fundamental problem of political theory: How does order emerge from the clash of human wills? Or, how are conflicting individual wills curbed? A classic answer to this problem would dichotomize the range of solutions into those based on power versus those based on authority. Thus one may curb a will by power (that is, by the exercise of force which acts as an external sanction) *or* by authority (that is, by the exercise of legitimacy which acts as an internal sanction). The contrast may be expressed as a contrast between 'physical versus moral' forces; or between 'material' versus 'ideological' forces. The dichotimization is parallel to the contrast in Durkheimian sociology between 'mechanical solidarity' (where people are useful to each other) and 'organic solidarity' (where people are bonded to each other). Finally, the dichotomization is cognate with a familiar division of the motors of human action: between, on one side, the calculation of self-interest, unconstrained by any consideration that does not bear (directly and indirectly) on one's self-interest; and on the other side, human action which is constrained or impelled by considerations not bearing (directly or indirectly) on one's self-interest (such as 'values' or 'passions').

The contrast between polities based on power and those based in authority obviously does not constitute a complete articulation of political forms. Legitimation is, after all, an exercise in value judgement, and there will be as many specimens of polities based on authority as there are different values. Thus '*ancien-régime*' polities that accommodated and resourced the values of *structure, honour* and *tradition* may be contrasted with the succeeding liberal polities legitimated by *freedom*, *welfare* and *rationality*. In their turn, both the *ancien régime* and liberal states have been menaced and sometimes destroyed by charismatic polities that have legitimated *self-extinction, power* and the *irrational.*

3 Leviathan, anarchy and truce: some economic modellings

Some economic concepts lend themselves easily to theorizing polities based on power. Indeed, the categories of monopoly and competition come easily to mind in contemplating such polities, as many 'species' of this type of polity may be distinguished as different locations along a spectrum measuring the dispersion of power. At one extreme on this spectrum is a total concentration of power on an individual (or a group of individuals with identical interests). In this 'Leviathan', all but one are slaves: there is 'no choice' but for the many to obey the one. This may be contrasted with its polar opposite of an infinite dispersion of power across persons. This mode of existence is denoted as 'anarchy', and is usually identified with chaos.

Both Leviathan and anarchy may be given clear articulations in terms of an equilibrium of rational actors; an economic modelling, in other words. The economic modelling of Leviathan would adopt the model of the optimizing firm – an agricultural firm – where a pastoralist manages some stock of animals so as to maximize the pastoralist's own income, or utility. Over the animals he dispenses care and neglect, and life and death, as he pleases, without the wills of the subjugated creatures having any significance. Mancur Olson (2000) has pursued such a modelling of Leviathan, and applied it in some detail to Stalin's economic system.

An economic modelling of anarchy has been supplied by Public Choice theorists. In this modelling anarchy is a game theory equilibrium between bandit-farmers able to prey on each other (Buchanan 1975, ch. 4). In the Nash equilibrium each bandit-farmer robs the amount that is utility maximizing given the other bandit-farmer's own utility maximizing amount of robbery. The analysis implications are not as dismal as might be expected; there is some useful division of labour, as the mutual robbery secures some of the 'gains to trade'!

But the theorizing of rational actor equilibrium suggests that the absence of some supreme power need not produce mutual chaotic assault and annexation ('anarchy'), but may instead yield order. One such form of order that can emerge from the dispersion of power may be referred to as a 'truce'; for if anarchy is a battlefield, one may also summon up a vision of life as a battlefield *with a truce declared.* In this vision the truce has nothing humanitarian or juridicial about it; in this vision power rules the truce as much as the battle. The truce is sustained solely by the fact that the terms of the truce are such that each side thinks it not worth their while to overpower the other. Not only might such a truce arise – as it sometimes has literally on the battlefield – but it may be argued (on the basis of a Hicks' model of the bargain; see Hicks 1932; Coleman 2010) that in the absence of informational errors – or wish to battle for battle's sake – such a truce *will* arise. A truce (of certain terms) is, in other words, the equilibrium. The terms of the truce consist of the distribution of resources such that neither side will find it profitable to seize the resources of the other (see Coleman 2010, 89–101). Further, the truce is not a mere state of peaceful coexistence, but would seem to include useful relations; just as there are sometimes useful relations between the two adversaries during truces on actual battlefields. Perhaps the most literal manifestations of the truce are those international orders that are based simply on a 'balance of power', such as the Cold War. Anarchy, by contrast, does not capture well the character of relations between states: for, despite the evident dispersal of power among the states of the world, international relations are usually not a matter of endemic mutual brigandage.[3] The real world correspondence of the truce may extend beyond international relations. We can at least conceive of the state of truce as characterizing domestic relations. In such a truce every person (or household) is their own enforcer. Corroborative of this possibility are examples of populations living in the shells of failed states that cannot be said to always live in anarchy. The truce, therefore, holds out the prospect of order without the state. There is, recall, no agency above decision-makers that in any way enforces the terms of the truce. The simultaneous presence of order and the absence of the state will appeal to libertarians ('your home is your castle'), and this marvel is solely from the calculus of power. But the very act that the truce involves order without a state leaves it trivially inadequate as an analysis of any society with a genuine state.

There is another type of order arising from a calculus of dispersed power (rather than 'authority'); and one which does exhibit the directed collective action characteristic of 'a state'. This political form is commonly known in political theory as 'association' (see Rawls 1993, 40–3), but I will refer to it here as 'the syndicate'. The choice of this sinister-sounding term is deliberate, since it summons up some of the best examples of an order based merely on power, but which also exhibits directed collective action: the Mafia, the bush ranger gang, the pirate ship.

This chapter will argue that the syndicate is promising not only as a modelling of the pirate ship, but also as an interpretation and rationalization of the popular despotism.

4 The syndicate

Like anarchy, the truce and Leviathan, the syndicate is based on power rather than legitimation. Unlike anarchy or truce, syndicate societies exhibit centrally organized collective action. But, unlike Leviathan, the collective action syndicate is not based on a massive concentration of power. Rather, the basis of that organized collective action is some deeply shared common project whose success depends upon collective action.[4]

Piracy illustrates the syndicate. The deeply shared common project of the members of a pirate ship is obvious: to not sink on the high seas, to successfully pillage other ships, and to evade the extreme punishment for that pillage. Further, defection in piracy is not a strategy: jumping into the rowing-boat is a suicidal action.

The obvious economic modelling of the syndicate turns on the concept of public good. Let the produced good be 'public' in that if the good is supplied to one person it is *ipso facto* supplied to all persons. The pirate ship constitutes a public good (for its crew). For the pirate ship either stays afloat for all the crew, or sinks for all the crew. A public good characterization of the syndicate provides a rationalization of a 'command-and-control' centre. Clearly some 'coordination' or organization is needed: we must all pull on the oars at the same time. Economists are, of course, highly familiar with the capacity for the invisible hand to coordinate without a coordinator, but one of the ironies of economic theory is that 'coordination without a coordinator' requires a conflict of wills. Consider the case where all private goods are free (due to satiation?), but that public goods are scarce. There is no conflict of wills here (assuming that preferences over the public goods are identical). There remains, however, a problem of the particular allocation of various resources among alternative public goods that maximizes utility. And how can the market secure that? It is a notorious theorem of economics that, barring particular conditions, the competitive market will not provide public goods.[5] Only a 'social planner' can secure that allocation. Thus the syndicate will require an organizing authority.

Yet the 'authority' centre in the syndicate is always provisional and conditional, and is based on the usefulness of the exercise of that authority to those under it. The *Bounty*, in its state of mutiny, illustrates the provisional character of the syndicate's authority. The *Bounty* was captained (competently) by Fletcher Christian. But as soon as the *Bounty* was beached and burnt at Pitcairn Island his authority dissolved; his seafaring expertise was henceforth irrelevant to the crew. This was not the case when the *Bounty* was under sail: then the crew's life depended on it.

The case of piracy illustrates the relative temperance of the exercise of authority in the syndicate. The pirate ship was no slave galley; it was administered with a measure of prudence, equity and even democratic processes. Some pirate ships stipulated by rule that 'Every man shall have an equal vote in affairs of moment'. This 'democracy' sometimes extended to electing the captain.

Thus the syndicate is no tyranny, and may constitute a simulacrum of a democracy. But I write only 'simulacrum', as the similarity with democracy is specious. In a genuine liberal democracy, democratic processes are accepted not because they serve an overwhelming common interest but because they accommodate liberal values. In a genuine democracy the democratic processes are the way in which you can assert yourself and pursue your own ends while respecting the right of others to pursue their own ends. In the syndicate the polity is endorsed, but that endorsement is based solely on gratification of interests, rather than on the gratification of democratic ideals. It is the lack of respect among members of the syndicate of the *right* of others to pursue their ends that makes the existence of some collective project so crucial to the syndicate.

5 The foundation of popular despotism

The thesis of this chapter is, evidently, that popular despotism – and, even more, illiberal democracy – may be modelled as a syndicate; an orderly, directed and popularly endorsed polity that is sustained solely by a calculus of power dispersed across the population. Thus the 'move' this chapter makes to explain a 'cooperative' society when there is no legitimate authority (but only a jumble of empowered wills) is a simple one: an overwhelming common shared interest is invoked. If you like, the conflict of wills is solved by not having a conflict of wills. Obviously the success of this move very much turns upon the reality of an overwhelming common collective project.

What might be that common collective project that is essential for a syndicate interpretation of popular despotism?

One answer that is likely to be proposed in answer to this question is, 'The economy'. This answer is doubtlessly stimulated by the huge economic success of China post 1979 that is coexistent with an apparent satisfaction of the great bulk of the population with a one-party state. But certain considerations weigh against this answer. As an empirical objection, one may instance the Putin state: for at least a decade it has constituted an outstanding example of popular despotism, yet its strength seems to have been only weakly underpinned by economic growth. A more fundamental objection to identifying the economy as the 'common project' of a syndicate society is that the economy is best seen as a terrain of *conflict* rather than as a common cause. Wealth is obviously an object of rivalry. And the management of the economy is beleaguered by prisoners' dilemmas, whereby each person would benefit by seizing an economic privilege in their favour at the cost of others. Thus the efficient management of the economy is not a common collective project. It is true that a totally economic incompetent stewardship is in nobody's interest (except possibly bailiffs, flea market dealers, etc.), but that consideration only rules out the totally incompetent stewardship; it does not make a common cause of efficiency, or maximize economic performance.

To obtain a clear example of that common collective project that is essential for popular despotism, we may return to piracy; not a pirate ship as such, but a pirate state, and its wars of booty. Let us consider France under Napoleon.

Ancien-régime France had a political system that elaborately served continuity, structure and honour, but by the time of the Revolution the fading of those values had left the old regime little legitimacy. At the same time notions of liberal polity had acquired little legitimacy; the insurgent ideology was an (anti-liberal) collectivist philosophy that turned on a Rousseauian 'general will', which by its very mythicality could never serve as an effective legitimizer. Thus, by 1789, not only had the former authority system lost its authority, but also no alternative system of legitimations had any grip. Thus there was an 'authority vacuum'. What could be the outcome of this but anarchy? The most notorious anarchy, indeed, in modern history: the Terror. This was epitomized in the Law of 22 *Prairial*, or *loi de la Grande Terreur*, which was enacted on 10 June 1794 and decreed, among other things, that the advocacy of the monarchy was a crime punishable by death, by a tribunal from which there was no appeal, and which was subject to no laws of evidence.

But consider: what spectacle would have greeted a visitor to Notre Dame Cathedral ten years later on 2 December 1804? They would witness the French Senate – having invited Napoleon to assume the title of Emperor – crowding with other notables into the cathedral in order to bow to their new emperor now bearing the crown of Charlemagne. This coronation inaugurated a decade of rule, which was despotic but also essentially popular. The Napoleonic regime always claimed that there was 'no opposition', and although this was an exaggeration, it was a forgivable one. From anarchy to despotism; from regiphobia to regimania in the space of ten years. How was this miracle achieved?

One might suggest that the 'Emperor of the French' offered the French a project that was a collective one: to establish a political and cultural French hegemony over Europe from Malaga to Moscow. This required everyone to contribute; certainly it required a *Grand Armee* based on a mass conscription unknown before Napoleon. And it rewarded everyone; a Marshall's baton was, of course, in every knapsack. (Why stop at a Marshall? Jean Bernadotte was translated from a sergeant at the outbreak of the Revolution to a King of Sweden; Joachim Murat from a haberdasher's clerk to the King of Naples.) It wasn't just that everyone was entitled to buy a ticket in life's great lottery (that was 'the career open to all talents'); there was, in addition, a prize for everyone: the stunning victories of Napoleon constituted what economists call a 'public good'. Their glory was essentially common enjoyment of the French people.

More generally, we can assert that great wars constitute a common project that provides a foundation for the syndicate. German nationalists rejoiced at the disappearance of 'egotism' upon the outbreak of war in August 1914, and this is understandable. But they somewhat misconstrued the phenomenon to which they were referring; it was not so much a disappearance of individual interests as individual interests assuming a new congruence in the face of the common enemy of the Triple Entente.

6 Some contemporary cases of popular despotism

The collective project of a syndicate need not, however, be a great war in the literal sense. Consider a leading illustration of 'popular despotism': Putin's Russia. The bogus nature of Russian democracy since Putin's ascent needs no argument. But until late 2011 there was 'no opposition' to speak of – despite the state being grossly corrupt and dysfunctional. The source of the public's long-time endorsement of the Putin regime is its perception that Russia's predicament is a national one, and therefore a collective one. It is not simply that Russia has problems; Russia has problems on account of it being Russia. The context of this perception is, of course, the conclusion of the Cold War with Russia's defeat; its empire torn away; several of its richest former provinces (Estonia, Latvia and Lithuania) joining (through NATO and the EU) the victorious West. Further, the defeated country remained under deadly attack from parts of the empire; most notoriously the Chechnyan terrorist atrocity at a Beslan school in 2004 that resulted in the deaths of 334 hostages The collective project that Putin offered the population was one of national reassertion, or 'counterattack'.

And there was a second distinct dimension to Putin's 'counterattack'. The Russian public is entirely in the grip of the mythology of its dispossession by

'Oligarchs' during the 1990s. The Oligarchs – who in the eyes of Russians are frequently 'non-Russians' – were the cause of Russian misfortune. Putin's undertaking concretely was to persecute those guilty of despoiling Russia (Mikhail Khodorkovsky and Boris Berezovsky) and, in the more abstract, offering Russians a 'national capitalism' as their economic saviour. In sum, terrorists and oligarchs are every Russian's awful enemies, and their destruction constitutes a common interest.[6]

Can the syndicate model be cogently applied to other popular despotisms instanced in the introduction?[7] What would be the common project for China? It is barely plausible to adopt for China the previous suggestion regarding Russia, and to construe this common project to be the national self-assertion of a beleaguered polity in the face of a (supposedly) hostile world. China is the exemplar of a rising power. There is, surely, a temptation here to invoke 'nationalism' as the common project. Indeed, the 'nationalism of spectacles' seems to provide the public good that is the stuff of the common project of the syndicate: the Olympic Games, lunar orbits and expeditions to Mars, the recurrent theatre of frontier disputes and 'incidents', the strut of chauvinistic media. But insofar as nationalism is understood as a manifestation of 'groupism' – a solidarity with one's own kind and 'visceral' hostility to the stranger – it sits awkwardly with a 'syndicate' interpretation of society. For such nationalism as 'groupism' is clearly inconsistent with the syndicate model's assumption of purely instrumental relations between human beings. This is not to deny that 'visceral' hostility to the stranger may be characteristic; perhaps such nationalism is, indeed, "the religion of modern China" (Townsend 1996, 5). The point is simply the logical one that such nationalism will do the syndicate rationalization of popular despotism no good, since that rationalization is an attempt to explain the social union in a society quite without any 'gods' or 'devils'.

Further, it is arguable whether genuine 'groupism' is, in fact, powerful in China. It is well known that recurrent bouts of Chinese self-denigration (e.g. Bo Yang 1992) are as familiar as self-applause. This alternation of self-disgust and self-exaltation is in parallel to the rapid oscillation between loving the foreigner and hating the foreigner. From the Goddess of Democracy (4 June 1989) to the Demon of Liberty (9 May 1999), all in the space of ten years. Hostile passions that are so mobile in shifting from one object to a completely opposite one suggest lack of a set of cultural rules of the game. Thus one analyst has suggested that in terms of "rules and norms for the behavior of leadership" the inspiration of the public China

> appears to be extraordinarily thin. There is little to compare with the substance of American nationalism with its mystique of the Declaration of Independence, the Constitution, the Bill of Rights, the Pledge of Allegiance and the whole body of values … that Samuel P Huntingdon has called the American creed.
>
> (Pye 1996, 86)

Of course, such a creedless society is exactly the terrain of the syndicate. But what is its common project?

Perhaps economic *growth* – as distinct from wealth – could constitute such a project. This chapter's earlier contention of the economic as a terrain of conflict did implicitly assume a static characterization of the economy. In such an economy of given factor supplies, the owners of each factor will strive to monopolize to benefit themselves at the cost of others. But once the possibility of growth appears – once the directing of one's energies towards the future becomes significant – then a degree of commonality of interest emerges. This is because the various monopolizing actions of labour, capital and natural resources will reduce the effective return on each interest's own saving, and that will clearly constitute a disincentive to monopolize. But how strong is this disincentive? There is no definite answer, but economic theory suggests circumstances when it could be strong. Economic models have demonstrated that a sufficiently low rate of 'time preference' (i.e. impatience) will entirely remove the private reward for socially costly monopolizations (see Coleman 2010, ch. 5). Thus a sufficiently low rate of time preference can leave economic actors acting 'as if' they are in the same boat. China's massive saving rates, in excess of 50 per cent (Ma and Yi 2010), bespeak a low rate of time preference, and we are left with the possibility that growth does indeed constitute a common project that sustains a syndicate. But the same economic models that demonstrate the elimination of the incentive to monopolize by a low rate of time preference also suggest that such a foundation for the syndicate will be precarious. A low rate of time preference will only cast its harmonizing magic with a 'sufficiently high' rate of return on saving, and the rate of return will certainly decline as capital accumulates. We are led to conclude that, with the passage of time, growth can no longer constitute a common project sufficient to sustain a syndicate, and conflict will emerge in a society based solely on a calculus of interest.

7 The fate of the syndicate: the totalitarian state?

The preceding section has laboured to advance some possible common projects which could provide unity for a population bereft of legality or values. Several of these candidates have some plausibility, but none may be said to quite match what is required of a common project to sustain a syndicate society. For much more is required from a 'common project' than merely everybody benefiting from some coordination. There must also be no possibility of benefiting from 'defection'. To illustrate: a pirate ship on the high seas was suggested as being possessed by a purely common cause. But such robbers can rob one another.[8] Defection seems to be the bugbear of collective action, unless all society is almost literally in the same boat. Napoleon's France was not literally a boat, and several of its crowned corporals – Bernadotte and Murat – defected as soon as Napoleon's state became metaphorically a sinking ship. Corruption – a form of defection – is notoriously an 'endemic infection' of societies based on instrumental relations.

Truly common causes, then, are rare, or, at best, passing. In contrast, the conflict of interests is enduring and fundamental. Thus this moderate success of the syndicate is passing or precarious. What then will supplant the syndicate in a universe of rationality and instrumental valuations of relationships? Will it end in a truce between rival interests, each not quite powerful enough to overwhelm the other? China's history is suggestive here, as the Treaty Port System from 1842 may be seen as consisting of truces between sovereign powers; the terms being such that neither the Manchu dynasty nor the West found it rewarding to overwhelm the other by force.[9] But, for reasons advanced in section 3, the truce is likely to be lacking in the benefits of coordinated collective action.

Is, then, Leviathan more likely to supplant a flagging syndicate on account of its greater capability to solve collective action problems? Not necessarily, as the conception of Leviathan advanced in this chapter also arguably has limited applicability. Has 'power' ever been perfectly concentrated in one will? There have certainly been tyrants with a 'power of life or death' over their subjects. But such power does not amount to the 'power' imputed to the Leviathan above since, in a world of solely instrumental relations, it is not a 'credible threat' to kill someone who is, in effect, your slave: you would be destroying your own property. It is hardly credible to threaten to destroy your own wealth unless you are granted your wish.[10] Thus the Leviathan rests on the possibility of inflicting punishment on subjects costlessly and undestructively. But techniques of punishment always have costs, both direct and indirect. We conclude that the pure Leviathan cannot exist in a world composed solely of rational instrumental relations.[11]

Given the vulnerabilities of actual (rather than ideal-form) syndicates and Leviathans, the thought arises that a mixed form of syndicate and Leviathan, where each reinforces the other, is more powerful than a pure syndicate (weakened by its inevitable deviation from the ideal form) or a pure Leviathan (also weakened by its inevitable deviation from its ideal form). The totalitarian state of the twentieth century might be interpreted as such a mixed polity: a Leviathan with an assimilation of the syndicate; a less than perfect concentration of power compensated by a commonality of cause. An upshot of this interpretation is that the totalitarian state had a dimension of popular despotism about it. The totalitarian state, indeed, differed from the 'tyranny' of the antique world, which seems to have been an uncomplicated relationship of master and slave. For, notwithstanding its oppressive and terroristic character, the totalitarian state received a significant degree of collaboration of the massed population.

Perhaps Nazi Germany had most of the colour of popular despotism. Like the Napoleonic state its origins may be said to lie in an authority crisis; the attempt of several generations to graft a liberal state onto an ancient regime state had ended with both liberalism and *ancien régime* being rejected in the wake of the traumas of World War and Depression. From the resulting chaos and violence there quickly emerged a totalitarian state that easily engaged the obedience of the population: an accomplishment that from the vantage point of Germany in 1932 must have seemed as impossible as the same accomplishment would have been in France in 1794. This unlikely achievement was undoubtedly built on the popularity of the regime.[12] But the fact of the regime's popularity begs the question as to the origin of that popularity. The stock answer is that the regime gave something to (almost) everyone. That answer in turn begs the question as to how such a politically desirable object was achieved. In any case, it evades the apparent necessity of conflict; they may have given 'something' to everyone, but did not (and could not) give 'everything to everyone'. The suggestion of this chapter is that of the regime's popularity turned on its syndicate aspect. As Napoleon did, the Nazi regime offered its subjects the common project of mastery of Europe. This mastery, it should be noted, included a grossly piratical aspect, in which the German populace at large benefited from the intensive looting of occupied Europe, and of course, the dispossession of Jewry (see Aly 2005).

8 The fate of syndicate: the propaganda state?

But must the fate of the syndicate in the face of the fading common project be recourse to Leviathan? Could not a struggling syndicate turn away from power, and instead attempt to sink its foundation in the phenomenon this chapter has so far avoided? Might it not seek legitimacy from authority; and seek aid from nationalism, religion and 'civic religion', a confected matrix of beliefs, rituals and sacred sites? Liberal societies also have such civic religions – the Constitution in the United States or parliamentarism in Westminster governments. But the purpose of civic religions in liberal societies is different: the purpose of civic religions in liberal societies is to accommodate and legitimate difference; in the faltering syndicate it is to promote a phony fusion of interests by preaching 'we are all of one'.

One of the more spectacular cases of recommending a delusive civic religion to hide social conflict and preserve rule is found at the dawn of political philosophy; the 'noble lie' that Plato proposes (in Book 3 of *The Republic*) to make secure the stratified society he favours. This lie, or myth, would have it that all citizens 'are brothers', but 'God has framed you differently'. Those with the power of command have had gold mingled in their physical creation; their auxiliaries have been imparted silver, while farmers and craftsmen have received only iron and brass. The "fostering of such a belief", writes Plato, "will make them care more for the city and for one another". The lie is easily interpretable as foreshadowing the mythologies of dictatorial regimes that justified their monopolization of power. Thus we are led back to *The Open Society*'s critique of method, but with a dogmatic attitude being the stuff of a saving expedient of failing syndicate rather than the siege engine of revolution.[13]

9 Conclusion and afterthought

The title of this chapter promised an economist's theory of popular despotism. The chapter has, however, sought to avoid invoking the 'economic success' that is commonly supposed to underwrite popular despotism. Nevertheless, it is an economist's theory because it supposes that popular despotism arises from the rational action of persons endowed only with interests, and lacking non-instrumental relationships. The theory, in other words, dispenses with the 'Russian soul' or the 'authoritarian mind' or 'Confucian morality' as rationalizations of popular despotism, but instead traces popular despotism to a utilitarian calculation of dispersed power, that finds use in a collective action over a common project. Given that, as a matter of historical record, the alleged cultural traits supposedly characteristic of popular despotism ('authoritarian mind', etc.) have coexisted with anarchy in only a short distance of time from despotism, this chapter's explanation of popular despotism without reference to values may prove cogent.

Nevertheless, it is unclear that anything in this chapter warrants giving the last word to power rather than authority (and legitimation and values). For having advanced an economist's theory of popular despotism, we are left asking: Can we advance an economist's theory of liberal democracy? One such theory has been long proposed by Public Choice theorists (Buchanan and Tullock 1962). It repudiates Rousseauan conceptions of democracy as an expression of a mythical 'general will', along with the Athenian (and Popperian) conception of 'democracy as discussion' – but instead conceives of democracy as no more or less than a system of competitive *political* exchange. But such an economistic conception only begs questions about how competition in 'political markets' is maintained in the face of the incentive to monopolize (i.e. de-democratize) political markets. The Public Choice theorist of democracy appears to have no recourse but to suppose that liberal democracy's ultimate foundation lies in values; a suite of value's that constrains each member's actions in the clash of interests by means of individual and political rights. But perhaps this is not the concession of the economist as it may seem, because even the economists' own favourite terrain – the market – is, in truth, also based to some degree on values. The market is dependent, in particular, on the value of honesty. But honesty is a relatively undemanding moral requirement; honesty is not benevolence, or self-sacrifice or brotherhood. Thus success of the market, then, is not greatly demanding of virtue. The wealth of nations does not require one to love one's neighbour as one's self, and the whole 'project' of economic growth is consequently sparing in its uses of the extant fund of virtue. The same may be said of a genuine liberal political system: it is a polity of authority rather than power, and therefore does not dispense with values, but relies on them. But it is sparing in its demand on them. By not making unreal demands of virtues, the liberal solution for the problem of solving the clash of wills is not beyond reasonable hope.

Notes

1 Despotism has attracted a number of adjectives from political philosophers, but not often the word 'popular'. The physiocrats of the 1760s favoured what they called 'legal despotism', which amounted to a strong central authority acting in accord with 'natural laws'. At about the same time Europe saw 'enlightened despotism', which

may be best illustrated by the reign of Emperor Joseph II over the Austrian Empire. Public choice theorists of the late twentieth century made much use of 'benevolent despotism' as a representation of the kind of rule for which economic reformers (such as the Physiocrats) have supposedly hoped. In none of these usages is there any pretence to popularity: the approval of the populace served no part of 'legal despotism'; enlightened despots such as Joseph II took little heed of 'the people', who abhorred him. And it is the very lack of popular approval for economic reform which occasions that long, wistful wait of some economic reformers for a 'benevolent despot'.

2 In Japan a single party (the Liberal Democratic Party) has been in power since 1955 save short stretches totalling four years. Might Sweden be a European example of 'illiberal democracy'? More than one observer has felt that there was something Singaporean about Sweden; that ambiguous hybrid of socialism and capitalism, for example. More to the point, the long hegemony of the Swedish Social Democratic Party has resulted in it ruling (at the time of writing) for sixty-five of the past eighty years, including one continuous forty-four-year stretch. Roland Huntford's *New Totalitarians* (Huntford 1971) supplies a well-known characterization of Swedish society as possessed by illiberal impulses.

3 Granted, 'endemic mutual brigandage' may be a just characterization of international relations in certain epochs, especially in the confrontations in history between 'empire' and 'barbary'. The Empire steals human beings (slavery) from Barbary, while Barbary steals material objects from the Empire. Sometimes it has been the other way around.

4 Some aspects of the concept of syndicate are also captured by the 'teleocracy' as developed by Oakeshott, and distinguished by him from 'nomocracy'. In a 'teleocracy', society has a single goal; a nomocracy has no such single goal. This difference is also captured in Hayek's contrast between a tribal society (a single goal) and 'the Great Society' (no single goal). The category of teleocracy, however, is more encompassing than the syndicate, since it will include Leviathan and, possibly, some societies based on authority rather than power.

5 Economic theorists have explored methods by which the market might internalize the 'positive externality' that the public good provides. But that itself still leaves open free-riding.

6 One particular aspect of Putin's Russia throws light on the lack of values in popular despotisms. Democracy died in Putin's Russia. But it did not die through the spread of some expressly anti-democratic 'ideal' or ideology among the population; it died through the sheer lack of public interest in democratic politics. It died of apathy. This apathy reflects the essentially instrumental attitude to any of the democratic processes that do manage to exist in syndicate societies, and the functionlessness of political competition in such societies. What would a pirate think of parties on a pirate ship? What would be their point? What would they represent? It is the common cause aspect of the syndicate that makes them redundant. In the syndicate democratic processes reduce to the selection of suitable human material for governance. In a liberal society political parties do have a point: they represent divergent interests and divergent values; the very things the syndicate lacks.

7 What would be the common project for Singapore? 'Survival' is a plausible answer. The viability of Singapore as an independent state was initially considered doubtful, and it remains fundamentally vulnerable.

8 It is recorded that Blackbeard marooned part of his crew "on a small sandy beach … where there was neither beast bird or herb" permitting a "vastly larger share for the men chosen to remain with the captain" (Lee 1974).

9 Tantalizingly, Fairbank (1953) proposes to describe the polity of the Treaty Ports as 'synarchy'; rule by several sovereigns. But Fairbank's explanation of this form of order is 'historical–genetic' rather than economistic.

10 That is, in a world of rationality and instrumental value of relationships, the subject

would not believe that the tyrant would exercise their threats. Granted: the subject might (rationally) believe such threats if the tyrant was irrational; or if the tyrant enjoyed killing people. But then we are outside the realm of rationality and instrumental valuations.

11 In the same way, 'the truce' as a political form rests on assumptions that are doubtful. The case that seems to best exemplify it – international relations – is also most menaced by the implausibility of the assumption that relations are purely instrumental. Are notoriously difficult international relations – India and Pakistan; Israel and Arabs; Greece and Turkey – passionless, instrumental ones? And – serving the same critical effect from the opposite direction – is it not also possible that successfully peaceful international orders are sustained not just by a calculus of power and interest, but also by a sense that the prevailing order is legitimate? Thus Kissinger (1957) argues at length that the international order that consolidated in the wake of the Congress of Vienna of 1814 was as much a matter of a resecured legitimacy as a restored balance of power.

12 Formal proofs of the popularity of the 'Third Reich' are inevitably difficult, but one that comes close is the 1935 League of Nations administered referendum in the Saar over that province's future, which recorded 91 per cent of voters supporting a union with Germany.

13 We are led to the thought that one can 'index' how much societies accommodate divergence – and how much they seek to frustrate it by blinding people to it – by the degree of contestability of opinion; ranging from zero in totalitarian states to almost complete in democratic ones. This is essentially the position of Karl Popper in *The Open Society and Its Enemies*, where he sought to construe liberalism as amounting to openness to criticism. He thereby underlined with polemical verve the 'democracy equals discussion' thesis that had been entertained at about the same time by Frank Knight and Henry Simons, and accommodated by John Start Mill in his vision of the legislature as the Congress of Opinions (Mill 1861).

Bibliography

Aly, G. 2005. *Hitler's Beneficiaries: Plunder, Racial War and the Nazi Welfare State.* New York: Metropolitan Books:

Bell, D.A. 1995. *Towards Illiberal Democracy in Pacific Asia.* Basingstoke: Macmillan.

Bell, D., D. Brown, K. Jayasuriya and D. Jones. 1995. *Towards Illiberal Democracy in Pacific Asia.* New York: St Martin's Press.

Bo Yang. 1992. *The Ugly Chinaman and the Crisis of Chinese Culture*, translated and edited by Don J. Cohn and Jing Qing. St Leonards, NSW: Allen & Unwin.

Buchanan, J. M. 1975. *The Limits of Liberty: Between Anarchy and Leviathan.* Chicago, IL: University of Chicago Pressd.

Buchanan, J.M. and G. Tullock. 1962. *The Calculus of Consent. The Logical Foundations of Constitutional Democracy.* Ann Arbor: University of Michagen Press.

Coleman, W. 2010. *The Political Economy of Wages and Unemployment: A Neoclassical Exploration.* Cheltenham: Edward Elgar.

Fairbank, J.K. 1953. *Trade and Diplomacy on the China Coast: The Opening of the Treaty Ports, 1842–1854.* Cambridge, MA: Harvard University Press.

Huntford, R. 1971. *The New Totalitarians.* London: Allen Lane.

Hicks. J.R. 1932. *The Theory of Wages.* London: Macmillan.

Kissinger, H. 1957. *The World Restored: Metternich, Castlereagh, and the Problems of Peace, 1812–22.* London: Weidenfeld & Nicolson.

Lee, R.E. 1974. *BlackBeard the Pirate: A Reappraisal of his Life and Times.* Winston Salem: J.F. Blair.

Ma, Guonan and Wang Yi. 2010. "China's High Saving Rate: Myth and Reality". *BIS Working Papers* No. 312.

Mill, J.S. 1861. *Considerations on Representative Government*. London: Parker, Son, and Bourne.

Pye, L.W. 1996. "How China's Nationalism was Shanghied". In J. Unger (ed.) *Chinese Nationalism*. London: M.E. Sharpe.

Olson, M. 2000. *Power and Prosperity: Outgrowing Communist and Capitalist Dictatorships*. New York: Basic Books.

Popper K.R. 1945. *The Open Society and Its Enemies*, 2 volumes. London: Routledge & Kegan Paul.

Rawls, J. 1993. *Political Liberalism*. New York: Columbia University Press.

Townsend, J. 1996. "Chinese Nationalism". In J. Unger (ed.) *Chinese Nationalism*. London: M.E. Sharpe.

Wintrobe, R. 1998. *The Political Economy of Dictatorship*. Cambridge: Cambridge University Press.

Index

Page numbers in *italics* denote tables, those in **bold** denote figures.

For Product Safety Concerns and Information please contact our EU representative GPSR@taylorandfrancis.com
Taylor & Francis Verlag GmbH, Kaufingerstraße 24, 80331 München, Germany

www.ingramcontent.com/pod-product-compliance
Lightning Source LLC
LaVergne TN
LVHW021107300926
849160LV00009B/646

* 9 7 8 1 0 3 2 9 2 8 7 9 1 *